FINNMARK

TROMS

NORDLAND

100
Natural Wonders
of Norway

100 Natural Wonders
of Norway

Tom Schandy · Tom Helgesen

© **Publisher: Tom & Tom 2007**

Tom Schandy and Tom Helgesen

Address:
Elgfaret 35
NO-3320 Vestfossen,
Norway
Tel: + 47 32 70 05 81
Fax: + 47 32 70 05 85
Mobile: + 47 95 97 91 95

E-Mail:
tschandy@online.no
tohelge2@online.no

www.tomogtom.no

English translation: Sandra A. G. Ulvær.

Front cover: Otertind Mountain. Photo: Torbjørn Moen.

Page 1:   Puffin in flight. Photo: Tom Schandy.
Pages 2-3:   Kjerag in Rogaland County. Photo: Tom Schandy.
Page 4:   The blue light of dusk in the Jotunheimen
               Mountains. Photo: Tom Schandy.
Page 208:   Full moon over Aurland. Photo: Tom Schandy.

Photos back cover:
Blindleia on the Southern Coast. Photo: Tom Schandy.
The Helgeland Coastline. Photo: Tom Schandy.
Jæren. Photo: Tom Schandy.
The Jostedalsbre Glacier. Photo: Tom Helgesen.
The Vettisfoss Waterfall. Photo: Tom Schandy.
Shags, Sklinna. Photo: Tom Schandy.

Design: Jostein Aas / Prinfo AS.
Reproduction: Capella Media.
Printing: Zoom Grafisk, Drammen.

ISBN: 978-82-92916-00-1
(Original title: 100 norske naturperler)

Tom Schandy has received support from
the Non-fiction Literature Fund.

Contents

Preface

If there is one thing Norway abounds in it is beautiful countryside. Few countries in the world can offer such a varied and magnificent nature with majestic mountains, dramatic fjords and coastal scenery, forested valleys and a multitude of traditional cultivated landscapes. This represents our joint natural heritage, something we Norwegians are extremely proud of. Nature and the countryside have been and still are a vital source of inspiration in sustaining our national identity.

We are particularly proud to have two of our most famous fjords inscribed on the World Heritage List: Geirangerfjorden and Nærøyfjorden. Many people want to experience Norwegian nature and the influx of tourists from abroad is increasing. We welcome our foreign guests as this creates a valuable foundation for jobs in the outlying districts. But there is an inherent paradox in tourism in that we must face: the ever increasing number of tourists from all around the world is of great importance in economic development and international understanding but it also entails environmental effects that need to be addressed, in particular emissions that can affect the worlds climate.

We must also take care lest the increased use of nature leads to a degradation of biodiversity - the very foundation of sustainable development. Action must be taken in order to ensure a continued rich environment - both in Norway and in the rest of the world.

This book is a gateway to many of our magnificent areas of nature. Many areas are vast and off the beaten track where you can spend several days trekking with a heavy rucksack. Other scenic areas are more accessible to the majority of people and are just as impressive. Nature is full of treasures just waiting to be explored!

Oslo, 22 October 2007

Erik Solheim
Minister of Environment and Development Cooperation

Photo: Tore Berntsen.

100 Natural Wonders of Norway

The diversity and beauty of Norwegian nature makes Norway probably one of the most beautiful countries in the world. The magnificent areas of fantastic scenery ranging from south to north and east to the west has presented us with an enormous challenge to choose "only" 100 of these natural wonders. The Norwegian Department of the Environment and each County Regional Commissioner's department for environment have provided tips and assistance for our selection.

"100 Natural Wonders in Norway" includes, of course, all the Norwegian National Parks. On the whole these are situated in mountain regions but the book also includes separate chapters and splendid photos from picturesque coastlines, fairytale forests, thundering waterfalls and deep fjords. Every county is represented from the coast of Østfold where the journey begins to its conclusion in Pasvik in Øst-Finnmark and on the way you will learn about the plants, birds, fish and mammals living in the different areas. Each chapter has an inset with facts including information about maps and access.

Despite our intention to choose the 100 best natural wonders in Norway, some people are bound to feel that their own favourite mountain, coastline or waterfall has been left out. Obviously with only 208 pages at our disposal it is impossible to include everything. We simply had to make a choice. However, we hope that this book will inspire you to discover and experience the fantastic places described here as well as other sights of natural scenic beauty in Norway.

"100 Natural Wonders in Norway" is also a small contribution to the conservation debate. Admittedly we have on the whole avoided the most controversial matters. We could, for example, have said more about the protection of coniferous forests, road planning, holiday cabin development and the larger predators, but we decided not to do so in this book. Instead we would like it to be a source of inspiration for people to travel and learn more about the values which have been preserved in this beautiful country. Knowledge is crucial for all forms of management and we hope the politicians will tread carefully as guardians of Norway's natural heritage in the future.

We would like to thank the Regional Commissioners in the various counties and their departments for environment, the local supervisors from the Norwegian Nature Inspectorate (SNO), as well as Professor Svein Dale at the Norwegian University of Life Sciences to whom we are much indebted for reading the manuscript. As the authors we are, of course, responsible for any possible mistakes or gaps in the text. We are also extremely grateful that we have had access to photographs from Norway's best nature photographers.

On these words it is time to start our journey in nature. We hope you like the route and stops we have made on our way from the fjords to the mountains! We wish you a pleasant trip!

Øvre Eiker/ Drammen September 2007

Tom Schandy and **Tom Helgesen**

Hvaler Islands
A summer paradise in Østfold County

This island paradise to the far south-east of Norway is a real pearl on the coastline and with its glorious sandy beaches, exciting islands, diverse flora, great coral reefs and abundant bird life it has something for everyone. Norway's first marine national park will be established here within the next few years.

Idyllic group of buildings at Kuvauen on the island of Vesterøy, Hvaler. Photo: Rolf Sørensen.

More than 800 islands, islets and skerries (ground area exceeding 20 square kilometres) cluster in the sea off the estuary of the Glomma River. Nearly all the islands belong to the Hvaler Municipality and form a holiday paradise which more than doubles its inhabitants in the summer months. Whereas people were previously dependent on boat transport to visit the islands, bridges and tunnels under the sea now provide connection to the mainland. From the west the first of the large islands you meet is Vesterøy, followed by Spjærøy, Asmaløy and Kirkøy, the latter being Hvaler's largest island containing the main town, Skjærhalden. Every island is a beauty spot, each with its own distinctive character, and if you do not have a boat yourself, there is a boat service with several daily departures to the charming islands of Nordre Sandøy and Søndre Sandøy, Herføl and Lauer.

The planned area of the marine national park totals 354 square kilometres and its conservational values concern the flora, fauna, types of beach and coastline, coastal coniferous forest, heaths and the magnificent, intact coastal landscape. Besides the plant life and wildlife, the reasons for conservation include the marine environment and the condition of the landscape. Among other things the tremendous coral reef 1,200 metres long at Tisler is quite a sensation and not only is it the largest coral reef in Norwegian sheltered water, it is extremely beautiful with a kaleidoscope of white, pink and yellow coral.

Special flora and protected areas

Despite a lot of nutrient poor bedrock, the mild coastal climate and some richer pockets of bedrock have given Hvaler the basis for an abundant flora. This includes Hvaler Municipality's official flower, sea wormwood, which you may be lucky enough to find near Brattestø on the island of Asmaløy. Sea wormwood has its only Norwegian habitats at Hvaler and at Kråkerøy in the neighbouring municipality, Fredrikstad. The plant has a strong taste and smell and has been used since the olden days as medicine for many complaints. Another plant which also has only a few habitats in Norway is the exclusive and critically endangered musk orchid.

There are several nature reserves among the Hvaler Islands. Arekilen, protected since 1976, contains one of Norway's largest, uninterrupted alder forests, as well as a rich bird life and wildlife. The reserve, measuring approximately 44 hectares (110 acres), is situated in the south of the island Kirkøy and is reached by a path starting from Road 108. Due to land rise after the last Ice Age, the lake lies almost 1 kilometre from the sea. As a result of the process of nature, parts of the lake are becoming overgrown, providing a home for reeds, several species of reed-mace and sedge as well as large quantities of alder. Almost 150 bird species have been registered here including Østfold County's largest and most stable stock of water rail, and it was in this area that the Eurasian reed warbler and bearded tit settled for the first time in Norway. In fact in many ways Arekilen functions as an area where south-eastern species can establish themselves.

Seabird sanctuary and ancient fort

In the sea approximately 1 kilometre south of Vesterøy and Spjærøy, the island of Akerøy lies. Although parts of this island along with Vesleøya and some smaller islets are

The sun goes down behind the Torbjørnskjær lighthouse at Hvaler.
Photo: Rolf Sørensen.

protected as a large seabird sanctuary totalling approximately 200 hectares (500 acres), the remainder of the group of islands is officially open to the public, with public amenities, drinking water and fantastic bathing beaches.

A number of gulls, terns, waders and ducks nest in this area, including redshanks, common snipes, ringed plovers and common shelducks, and due to the bird life any form of traffic is prohibited on the reserve between 15 April and 15 July. In the spring and autumn migratory birds visit Akerøya and since 1961 extensive migratory bird studies have been carried out here.

As well as its beautiful scenery, Akerøy has a small fortress from the1660's, Akerøy Fort, which is an exciting place to visit where it sits on the far edge of the Hvaler Islands. However, this coastal fortress is not the oldest cultural monument in the island group, there being several Bronze Age burial mounds on one of the highest hills.

2 ▶ Øra Wetlands at Fredrikstad
Rich biological diversity in the Glomma Estuary

On the east side of the Glomma Estuary, directly south of the town of Fredrikstad, lie the vast Øra Wetlands. Despite the proximity of Østfold County's largest town and several industrial estates, an abundance of birds, plants and fish exists here.

In total the Øra Nature Reserve covers 15.6 square kilometres of which 2.3 square kilometres are land based. In other words, this is an extremely large nature reserve, especially considering the dense population nearby. The protected area includes Gansrødbukta, Neskilen and outlying islets and marine areas. To the north-east and east the reserve borders on rolling, forested hills, pasture and cultivated fields, and to the south and west is the sea. This landscape, full of idyllic promontories, deep inlets and islets, resembles a skerry coastline.

View of the wetlands at Øra with islands and water. Photo: Rolf Sørensen.

Several hundred nesting pairs of cormorants have settled at Øra. Photo: Rolf Sørensen.

Øra is also interesting because Norway's largest river, the Glomma, meets the sea here. The sediment accumulates in large areas of shallow water and wetlands. The brackish water has resulted in very special biotopes for many species of flora and fauna. There are now plans to expand the reserve by a total of over 100 hectares (250 acres), more or less equally divided between land and sea.

Varied bird life
Bird enthusiasts have known about the birdlife at Øra for a long time and already in the 1800's the amateur ornithologist J. A. Thome was working here. Since then several well-known Norwegian ornithologists have visited Øra, but it was only in the 1960's that the area's rich bird life first came into focus. This was mainly because of the large concentrations of whooper swans and mute swans that over-wintered and up to 1,000 individuals could be observed at any one time. As early as 1937 nesting mute swans were recorded at Øra, as one of the two sites for this in Norway. The nature reserve was established in 1979 and in 1985 it was declared a Ramsar region. The Ramsar Convention is an international agreement with the purpose of protecting the world's wetlands generally, and in particular as habitats for wetland birds.

During the migration period every spring and autumn many rare visitors are observed in the Øra reserve. The white-fronted goose, barnacle goose (now a nesting bird in Øra), brent goose and white-billed diver are found here as well as birds of prey such as the golden eagle and red-footed falcon. Colourful and exotic species such as the kingfisher and goldfinch have also been observed, the latter even nesting beside the Øraveien road. Some years ago a colony of more than 700 pairs of great cormorants was established at Øra and this was the first of its kind in the Oslofjord. The majority of these birds however do not belong to the north Atlantic subspecies that nests in Northern Norway, but to a subspecies Phalacrocorax carbo "sinensis", which nests in freshwater in Sweden and Denmark and further south towards the Mediterranean. It has more white on its throat, neck and head than the cormorant species in Northern Norway.

Altogether there are over 250 bird species registered at Øra, and a new bird observation tower provides bird enthusiasts with a much better vantage point over this relatively flat area. The observation tower lies in a buffer zone between established factories and the nature reserve at the mouth of the Glomma River.

41 different types of fish
Nature-lovers also associate Øra with a rich fish life as well as distinctive countryside. The large areas of shallow water and the special environment which arises where freshwater meets the sea are essential for the biological life. The water vegetation is dominated by plant species such as reed, soft stem bulrush and seaside bulrush, much appreciated by all the warblers.

Øra's fish life is quite unique. The salt content in the water can vary greatly, often dependent on the periods of flooding in the Glomma River. Saltwater fish like cod and whiting are generally caught during the winter, while perch, roach and bream are more usual when the level of freshwater rises. The fascinating thing is that at certain times of the year it is possible to catch freshwater and saltwater fish in the same net. Altogether 41 different types of fish are recorded at Øra.

Jeløya
A unique piece of Østfold County

To the west of Moss lies Jeløya, an island known for its wonderful beaches, teeming boat life, beautiful traditional cultivated landscapes, manor houses, lush nature and art galleries. Søndre Jeløy, at the southern end of the island, is a landscape protection area totalling over 400 hectares (1,000 acres) and an area of real natural beauty.

The whole of the south-west tip of Jeløya belongs to this landscape protection area and due to its warm, coastal climate there are several types of forest which thrive here. Hardwood forest grows in favourable light conditions in the transition between cultivated soil and coniferous forest, and in good soil towards the sea. Examples of such forests are: grey alder and ash; alder and wetland forest; wych elm and small-leaved lime. A pine and coastal forest dominates on the dry and exposed beaches on the west coast and is a so-called protective forest, playing an important part in sheltering other vegetation. In the spring, before the trees leaf and shut out

Coastal landscape on Jeløya. Photo: Øystein Søbye/NN/Samfoto.

Røed Country Manor is an attraction on Jeløya. Photo: Øystein Søbye/NN/Samfoto.

~ FACTS ~

Island of 19 square kilometres in the Oslofjord with connecting bridge to the mainland. Part of Moss Municipality in Østfold County.

Attractions:
- Søndre Jeløy Landscape Protection Area
- Country manors (Alby and Røed are open to the public)
- Gallery F 15 at Alby

Map:
1813 I Horten 1:50 000.

Access:
Leave Road E6 and follow the signs to Moss. Jeløya is west of the town of Moss and is connected by a bridge. There is also a ferry service between Horten and Moss.

the light, the floors of the hardwood forests mentioned above are covered with a carpet of blue hepatica anemone and white wood anemones.

The blue hepatica anemone is a recognised sign of spring on luxuriant Jeløya. Photo: Tom Schandy.

The purpose of protecting the Søndre Jeløy landscape is to preserve the geology, botany, zoology and cultural history of the unique nature and traditional cultivated landscape. On the southernmost tip of the landscape protection area, exposed to the Oslofjord and Norway's warmest summers, the Rødsåsen Nature Reserve lies totalling approximately 31.8 hectares (80 acres) with the purpose of protecting an area of forest lying on Permian rock, and all its natural plant life.

Plans exist to establish two new nature reserves in the landscape protection areas, Grønliparken (4.1 hectares/10 acres) and Reieråsen (8.2 hectares/20 acres). Both areas are dominated by hardwood forest.

Country manors and biological diversity

In a landscape where avenues, stone walls, large country manors and gardens are dominant features, the walks in many places go quite near the sea. In the 1700's and 1800's the farm properties on Jeløya were purchased by wealthy town families and government officials, and then developed into country homes with parks and avenues. This landscape of country manors, including Røed and Alby (which houses Gallery F 15) is lusher than much of the rest of Østfold County. This is due to the island's volcanic rock which disintegrates easily and is richer in nutrients than the more common gneiss and granite found on the mainland. Geologically Jeløya is part of the Oslo Field and consists of young lava rock from the Permian Period.

Varied vegetation often leads to biological diversity. Jeløya lies in the centre of the important bird migration flyways along the Oslofjord, and not surprisingly a total of 220 bird species have been recorded. People walking in the area will often get a glimpse of a roe deer, but many insect species have also found their ideal habitat here.

The Islands in the Inner Oslofjord
Botanical and geological jewels

One of Norway's most splendid areas of natural beauty lies in fact right on the doorstep of the capital city's inhabitants. The islands in the Inner Oslofjord are botanical and geological gems with a rich bird life and extensive recreational possibilities.

The municipalities, the organisations for recreational activities and the environmental authorities have deliberately avoided development in this area. Oslo Municipality alone owns 40 islands and 37 kilometres of shoreline. There are many forms of access to the various islands, some being connected to the mainland, some having ferry services, while others can only be reached if you have your own boat.

The islands consist of stratified Cambrian-Silurian rocks which provide a fertile soil and an exceptional flora. The island plant life depends on limestone and warmth at the same time as it has to tolerate periods of drought.

Aerial view of Hovedøya with Lindøya behind to the right, followed by Gressholmen/Rambergøya and Langøyene. To the left we glimpse a corner of Bleikøya. Photo: Tom Schandy.

The Inner Oslofjord has a number of islands which consist of stratified Cambrian-Silurian rocks, an exciting flora and a diverse bird life.

Attractions:
· Seabirds
· Coastal flora
· Geology including fossils
· Bathing beaches
· Hovedøya
· Brønnøya with self-service cable ferry

Maps:
1814 I Asker and 1914 IV Oslo 1 : 50 000.

Access:
Ferry service to Hovedøya, Bleikøya, Gressholmen, Lindøya and Nakholmen, as well as to the Langøyene Islands. Self-service cable ferry or floating bridge to Brønnøya from Nesøya.

Vendelsundet separates Nesøya and Brønnøya. In the foreground we see the characteristic Cambrian-Silurian rocks which typify Brønnøya. Photo: Tom Helgesen.

Several species are at their northernmost limit in Eastern Norway and along the Oslofjord. Hovedøya Island alone is home to 400 different plants, including the pasque flower and Oslo County's own flower, the mountain clover (mountain trefoil). Mountain clover is considered extremely rare and this is the only place it grows in Norway. The beautiful blue dragon flower is protected and thrives on several of the islands in the Oslofjord.

Many jewels

In addition to the rare flowers, the island of Hovedøya is considered to have the most cultural history. Among other things there are cloister ruins (building was started in 1147), a shipbuilding yard, a stone quarry, military housing and there are still twelve canons at the Vestre Kruttårn (an old gunpowder storehouse). Furthermore the island's south-west shore has a large bathing beach, so here is something to suit everyone. In order to keep the vegetation under control and to preserve the traditional cultivated landscape, sheep belonging to the municipality are brought from Bogstad Open Farm to Hovedøya to graze each summer. This aids the survival of plants which need plenty of light.

Originally three separate islands, Gressholmen, Heggholmen and Rambergøya are now linked together. They lie to the southeast of Hovedøya and can offer good bathing facilities, an inn serving food and not least, masses of nature and history to explore. The nature reserve on Gressholmen and Rambergøya was established in 1992 for the protection of an area of shallow water as well as the rich plant and animal life. Gressholmen and Rambergøya are also important resting places for the migratory birds that come to Norway via the Oslofjord. Many birds stay here during the winter and over 180 different bird species have been observed.

Holiday cabins and abundant nature

Brønnøya in the Asker Municipality has always been an idyll in the Oslofjord, and more so when the Oslo Airport and associated aeroplane noise was moved to Gardermoen. Some people live permanently on Brønnøya but there are also many holiday cabins. Those that do not have their own boat can use a floating bridge, a self-service cable ferry or coastal steamer as means of transport. The island is completely free of cars and has a wonderful network of narrow gravel paths, ideal for cycling and exploring the dry lime-rich meadows full of flowers, or for finding a good place to bathe.

At present a conservation plan for the Inner Oslofjord and a separate management plan for Hovedøya are under political hearing. Their purpose is to provide better conservation of the approximately 40 islands and in May 2006 the government established two nature reserves as well as a landscape protection area for conservation of the plant life on unique Hovedøya. There can be few other capital cities in the world that have such fantastic recreational possibilities right on their doorstep.

5 ▸ Østensjøvann Lake
Nature reserve in the middle of Oslo

The 1.8 kilometre long lake, Østensjøvann, lies in the middle of one of Oslo's satellite towns. Over 215 bird species and 460 plant species are registered only a stone's throw from a dense population that also appreciates the near presence of this nutrient rich lake. The entire lake is surrounded by a network of excellent paths where people exercise, or take their dog for a walk.

Marine sediments left behind from the ocean which covered the area after the last Ice Age have formed the basis for the lushness of Østensjøvann Lake, not least assisted over the last decades by the artificial drainage of nutrients in the form of fertilizer and sewage. The biological wealth in and around the lake is enormous and it contains for example between 35,000 and 70,000 invertebrates per square metre, including findings of 12 of Norway's 27 freshwater snails. With more than 460 registered plant species the lake has enjoyed renown as a classic plant location since the middle of the 1800's. The bulrush, lesser bulrush, yellow iris and sweet flag all grow here, not

In the middle of one of Oslo's satellite towns lies the idyllic Østensjøvann Lake. Photo: Tom Schandy.

to mention the reeds that form picturesque "forests" around the lake.

Culture is found not far from the lake in the form of Abildsø Gård enthroned on a gigantic island of arable land with oak and hazel trees. In Almedalen (Elm Valley) beside Østensjø Gård the vegetation is luxuriant, elm trees of course being the main feature. Similarly oak trees dominate in Eikelunden (Oak Grove).

There has been a long struggle to preserve Østensjøvann Lake for future generations but in 1992 the area was finally given the status of a nature reserve. The organisation, Friends of Østensjøvann Lake, has been active in safeguarding the natural and cultural environments surrounding the lake and this has led to Oslo Municipality establishing the Østensjøvann District Environment Park.

The great crested grebe is a characteristic species at Østensjøvann Lake. Photo: Tom Schandy.

A vitamin boost

More than 215 registered bird species makes Østensjøvann Lake one of Norway's most renowned bird lakes. A visit here on a spring day with screeching black-headed gulls, fighting coots and courting great crested grebes is a vitamin boost. The sharp screams of the black-headed gulls leave an audible mark on the surroundings and a vast colony of up to 1,500 pairs has made the lake its home for many years, although the numbers have declined substantially more recently.

When the ice breaks up in the spring the birds gather in some of the small holes in the ice under the bridge at the southern end, and at the outlet of the small river, Bølerbekken. At this time of the year one can make close early morning studies of the common goldeneye's courtship display, the male throwing back his head and kicking up a spray of water. The black coots with their white foreheads are hotblooded now and one can often witness them chasing each other and even attacking front on, lying and splashing in the water with their feet facing. A close relative of the coot is the moorhen, who is a little smaller, has a red bill and thrives among the reeds. Tufted ducks with their distinctive crests are calmer and more interested in diving for food than begging bread from people passing by.

The Penguin Dance

Great crested grebes arrive on the lake during April. This is the characteristic species of the lake and hundreds can be observed. It is a splendid bird which first nested at the lake in 1972 and if one is lucky one can observe its romantic courtship which after some introductory shakes of the head ends in a "penguin dance". The birds rise out of the water, chest against chest, paddling eagerly with their feet and swinging their bills, which are full of water plants, from side to side. The great crested grebe often builds its floating nest made of water plants on one of the many artificial islands dug out in the 1960's.

A coot with nesting material in early spring. Photo: Tom Schandy.

Nordmarka
Large lakes and thick forests

Nordmarka has nearly everything ranging from amazing skiing, good biking trails, numerous fishing lakes of various sizes and an extensive network of trails. Large lakes and long spruce valleys dominate the countryside alongside scanty pine forests and lush meadows of flowers.

Nordmarka has many natural beauty spots with several areas being protected as nature reserves where the forest lives its own life untouched by human interference. Most people connect Nordmarka with Oslo but in fact four counties share this wonderful countryside – Oslo, Akershus, Buskerud and Oppland – the latter containing Nordmarka's highest hill, Svarttjernshøgda at 717 metres amsl.

A 25-year fight for conservation

The Spålen-Katnosa Nature Reserve was established in 1995 and today this 18.4 square kilometre protected area contains enormous, unspoiled landscapes, several lakes, rivers and streams, bearded spruces and twisted pines. The capercaillie holds its courtship displays in the pine forests and tracks of pine marten and lynx can be found on the spruce clad slopes. Old summer dairy farms and evidence of timber floating remind us that cultural history is close at hand. If you want to visit the reserve the best approach is the road through Nordmarka, from Jevnaker to Tverrsjøstallen and further on to the parking area under the hill Pershusfjellet. On a tour like this the distance walked is not as important as what you experience on your way, especially if you walk slowly and use all your senses to search for the small details hidden in the forest. Remember this is nature's own cathedral!

A little further south in Nordmarka the Oppkuven-Smeddalen Nature Reserve lies, where around 400 hectares (1,000 acres) are protected in this reserve dominated by coniferous forest. The environment on the hills north of Oppkuven is reminiscent of primeval forest with spruces more than 400 years old being found here. In addition to old-growth forest, Oppkuven (704 metres amsl) is a splendid vantage point with its own observation tower. Krokskogen, the western part of Nordmarka, is known for sites of old mountain summer farms and Finnish settlements, as well as the author of fairy-tales Peter Christen Asbjørnsen's legendary description of his experiences there during a summer evening 180 years ago.

Sunset over the mountain forest at Bislingen. Tracks of a solitary fox out hunting. Photo: Tom Schandy.

All-round use

There are good opportunities to

Nordmarka is a paradise for cycling, here at Katnosa Farm. Photo: Tom Helgesen.

Nordmarka, the dam warden's house has no provisions and is locked with the Norwegian Trekking Association's master key.

The roof of Nordmarka

Even if Svarttjernshøgda is Nordmarka's highest point, Bislingen (in the Lunner Municipality to the north) is one of few areas in this large forest complex that contains some mountainous features, which is why Nordmarka's only mountain lodge, Bislingen Fjellstue, is here. Even during the winter the ptarmigan thrives in this tempting natural habitat of open mountain plains, dense spruce thickets, marshes and small lakes. A January day in low sunshine, with snow-covered trees and glistening ski conditions is a winter dream and ski enthusiasts can enjoy the long trail through Nordmarka from Bislingen Fjellstue to Frognerseter in Oslo, a tour of 35 kilometres which is undoubtedly the main route south for most skiers.

catch trout in the lakes and this provides the makings of a delicious meal if you have the means to prepare and cook the fish beside a quiet forest lake. Remember that the use of an open fire is prohibited during the summer months.

Fishing is permitted all year round in Nordmarka except for certain restrictions in running water in October when the trout are spawning. Catching crayfish using bait, a torch and quick hands is a special and exciting form of fishing on several of the lakes in the dark august evenings. A fishing permit is necessary for all fishing and crayfish fishing, the latter needing a separate permit.

A great deal of Nordmarka is riddled with forest roads, but luckily for outdoor enthusiasts much of this road network is closed for motor traffic, thus providing endless and varied possibilities for cycling during the summer.

Nordmarka's watercourses still bears traces of the timber floating which was carried out here for several centuries. In connection with the negotiations concerning transfer of the water rights in 1875, 24 dams were described in this water system. At Katnos Dam the dam warden's house from the 1880's is now a popular place for an overnight stay with 15 beds and electricity, and there are three canoes and life jackets on loan for daytrips on the Katnosa Lake. As with the other no-service cabins in

A spring day and fresh green leaves adorn a birch on an island in Spålen Lake, included in the Spålen-Katnosa Nature Reserve since 1995. Photo: Tom Schandy.

> ### ❧ FACTS ❧
>
> Area of forest between Oslo and Hadeland
>
> **Attractions:**
> · Spålen-Katnosa Nature Reserve
> · Norway's densest network of prepared skiing trails
> · Numerous fishing lakes
> · Svarttjernshøgda (717 metres amsl)
>
> **Maps:**
> Touring maps Oslo Nordmark summer 1: 50 000 and Oslo Nordmark winter 1: 50 000.
>
> **Access:**
> Sognsvann Lake, Frognerseter, Maridal, Sørkedal, Lommedal, as well as Sollihøgda, Kleivstua, Ringkollen, Tverrsjø Lake, Bislingen and Mylla.

Nordre Øyeren
Scandinavia's largest inland delta

Nordre Øyeren is a unique nature reserve. The three rivers, Nitelva, Leira and not least the Glomma create Scandinavia's largest inland delta featuring long promontories, islands, shallows and a tangle of old and new river courses. The lake holds the record for the number of fish species, exciting water plants and in particular an extremely varied bird life.

The rivers transport enormous volumes of sand and mud which are deposited where the river water loses speed as it enters the great lake. The supply of new material builds up new islands while breaking down others. The swift current gouges out the earthy banks and deposits the mass in calmer stretches. In other words the delta landscape constantly changes and is in fact moving south into the lake. By studying old maps one can ascertain that the delta's land area has increased by more than 100 per cent in the period between 1875 and 1956. All the islands have given the lake its name. Øyeren comes from the Norse Øyir which is a derivative for the word Øy, meaning island.

The special natural conditions give origin to a very distinctive plant and animal life. Not surprisingly

The delta in Nordre Øyeren is Scandinavia's largest inland delta. Photo: Tom Schandy.

The osprey snatches fish in the delta during the summer season. Photo: Tom Schandy.

FACTS

Nordre Øyeren Nature Reserve, Scandinavia's largest delta. Ramsar region. Situated near Lillestrøm in Akershus County.

Attractions:
- Striking landscape
- Unique botany
- Varied bird life
- Beaver

Maps:
1914 I Fet and 1914 IV Oslo 1: 50 000. Boating and recreation map for Øyeren, Glomma, Vorma (1: 50 000).

Access:
Drive Road 120 south from Lillestrøm, on the west side of Øyeren. Turn off for Årnes. You can park here and walk out over Årnestangen. You can also reach the delta from the east side by taking Road 22 towards Fetsund.

Nordre Øyeren is an aqua-botanical jewel offering everything from extremely abundant localities to cold groundwater environments giving life to more than 325 registered swamp and water plants. Grey alder forest grows at Øyeren and there is also a locality supporting an almost pure almond willow forest.

Nordre Øyeren was protected as a nature reserve in 1975 and in 1992 expanded to include Sørumsneset. The reserve covers 64 square kilometres and in 1985 the area was given formal status as a Ramsar region, which is to say an area internationally considered worthy of preservation.

Fishing record

Fish life at Øyeren is in a class of its own as no other place in Norway has so many different species. All the 25 different freshwater fish registered here have their own special niches in the lake.

Roach is most numerous in the lake's shallow bays but also has the company of ide, perch, bream and pike. White bream, bream, bleak, ruffe and roach are all species which tolerate the earthy water in the open areas exposed to the wind. Perch, roach, dace, grayling, common whitefish and burbot live in the cold water from the Glomma River, while, burbot and smelt thrive in the deep water in the south of the lake. In other words one can catch quite a variety although it might not always be easy to identify the species. The king of the fish species is the zander or pike perch, which can reach 3 to 4, and even 10 kilograms. For fishermen casting from land with dead bleak as bate it provides popular fishing in May-June on its way up river to spawn.

Nearly all the Norwegian species of amphibians are found around the lake, including moor frog, common frog, toad and common and crested newts. 26 species of mammals have been observed in the area. Moose and roe deer graze on the rich vegetation and the numerous canals are home to beavers.

Abundant bird life

All the same Nordre Øyeren is best known as a bird locality. More than 260 species have been observed and 133 of these are attached to wetlands. The large variations in the water level result in relatively few nesting birds in the delta, so it is mainly in the migration periods April-May and July-October that the delta is full to the brim with a wide variety of wetland species. Common teal, mallard and wigeon are the most usual of the thousands of duck species enjoying themselves here. At low water large mud flats appear to the joy of the waders. The mud contains volumes of food which can total over 100,000 microscopic creatures per square metre of mud flat. Roundworms, annelid worms and non-biting midges comprise 95 per cent of the menu. All summer several osprey pairs fish in the delta and on seldom occasions the magnificent kingfisher has nested in or beside the reserve. In the winter, as long as there is no ice, a possible 1,500 whooper swans party in Øyeren and this makes the area one of the most important winter habitats in Norway for this species.

Nordre Øyeren is a popular recreational area, not only for boating people, but also walkers who especially enjoy hiking on the long tongue of land called Årnestangen. A walk here in the bird migration periods provides an opportunity to observe many ornithologists with telescopes, and on the outermost tip of the tongue on the east side of the delta there is a bird observation tower.

Finnskogen
Desolate forests in the border districts

Vast forested hills, old Finnish settlements and large predators. As well as seeming desolate and wild, there is an air of history over Finnskogen. This is an exciting area of nature and culture on both sides of the border between Norway (Hedmark) and Sweden (Värmland).

Simplistically stated, Finnskogen is a forest region stretching between Magnor and Trysil, and bordering Sweden in the East. Locally the area is divided into Brandval Finnskog, Grue Finnskog, Åsnes Finnskog and Våler Finnskog. The Finnskogen name derives from the Finnish immigrants during the first half of the 1600's. They settled on both sides of the international boundary and therefore the description of this natural oasis covers the natural conditions and history on both Norwegian and Swedish sides of the border. It made no difference to the Finns whether they had their home or made their living in Norway or Sweden.

Forested hills and walking trails

The nature in Finnskogen features rolling, forested hills with river valleys, large and small lakes and marshlands. The region has many old cultural monuments from the Finns who lived in the forest, as well as a rich animal and bird life. This makes Finnskogen an exciting place to walk both for those who want to cover distance and for families with small children.

The Finnskogen Trekking Association along with a number of collaborators can offer a total of 1,100 kilometres of marked trails, the best known of which is the Finnskogleden which starts at Morokulien (Magnor) in the south and ends at the southern end of Osensjø Lake in the north. This trail covers approximately 240 kilometres travelling along old paths and trafficking routes in Norway

There is something desolate and wild about Finnskogen. Photo: Øystein Søbye/NN/Samfoto.

Since the 1980's Finnskogen has been the best habitat for wolves. Here a wolf has killed a moose calf.
Photo: Tom Schandy.

and Sweden, traversing the vast forests, following lake shorelines, over peaks and past the old Finnish settlements. Despite several hundred years of habitation and somewhat extensive forestry, Finnskogen homes the large predators, bears and wolves. Although the probability of seeing these animals is quite remote, it is possible to find their tracks. Following wolf tracks in the snow can be exciting and lead to a moose carcass, but a real taste of the wilderness can be experienced if you are in the right place at the right time – a moonlit, winter night when the wolves' sustained howls fill the air.

Around 1980, one believed that wolves were almost wiped out in Scandinavia but in 1983 researchers ascertained that there was breeding for the first time in Finnskogen, which resulted in the birth of a total of six cubs. The pack did not expand until 1990 when new blood came in, and since then Finnskogen has been one of the best habitats for the species in Norway. As of 2006 the so-called Kynna pack, consisting of five individuals, has been living in Finnskogen and the large moose population here means that there is plenty of prey, which is why the wolves thrive. Indeed, Finnskogen is considered to be one of the areas in the world with the highest density of moose.

The fact that many of the forest roads are closed to ordinary traffic makes Finnskogen a wonderful place to cycle, and canoeing and kayaking is possible on many of the lakes. The variation of outdoor activities is wide in this natural El Dorado in Hedmark.

Traces of Finnish culture

There were several reasons for the immigration of Finns to Norway, but perhaps the most crucial were years of bad harvests, war and starvation in the Savolax district around the 1600's. The Finns from the forested regions first settled in Värmland and moved steadily westwards. In the vast forests around the border region they practiced slash-and-burn agriculture. Simply explained, they cut down forest which was then dried on the forest floor. When the wood was dry enough it was burned and rye or turnips were sown in the ashes. This form of agriculture demanded vast forested areas and came into conflict with forestry when the price of timber increased. Today there is no clear trace of the Finns' agricultural activities but many of the rye fields became crop fields for the smallholdings in Finnskogen.

Otherwise the names in this area tell the story of the Finns and reflect their special method of cultivation, for example, vål (Våler), ris (Risberget) and bråte (Bråten), are all names for areas of burnt-off forest. In addition many place names have a Finnish background. Apparently right up until 1960 a number of the older people in Finnskogen still spoke Finnish, and the culture of smoking ovens and saunas comes from the Finns. The saunas were so-called smoke saunas because the smoke came out into the room. After a while, stoking the fire was stopped, the smoke gradually cleared and the sauna was ready for use. The smoke ovens also led the smoke out into the room (in order to make maximum use of the warmth), the smoke then exiting through a hole in the roof. Smoke saunas and smoke ovens are preserved at several of the old Finnish settlements in Finnskogen.

🙩 FACTS 🙩

Vast forest area in Hedmark County in the border districts between Norway and Sweden. Given this name following immigration of Finns at the beginning of the 1600's.

Attractions:
· Old Finnish settlements
· Desolate forests
· Bears and wolves

Maps:
Individual maps in the main map series for Norway 1: 50 000.
Map folder Finnskogleden 1: 50 000.

Access:
Søre Osen, Gravberget, Kirkenær, Svullrya, Øiermoen and Morokulien are good starting points for walks along the Finnskogleden. Roads 21 and 25 frame Finnskogen in the south and north.

9 ▶ Sølen
Beautiful mountain district and inland fishing village

Rendalssølen (1,755 metres amsl) is the "big chief" of the Sølen Massif at Rendalen, Hedmark, while the "Sølen Kings" live beside the beautiful mountain lake, Sølensjø, a little more to the east. The presence of char and common whitefish make the lake an adventure for fishermen.

The Sølen Massif in Rendalen is a well-known landmark. Photo: Øystein Søbye/NN/Samfoto.

 **FACTS**

Beautiful mountain district east of Rendalen in Hedmark County. Currently of interest as a new landscape conservation area in Norway.

Attractions:
· Rendalssølen (1,755 metres amsl)
· Sølensjø Lake
· Mistra Watercourse

Maps:
Touring map Femunden 1: 100 000, and individual maps in the main map series for Norway 1: 50 000.

Access:
Bus or car via Road 30 to Øvre Rendal. Follow the mountain road, Road 37, from Bygdebrua eastwards to Fiskevollen beside Sølensjø Lake. Mistdal and Grøndal are popular starting points for summit ascents on Rendalssølen.

Fiskevollen is a unique inland fishing village on the shores of the Sølensjø Lake. Photo: Øystein Søbye/NN/Samfoto.

Rendalen Municipality is the largest in Southern Norway and contains many areas of natural scenic beauty. The most well-known is the above-mentioned Sølen Massif, hosting its own reindeer herd and the legend-spun lake, Sølensjø, with an inland fishing village. Perhaps less well-known is the permanently protected Mistra Watercourse west of Sølen and the wetlands along the Sølna River north of the Sølensjø Lake.

A landmark

The relatively low mountains surrounding the Sølen Massif make it a real landmark. There are in fact three peaks, Rendalssølen (1,755 metres amsl), the northern summit (1,699 metres amsl) and the southern summit (1,688 metres amsl). In addition to an absolutely magnificent view, said to be the most panoramic in the whole of Southern Norway, the special feature of the mountain is a V-shaped pass which slices right through the massif. At 1,250 metres amsl the pass has a dimension which is clearly visible for miles and it more or less divides Rendalssølen and the southern summit in two. The pass gives the mountain the shape of a saddle and this is the background for the mountain's name. Sølen comes from Norse and means quite simply, saddle.

Originally in Southern Norway there were one or perhaps two large herds of wild reindeer which wandered enormous distances between their summer and winter grazing. Human encroachment has divided the herds into a number of smaller and more vulnerable herds. Intense hunting led to the disappearance of the wild reindeer in the Sølen district at the beginning of the 1900's. The inhabitants of Rendalen introduced domestic reindeer in the 1920's and today a company called Rendalen Renselskap manages its own reindeer herd, which numbers at present approximately 1,300 animals, on the Østfjell Mountain (the Sølen district). The reindeer at Rendalen are rather special as it is the only reindeer herd in Norway which is owned by the landowners in the district. Outdoor enthusiasts walking in the Sølen district must not disturb the reindeer should they appear, just enjoy the sight.

Traditional fishing

The Sølensjø Lake (688 metres amsl) is situated east of Rendalssølen, and has a water surface area of approximately 21 square kilometres. At the northern end of the lake lies Fiskevollen with the atmosphere of a genuine fishing village. Many old sun-scorched boathouses and fishermen's shacks decorate the shoreline. The fishing here has long and rich traditions, dating originally back to the time of the Vikings, and legend has it that this was the "fishing realm" of the Sølensjø Kings. The main fishing has previously been for char in the autumn at the southern end of the lake, but now common whitefish dominate with catches of up to approximately 15 tons annually. Originally there were 20 farms in Øvre Rendal with complete fishing shares in Sølensjø Lake. Some of these have later been divided and at present there are 40 share fishermen. The Share Fishermen's Association sells permits for fishing with rod, otter and net.

Jutulhogget
Canyon steeped in legends in Hedmark County

Due to its situation off the beaten track, not many people have visited Jutulhogget. This remarkable natural phenomenon is a 2.5 kilometre long and up to 200 metre deep canyon which knifes its way through the mountain area between the Østerdalen and Rendalen.

Jutulhogget slices its way through the mountains between the Østerdalen and Rendalen. Photo: Dag Røttereng/NN/Samfoto.

This gigantic mountain cleft in Hedmark has of course been the subject of wild imagination through the centuries. In the olden days people lacked the knowledge of geology and the Ice Age to understand how Jutulhogget was formed and several tales grew up around the origins of the canyon. One legend tells of the giant of Rendalen who split the mountain with his enormous axe so that the Glomma River would flow into Rendalen. He did not complete the work before the sun rose in the east and he burst. Trolls do not tolerate the sun's rays. Another legend includes the giant of Glåmdal who became enraged with the Rendalen water thief, the latter subsequently dying after being hit on the head with a stone.

Glacial dams and huge volumes of water

The Quaternary geological explanation is more factual but nonetheless dramatic. Towards the end of the last Ice Age (approximately 9,000 years ago) the last remains of the inland ice were melting. In many places the ensuing enormous volumes of water were withheld by glacial dams, and such a glacial dam lay right across the upper regions of the Østerdal Valley and Rendalen. Suddenly the ice broke and huge volumes of water roared down with a tremendous force and in a relatively short time the water had gouged 200 metres into the sparagmite (sandstone). Jutulhogget was born. Sparagmite can create flat rock slabs that often crack at right angles, which explains the canyon's steep perpendicular sides.

Jutulhogget is exceptional in Norwegian terms and the area is therefore protected as a nature

Yellow lichen covers a rock face in the depths of Jutulhogget.
Photo: Bård Løken/NN/Samfoto.

reserve. The purpose is to preserve a distinctive landscape where formations from the Quaternary Age, especially the canyon characteristically hewn out by the disgorged water masses, comprise areas of considerable value regarding natural history. The conservati-

on area is 3.4 square kilometres and is situated in the Alvdal and Rendalen Municipalities.

A special flora

The flora down in the canyon is also exceptional, including both southern and alpine species. 100

Jutulhogget is a special natural phenomenon between Østerdalen and Rendalen in Hedmark County. The canyon is 2.5 kilometres long with perpendicular walls reaching 200 metres.

Attractions:
· The high perpendicular sides of the gorge
· A special plant life
· Enormous stone screes

Maps:
1918 IV Hanestad and 1619 II Tylldal 1: 50 000.

Access:
Turn off Road 3 at Barkald in the Østerdal Valley. A short while later you reach a car park. Follow the marked path to the entrance of the gorge.

years ago the warmth-loving deciduous tree, the elm, was discovered in Jutulhogget, the only place in the whole of Alvdal where it grows. Other species found here and not otherwise common in Hedmark are angular Solomon's seal, lily of the valley, maiden saxifrage and the lady's slipper orchid. A wide variety of flowers cling to the warm and sheltered sunny side of this natural wonder, while ferns and moss dominate on the side in shadow.

Several good vantage points along the edge give a fantastic view down into the gorge. Some people choose to walk through the gorge from east to west, a tough and exhausting trip not because of the distance which in itself is not long, but rather due to the many challenges provided by the rough and mysterious stone screes. You must allow four to six hours to walk through this spectacular natural beauty spot.

Gutulia
Forest of huge pine trees

A wild and bewitching primeval forest is the main feature in the national park at Gutulia. This is Femundmarka's little cousin in the south and its lack of marked trails makes it less accessible for recreational activities.

Cattle and sheep were tended at the mountain dairy farms at Gutulisetra for 200 years. Photo: Svein Grønvold/NN/Samfoto.

This forest of huge pine trees was the main reason that Gutulia was recommended for conservation as long ago as 1918. However 50 years passed before conservation was a reality and in 2004 the national park was expanded. The present protected area measures 23 square kilometres and the expansion led to conservation of more primeval forest. The trees in Gutulia are unusually large and many are several hundred years old. The expansion brought with it an increased variety of nature, including a mountain and marsh landscape, which is typical for this region. The Gutulia National Park is situated east of the Gutulisjø Lake and the Swedish border.

In the middle of the park, Gutulivola Mountain protrudes out of the primeval forest. The top is 949 metres amsl with a wonderful panorama over Gutulisjø Lake to the south, as well as the mountains lying in Femundsmarka and to the west of Femunden Lake in the north. The finest primeval forest in the park lies to the east of this majestic, round mountain ridge.

Old-growth forest

Old-growth forest is characterised by a large element of dead trees and in Gutulia approximately 10 per cent of the trees still standing are dead. This applies particularly to the pines which can remain standing up to 100 years after they have died. Spruce trees arrived several thousand years after the birches and pines and, because the spruce is more competitive, it gradually took over the areas of nutrient rich and continuously moist soil. The dynamics of the pine and spruce forests are due to natural forest

Gutulia is mainly recognised for its primeval forest. Photo: Steinar Myhr/NN/Samfoto.

fires (started by lightning) and there are traces of old fires in several places. Four large forest fires have been recorded in what is now the national park, in 1700, 1720, 1800 and 1860.

The strong contrast between Gutulia's forest and the open pine forests around Femunden Lake and large areas of Femundsmarka is due mainly to the Røros Copper Works' rough handling of the countryside. The works cleared extensive areas of forest to feed their melting furnaces, but luckily the loggers never reached far enough south to Gutulia and we can therefore find 400 year old pines in the national park. Some of the spruces have also reached an impressive age, among which is the 300 year old large spruce called "Storgrana", standing 500 metres north of Gutulia Seter mountain dairy farm. Due to the mature ages of the trees several species of fungus and lichen can survive in Gutulia. Modern forestry cuts down trees before they reach these ages, thus depleting the variety of species found in the forest. One of the park's spe-

cial fungi is a rare species of bracket fungus which is used by biologists as an indicator species concerning long term development of primeval forest.

Mountain dairy farming

Apart from a limited area in the south there has never been any regular forestry in Gutulia National Park, although it is certain that both firewood and building material for the summer mountain farms have been extracted. From 1750 to 1950 three farms ran their summer dairy farms at the Gutulia mountain dairy farms, without greatly affecting the character of the original vegetation. When the area was preserved nearly 40 years ago, its natural qualities were of course a decisive factor. Gradually people became aware of the cultural monuments in Gutulia especially the old mountain farm buildings. At present there are altogether 13 restored mountain farm buildings in the national park and one of them serves refreshments during July. The old cheese store at Oppåvollen is now an open

"guest house" and to reach it there is a 3 kilometre hike from the nearest car park.

Gutulia's wildlife is not especially abundant, but some species are numerous. One thousand birds were registered nesting in the park one summer. Half of these were brambling, tree pipit and willow warbler, the brambling with 300 pairs being decidedly the most common. However the richest bird life is found on the east side of the park at Valsjø Lake where small tarns, streams and marshes create a paradise for ducks and waders.

Visitors to the national park will have a good chance of seeing moose, roe deer, foxes, pine martens or mink. Otters can also be observed in Gutulia as well as beavers that have their haunts at Gutua and Valsjø Lake. Otherwise, there is only a remote chance of meeting any of the four large predators – bears, wolves, wolverines and lynxes – but they have been known to wander through the park occasionally.

Femundsmarka
Unspoiled wilderness bordering Sweden

What Femundsmarka lacks in steep mountains and thundering waterfalls it makes up for in its sheer vastness reaching towards the Swedish border. Primeval forests, rocky ground, gentle mountain tops and numerous lakes and rivers in an undulating countryside.

Autumn day in the national park. Photo: Bård Løken/NN/Samfoto.

Femunden Lake, 60 kilometres long and covering an area of 201 square kilometres, is Norway's third largest inland lake. Femunden Lake has lent its name to the enormous forests and plains which spread around the shores of the lake and towards the Swedish border. The national park was established in 1971 and after expansion in 2003 now measures 573 square kilometres. Together with the protected areas on the Swedish side, Femunds marka is one of the largest uninterrupted "wilderness areas" in the whole of Southern Scandinavia. The Landscape Protection Areas Femundslia and Langtjønna have been established as two buffer zones on the west side of the national park.

Pine forest and rounded mountain tops

Low winter temperatures and little precipitation has favoured the pine forest in Femundsmarka giving domination of old, twisted pines in some areas. A gently undulating, hilly landscape reaches up to 800-900 metres from Femunden Lake's 662 metres amsl, with a number of peaks stretching over 1,000 metres, the highest in the far north being Storvigelen (1,561 metres amsl). In the south are Store Svuku (1,415 metres amsl), Grøthogna (1,401

A fisherman has pitched his tent beside Femunden Lake and admires the sunset over the water. Around half of the visitors to Femundsmarka come to fish or canoe. Photo: Svein Grønvold/NN/Samfoto.

Abundant wildlife and bird life

Despite its barren appearance, there is an exciting fauna in the protected area, where wolverines live and bears and lynxes pass through. Moose have a winter grazing paradise in parts of Femundsmarka and a herd of musk oxen, which have wandered from the Dovre herd, regularly visit the park. If you see any reindeer they are domesticated and Elgå (in the middle of the eastern shore of Femunden Lake) is the southernmost area in Norway that Lapps keep domesticated reindeer. Otters and beavers have also found ideal habitats along some of the watercourses in the park.

The bird life includes many interesting species, one of them being the osprey, with all the old flat-topped pines in the national park providing perfect nesting sites. This combined with shallow lakes rich in fish has resulted in many nesting pairs of osprey inside the protected area, which in addition supports nesting pairs of golden eagle, gyrfalcon, northern goshawk and eagle owl.

❧ FACTS ❧

Area of wilderness east of the Femunden Lake in the counties of Sør-Trøndelag and Hedmark.

Attractions:
- Vast area of wilderness
- Canoeing
- Density of good fishing lakes
- Storvigelen (1,561 metres amsl)
- Boat service M/S Fæmund II

Map:
Touring map Femunden
1: 100 000.

Access:
Bus or car from Elverum, Rena or Koppang. County road from Røros to Synnervika/Langen Tourist Station. Road 221 to Elgå. In the summer there is a boat service over Femunden Lake from Synnervika, Femundshytta (tourist lodge), Jonasvollen or Elgå, disembark at Røosen, Haugen or Revlingen.

metres amsl) and Elgåhogna (1,460 metres amsl) the highest summits. Otherwise the nature in these border regions with Sweden has features dating from the end of the Ice Age approximately 10,000 years ago in the form of an endless number of huge stone blocks and quantities of stone and gravel strewn about in Femundsmarka.

Plenty of canoeing and fishing

Approximately half of the people who visit Femundsmarka do so to fish or go canoeing. The possibilities are diverse and a combination of canoeing and fishing is quite popular, especially recommendable being the system of lakes in the centre of the national park. The upper regions of Røa, Reva, Revsjø, Styggsjø and bordering areas on the Swedish side are marvellous for canoeing adventures, and if you do not have your own equipment, this can be hired on both sides of the border. The Norwegian Trekking Association has several hiking trails in the national park with some of the paths crossing over into Sweden. Accommodation is available in tourist cabins, some without provisions and some self-service, with provisions, run either by the Norwegian Trekking Association or privately.

Large areas of Femundsmarka are splendid for canoeing. Here a group pass the little hamlet Sorken on the south-east shores of the Femunden Lake. Photo: Øystein Søbye/NN/Samfoto.

Forollhogna
The home of the great reindeer bucks

Just before Christmas 2001 the Forollhogna National Park was established, rescuing the large natural treasures in the area north of Tynset and Tolga, west for Røros, south of Støren and east of Kvikne for future generations. This almost unspoiled mountain region is the home of Norway's biggest reindeer bucks.

Forollhogna at 1,332 metres amsl is the highest point in the protected area and has given its name to the national park. Indeed it is also a central point where it lies on the border between the counties Sør-Trøndelag and Hedmark, its pyramid shape towering over the surrounding terrain. In fine weather it is well worth the walk to the top of Forollhogna to appreciate the best view of the national park and perhaps also to get one's bearings in the landscape. For centuries it has been a landmark and guide for hunters, fishermen and other outdoor enthusiasts, even pilgrims on their way to Nidaros Cathedral in Trondheim. The easiest route to the top starts in picturesque Dalsbygda, and as you leave the lush Vangrøftdal Valley, Forollhogna's mighty silhouette appears in front of you.

Norway's largest reindeer bucks live on Forollhogna. The bucks are a magnificent sight in the mating season at the end of September. Photo: Tom Schandy.

Norway's best area for wild reindeer

Forollhogna is Norway's northernmost habitat for wild reindeer, the herd being in good condition with some of the bucks when slaughtered weighing in at around 140 kilograms. Plentiful winter grazing combined with good spring and summer grazing on lime-rich soil is most probably the main reason for this as well as there being little outside interference in the area with nearly no organised recreational activities, and this leaves the reindeer in peace. Many people consider Forollhogna to be the best area for wild reindeer in Norway, and a lot of the bucks develop magnificent antlers. Each year approximately 300 animals are felled in the hunting season with the aim of keeping the herd to around 1,700 to 1,800 animals. Although this is an old area for wild reindeer, the hunting has not always been good as the herd was almost wiped out a century ago and the present day herd on Forollhogna has descended from herds of domesticated reindeer. People from the Østerdal Valley and Trøndelag could resume hunting in 1956 and the herd is now managed well. Norway has an international responsibility to look after the habitats for reindeer.

Named after trout?

There is disagreement about the origins of the name Forollhogna. "Hogna" is the local dialect for mountain summit, but there are several opinions about the first part of the name. Some say that it comes from "fårrå" which means to pass by, while others think that it comes from the German word for trout, "forelle", many Germans having been employed at the cop-

The birch forest in its autumn colours beside Svartsjø Lake. Photo: Tom Schandy.

per mines at Røros in the mines' time of prosperity. Forollsjø Lake is rich in trout and is considered to be one of Hedmark's best trout lakes. There are many fishing huts on the shores of the lake and these belong to mountain farms further down in the valley, the landowners being allowed to set out ten nets each. It is forbidden to put out fish in the Forollsjø Lake, to prevent destroying the fine old breed already there.

Landscape protection areas in valleys with upland summer pasture

In many ways Forollhogna is the mountain area where the valley of Østerdal ends and goes over into Trøndelag on the other side of the mountain. The great open plains do not have the dramatic scenery found elsewhere in the country and thus provide easy walking ter-

rain. However Forollhogna contains more than mountains and desolate plains, as when the national park was established eight landscape protection areas totalling 452 square kilometres were included. All these areas are valleys with lush upland summer pasture and lead in towards the mountains. In this characteristic natural and cultivated landscape, used for mountain dairy farming since the 1600's, there are still a few active summer mountain farms, some even keeping up the traditional methods of grass cutting and cattle grazing. In order that the culturally dependent biological qualities do not deteriorate, it is important that this old method of using the summer pasture valleys continues. There are many complete mountain dairy farm environments with old buildings of great cultural-historic value.

Dovrefjell-Sunndalsfjell National Park
The most intact mountain eco-system in Europe

2002 saw a new Norwegian record in nature conservation when Dovrefjell National Park became more than six times larger and was renamed Dovrefjell-Sunndalsfjell National Park. Seven new landscape protection areas were established – in addition to expansion of the Fokstumyra Nature Reserve. Hunters, fishermen, outdoor enthusiasts, trolls and the fairy-tale giant Dovregubben were thereby given 4,367 square kilometres of protected land for their enjoyment!

This new conservation area means that most of the mountain region between Dombås, Hjerkinn, Oppdal, Sunndalsøra and Åndalsnes is protected in one way or another. Nowhere else in Norway is there such a large uninterrupted protected area. The nature varies tremendously from the gently sloping plains in the east to the jagged mountain scenery in the west.

Snøhetta at 2,286 metres amsl towers in the centre of the park and consists of several summits. Stortoppen is the easiest to climb, while Vesttoppen is steeper and wilder.

Snøhetta is a landmark on the Dovrefjell Mountains. Photo: Tom Schandy.

Both peaks give a fantastic panorama stretching from Rondane in the south to Trollheimen in the north. Snøhetta's great mountain face is a sheer drop with perpendicular rock walls and a glacier which calves into Istjønni Lake.

Unique flora
Knutshø and the Dovrefjell Mountains are famous internationally for their alpine flora. The German professor Georg Christian Oeder discovered Dovre's plant life in 1756, and this led to a pilgrimage of Norwegian and foreign botanists visiting Knutshø to collect plants.

Easily disintegrated rock rich in minerals, dry summer climate and talus slopes are important contributions to the diversity of plant life on Dovre. Oeder's lousewort, the Dovre poppy (Papaver radicatum ssp. ovatilobum – a subspecies of the arctic poppy) and Scottish wormwood were all discovered by the German botanist Georg Christian Oeder. All three species can be easily observed alongside the main E6 road over Dovre. The list of mountain plants found on Dovre is long and many of them deserve to be mentioned. Those which are a little more exceptional are the endemic species found here; the

Dovre dandelion (Taraxacum dovrense), a Scandinavian subspecies of the rock whitlow-grass (Draba cacuminum), and the Knutshø meadowgrass (Poa arctica ssp. stricta).

Wild reindeer
Dovre is a respected symbol of Norway's Constitution, and when this was signed at Eidsvoll in 1814 the officials present shook hands and swore to be "united and loyal until the Dovre Mountains fall", thus making this region Norway's national mountain. This is the home of trolls and spirits, and archaeological findings have revealed that for thousands of years our ancestors have exploited the mountain's natural resources. Several places in the mountain region bear signs of human-made systems and ditches for catching reindeer, and even grave sites have been found dating back to the period 300 to 1700 AD. Investigation has revealed that the reindeer here are genetically the most indigenous reindeer in Norway. While other reindeer herds have been crossbred with domestic reindeer, the Snøhetta reindeer have nearly none of these hybrid genes.

Predators
The interplay between the wild

reindeer and other animals makes the Dovrefjell Mountains unique. Arctic foxes and wolverines as well as winged predators such as the golden eagle and gyrfalcon are also part of the wildlife and Dovrefjell is therefore the most intact mountain eco-system in Norway and Europe. The predator at the top of the chain is the wolverine, while the arctic fox lives off the remains of the wolverine's kill in the winter. Apart from the gyrfalcon which hunts ptarmigan all year and the golden eagle which hunts ptarmigan and hares, all other birds of prey leave the mountain region in the autumn, when the small rodents become inaccessible.

The Musk Ox
Despite the wild reindeer, wolverines and arctic foxes, the real symbol of the Dovrefjell Mountains is the musk ox. Musk oxen are on the whole peaceful herbivores so it is easy to get quite close to them. However, one should be careful because the musk oxen can attack. People have been killed and it is therefore strongly recommended not to get closer than 200 metres.

The musk oxen were part of the Dovrefjell Mountain fauna before the Ice Age, but disappeared when

glaciers formed. During the building of the Dovre Railway, dorsal vertebrae from musk oxen were found and the idea of reintroducing these animals to Dovrefjell was born. In 1932 two calves were imported from Greenland. They bred, but the animals were shot during the war. Several groups totalling 27 calves were introduced to the region from 1947-1953. This time they succeeded in establishing themselves and at present the population numbers over 200 animals.

Musk oxen are Dovrefjell's prime trademark. Here is a winter herd lined up on a snowy mountain ridge. Photo: Tom Schandy.

Fokstumyra
Norway's first bird sanctuary

Fokstumyra on the Dovrefjell Mountains is possibly the most well-known bird sanctuary in Norway. European bird watchers make pilgrimages here to see some of the best of the Scandinavian mountain bird fauna.

As long ago as 1816 Professor Sven Nilsson wrote about this 10 kilometre-long marshland and from 1832 Norwegian natural scientists, among them the Professors L. M. Esmarch and H. H. Rasch, worked at Fokstua. Jacob Bøckmann Barth wrote in his book "Norwegian Nature" from 1856 that Fokstumyra *"does not need to fear that the noise of a high-speed steam carriage will disturb its natural peace and frighten away the wildlife that we are entrusted to support"*.

Disturbance from steam carriages

Barth was wrong. In 1916-17 the Dovre Railway was built across the mountain region passing straight through the marshland and had great consequences for the bird life.

In 1907, 41 nesting bird species were registered on the marshlands, but by 1917 the conservationist H. Th. L. Schaaning found only 19 species. Among other things the railway line destroyed the great snipe's two established display grounds as

Fokstumyra was protected as Norway's first bird sanctuary in 1923. Photo: Tom Schandy.

The bluethroat thrives in the willow thickets at Fokstumyra. Photo: Tom Schandy.

well as the nesting sites of the rare broad-billed sandpiper.

Schaaning's alarming report led to the protection of Fokstumyra in 1923 as Norway's first bird sanctuary. Conservation helped and the bird life has returned despite the fact that "high-speed steam carriages" pass several times a day. On 23 May 1969 a royal decree declared the area a nature reserve and in 2002 the reserve was expanded from 7.5 square kilometres to approximately 18 square kilometres. At the same time the reserve was named a Ramsar region, that is to say, wetlands of great international significance. By 2005 163 bird species have been observed, 78 of which were registered as nesting.

Mountain birds

The nature reserve has a good cross-section of Norway's mountain birds. From the willow thickets lining the paths the song of the bluethroat can be heard, while the common snipes shear through the sky with a type of bleating sound which comes from the air vibrating in their outer tail feathers. At Horrtjernene Lake there is a good chance of seeing the courtship display of the ruff, and this is one of the characteristic species found in the reserve. The ruff disappeared in 1897, but returned in 1958. As many as 30 displaying ruffs have been observed on tussocks and islands in Horrtjernene Lake and in the 1970's, the author and photographer Mathias Kværne, captured these birds on film from his cabin beside the reserve. Unfortunately the ruffs are substantially depleted in numbers within the protected area and there are only a few individuals left. This applies not only to Fokstumyra but reflects a general trend over the whole of Norway.

The marshes are a paradise for the various species of waders. Redshanks, wood sandpipers, greenshanks, common sandpipers and red-necked phalaropes are quite common in addition to the ruffs and common snipes. Northern lapwings, whimbrels and curlews also nest here alongside some great snipes who have returned to the area. The marshland's shyest bird is the common crane, with one or two pairs nesting here every year and if you are lucky you will see this handsome bird on your way through the reserve. All sorts of ducks swim around on the lakes including mallards, common teals, tufted ducks, wigeons and northern pintails. In addition the black-throated diver has its haunts on Horrtjernene Lake.

Fokstumyra is also the place to spot exciting birds of prey. The merlin nests in the mountain birch forest and the beautiful hen harrier can be seen suspended in the sky over the marshes. This bird of prey nests few and far between in the central regions of Southern Norway from Røros to Hallingdal, and Fokstumyra is the most well-known breeding site, with nesting being ascertained here as long ago as 1884. In years with large quantities of small rodents as many as 9 nesting pairs of hen harriers have been registered at Fokstumyra.

With a bit of luck one can witness the hen harrier's handing over of prey. The male gives the prey to the female with a spectacular air show. He drops the prey in the air and the female catches it. The short-eared owl is also a characteristic species and in years with a good supply of small rodents there can be 4 or 5 pairs nesting in the marshlands. 1963 was a good year for small rodents and 12 short-eared owl nests were found in the area.

If you are going to get the most out of your visit to the reserve the best time is the beginning of June when the birds are still singing and displaying. A visit to the reserve can be strongly recommended as there are not many places where you can observe so many mountain birds in the course of just a short walk.

16 ▶ **Dovre National Park**
Palsa mires, wild reindeer and rare plants

The name can be confusing, but the Dovre National Park is a separate national park on the southern side of the E6 road over the Dovrefjell Mountains. This is the home of wild reindeer, Norway's southernmost palsa mires (permafrost peat bogs) and many rare species of plants.

The Dovre National Park came into existence in 2003 and it lies between the vast Dovrefjell-Sunn- dalsfjell National Park to the north and the Rondane National Park to the south. A characteristic feature of the park is the rounded hilltops and contours each with a name ending in "høe" which basically means dome-shaped, for example, Gråhøe, Fokstuguhøe and Mæsæterhøe. The area surroun-

The mountains in the Dovre National Park mirror themselves in Avsjø Lake which lies beside Road E6 over Dovrefjell. Photo: Tom Schandy.

ding the summits almost bears the mark of an arctic steppe with traces of permafrost.

The landscape in Dovre National Park was formed when the inland ice melted away after the last Ice Age. Large volumes of meltwater were released and this led to a strange build up of deposits along and under the edge of the glacier and in cavities in the ice. Examples of this are the striking meltwater terraces with kettles and long, narrow ridges or eskers, of sand and gravel.

Primeval reindeer and rare plants

One of the main purposes of establishing the Dovre National Park is to safeguard the habitats of the wild reindeer. As in the Dovrefjell-Sunndalsfjell and Rondane national parks the original wild mountain reindeer, descendants of the primeval reindeer, also live here. The animals in the park are therefore extremely shy and due to this people are asked to show consideration should they spot the reindeer.

Dovre National Park lies on Cambrian-Silurian rocks which disintegrate easily and produce good soil, which in turn positively influences the flora. This includes the only occurrence in Southern Norway mountain regions of the Lapland reedgrass as well as the rare and endemic Dovre poppy and Dovre dandelion. There are also vast quantities of drooping saxifrage which loves to grow on the slightly damp irrigated surfaces at the edge of snowdrifts. Along the stem of the plant there are a number of small grain-like buds which are clones of the mother plant. They are fertile and can commence photosynthesis immediately they find a suitable place to grow.

Palsa mires and bird life

The national park is known for having the southernmost occurrence of palsa mires in Norway. These bogs consist of peat mounds with permafrost structures, that is to say that the bog is frozen all year. The principle behind these palsa mires or permafrost peat bogs is quite simple: when the water freezes it expands and lifts the soil layers lying above it. In marshy areas with little snow coverage, as is the case on Dovre, the frost can reach deep down into the bog and

lift the surface accordingly. If the summer is not too warm and the peat layer is thick enough, only the top layers will thaw, while the deeper layers in the bog will remain frozen, as in the tundra. When this repeats itself over several years, a rounded elevation (palsa) is created in the bog, and when this has reached a certain size the peat layer over it splits and exposes the ice core which then melts. The process then repeats itself. These palsa can live up to 400-500 years. Photographic studies show that some of these palsas reduced their size between 1974 and 1996, which can correlate with climatic changes.

Within the Dovre National Park there is one nature reserve with palsa mires and that is Veslehjerkinntjønnin which lies approximately five kilometres southwards along the path between the cabins Hageseter and Grimsdalshytta. There are two lakes and several small tarns here encircled by lush swamps and palsa mires with permafrost ice cores. With a total of

FACTS

Dovre National Park, 290 square kilometres, situated in the counties of Oppland and Hedmark.

Attractions:
· Wild reindeer
· Palsa mires (permafrost peat bogs)
· Mountain birds
· Mountain plants

Map:
Touring map for Dovrefjell 1: 100 000.

Access:
Easily accessible. Train or car to Hjerkinn on Dovrefjell and follow the red marked trail to Grimsdalshytta where you can stay overnight. You can also drive your car to Grimsdalshytta.

40 bird species of which 26 are registered as nesting, the reserve is also interesting from the ornithological point of view. Wetland bird species dominate including six different duck species, 13 species of waders and 2 species of gulls.

The Dovre poppy is one of the many rare plant species in the national park. Photo: Børre Dervo.

Rondane
Norway's first national park

Colossal and powerful with soaring peaks, deep cirques, long valleys and wide expanses, Rondane resembles a fairy-tale castle nestling in Norwegian mountain scenery. No wonder it was established as Norway's first national park in 1962 comprising 572 square kilometres, which in 2003 was substantially enlarged to cover the present day's 964 square kilometres.

The national park contains 10 mountain summits towering over 2,000 metres with Rondslottet's 2,178 metres soaring highest in the east on the Hedmark County border, neighboured by Vinjeronden (2,044 metres amsl) and Storronden (2,138 metres amsl).

Despite these lofty elevations there are almost no glaciers within the park boundaries and this is due to the extremely dry climate in Rondane with little precipitation and hot summers. However, the immense cirques and U-shaped valleys on the shady north side of the mountain indicate that Rondane was in fact covered in ice during the last Ice Age and this formed the dramatic contours of these mountain regions. The small, short, U-shaped valleys with flat bottoms and vertical rock faces emerged after the glaciers ploughed their course and fingers of water that froze in rock crevices loosened large boulders, gouging out cirques almost at right angles in the oblique sandstone.

Skranglehaugen, a so-called kettle landscape with gravel ridges and large depressions in the ground resembling shell impacts, lies in the Døråldal Valley, in the north of the national park. When the ice melted at the end of the last Ice Age, a number of glacier-dammed lakes formed in this area and in several places the water burrowed under the ice creating long tunnels where volumes of gravel and sand were deposited. As the ice disappeared these deposits remained in the landscape as long ridges, called eskers by the experts, and because the ice melted in stages, several levels of gravel terraces are visible. These ice-fronted deltas indicate where the dammed meltwater lay for considerable periods while the icecap melted and in some places the ice was buried in clumps under sand and gravel. These clumps of ice melted gradually, which led to hollows in the gravel and their subsequent collapse creating large depressions and pits, called kettles, in the landscape. Today some of these kettles are small, idyllic tarns adorned perhaps with a lonely mountain birch.

Døråldal is one of Norway's prettiest valleys. The summits of Høgronden, Midtronden and Digerronden display autumn's first dusting of snow. Photo: Tom Schandy.

The rock ptarmigan is in its element in Rondane's barren surroundings. Photo: Tom Schandy.

This strange Ice Age landscape is constantly watched over by Rondane's row of mighty summits. From the east there is Høgronden at 2,114 metres amsl, then Midtronden at 2,060 metres amsl and Digerronden at 2,016 metres amsl. In September, when the birch forest is clad in gold and the mountains have been dusted in the first fall of snow, Rondane is at its most glorious, and is a popular motif for Norway's nature photographers.

In the west wild scenery embraces Smiubelgen with its complex of ridges and jagged spires, Storsmeden being the highest at 2,016 metres amsl. Vertical rock faces several hundred metres high overshadow deep cirques. The easiest way to experience this remarkable landscape is to follow the path from Rondvassbu to Veslesmeden (2,015 metres amsl). The whole family will

enjoy this tour which takes three hours up and two hours down.

Lichen and reindeer

There are masses of stones in Rondane, all patterned with clinging corrosive map lichen which gives the region its characteristic yellowy green colour. No other mountain region in Norway has so much map lichen and this is due to the dry climate and the hard rock which favours species that tolerate arid conditions.

Map lichen is pretty, but the reindeer need other species of lichen in order to stay alive, and these are reindeer lichen, crinkled snow lichen and Iceland lichen. If you do spot reindeer then remember that, alongside the Dovre reindeer, these animals are the most genuine strain that is found in Norway. That is to say, these are original wild moun-

tain reindeer not crossbred with domestic reindeer, which can be the case with most other Norwegian wild reindeer herds.

The reindeer were significant for the old hunting and trapping culture in Norway and evidence of this is prolific in Rondane. Trapping systems and pit traps can be seen along the reindeer trekking routes and remains of extensive mass trapping systems have been found in the Verkilsdal Valley in the middle of Rondane, Storgrava in the Haverdal Valley and at Einsethø in the Grimsdal Valley. There is also a trapping system 1 kilometre east of Rondvassbu Mountain Lodge in the Illmanndal Valley, along the path to Bjørnhollia, as well as beside the car park at Spranget near Mysusæter. The reindeer hunt in Rondane is still quite an event and 980 animals were felled in the autumn of 2005.

Rondane also provides a home for the wolverine, golden eagle and gyrfalcon. However, the bird fauna is relatively sparse with only around 35 nesting species. The majority of species found here are those which thrive in dry and barren terrain such as rock ptarmigan, Eurasian dotterel, golden plover, northern wheatear, meadow pipit, horned lark and snow bunting.

Today Rondane is one of Norway's most popular areas for hiking. The network of tourist cabins and marked trails is excellent and particularly the routes between the cabins Bjørnhollia, Rondvassbu and Døralseter are some of the most used, the cabins being ideal starting points for enthusiasts collecting summit ascents over 2,000 metres elevation.

Reinheimen
Wild reindeer and wilderness

This fantastic wilderness on the border between the counties of Oppland and Møre and Romsdal has now been made a national park. Apart from the Hardangervidda Mountain Plain, Reinheimen is the largest area in Southern Norway with an air of wilderness.

The national park, spreading over almost 2,000 square kilometres, embraces a vast, uninterrupted wilderness-like mountain region which comprises the habitat for the wild reindeer stock in Ottadalen Nord. These reindeer are known for being some of the most productive in the country, with good body weight and calf yield. The landscape in the national park and landscape protection areas varies from lush farming valleys, via plains, watercourses and lakes to jagged mountains towards the west.

Simplistically explained, the area lies between the Ottadal Valley, Lesja in the upper reaches of the Gudbrandsdal Valley, the Romsdal Valley and Tafjord, and Reinheimen's natural grandeur is divided between the municipalities of Vågå, Lom, Lesja and Skjåk in Oppland County and Norddal and Rauma in the county of Møre and Romsdal. When it comes to conservation, Olaf Heitkøtter must be mentioned. He is a mountain warden, nature conservationist, nature photographer and writer from Lesja and has written several books and articles, held talks and made films for television concerning his wilderness realm. In particular, his book, "Reinheimen. From a mountain warden's diary" from 1974 made a great impression on many people and became known all over the country.

Varied mountain nature

Reinheimen contains many valuable localities as well as interesting and endangered species, especially the above-mentioned wild reindeer herd. While the birth grounds and the majority of the winter grazing are in Oppland County, some of the summer grazing is found in the county of Møre and Romsdal. Numbering approximately 2,200 winter animals, the wild reindeer here belong to the district called Ottadalen Nord. Other key species in Reinheimen's ecosystem are wolverine, golden eagle, gyrfalcon and ptarmigan, with moose, deer, roe deer and lynx also making these regions their home. The bird life is abundant and this is an essential area in Southern Norway for the long-tailed duck and purple sandpiper, as well as an attractive mountain habitat for the velvet scoter, ringed plover, Temminck's stint, Eurasian dotterel and horned lark. Reinheimen's flora is quite diverse, which is not surprising considering the variety of bedrock and varied climate, with, for example, the annual precipitation at Skjåk being often ten times less than in the Romsdalsfjell Mountains in the west. Such a vast and untouched central area with little disturbance provides a mountain ecosystem significant for research and management.

Area of conservation

In the autumn of 2006 a large conservation area was established and consists of the Reinheimen

A reindeer bull in Reinheimen. Photo: Olaf Heitkøtter.

The majority of Reinheimen is an area of wilderness with little organisation for outdoor pursuits. Photo: Olav Heitkøtter.

✨ FACTS ✨

Reinheimen is a wilderness-like mountain region on the border between Oppland County and the county of Møre and Romsdal. Norway's third largest national park, protected since the autumn 2006.

Attractions
- The summits Gråhø (2,014 metres amsl), Pyttegga (1,999 metres amsl), Karitind (1,982 metres amsl) and Storhø (1,924 metres amsl)
- Wolverine
- Golden eagle and gyrfalcon
- The watercourses

Maps:
Individual maps in the main map series for Norway 1: 50 000.

Access:
From Road 15 at Billingen and Grotli. Several possibilities to start a hike from Road 63 between Valldal and Åndalsnes, as well as Tafjord, a good starting point for entering Reinheimen from the west.

National Park together with the landscape protection areas of Romsdalen, Trollstigen, Tafjord-Reindalen, Ottadalen, Finndalen and Lordalen which are spread between the municipalities of Lesja, Skjåk, Vågå and Lom in Oppland County, and the municipalities of Rauma and Norddal in the county of Møre and Romsdal. The total expanse is approximately 2,600 square kilometres and it is important to remember that a lot of Reinheimen is also traditional grazing ground for thousands of sheep and cattle every year. Many of the summer mountain farms are still in use and cultural monuments from hunting and trapping dominate in the mountains. The farmers in some places still use extensive and ingenious devices for leading the water from deep in the mountains down to the fields and meadows. As long ago as 1798 the farmers in Skjåk bought the common pasture land there (Skjåk Almenning) and they have exploited Reinheimen for several centuries.

The region contains several valuable watercourses of which Rauma, Ista, Valldøla, Lora and Finna are permanently protected against hydro-electric power development. Furthermore, Reinheimen has an abundance of cultural monuments and traditional cultivated landscapes and these combined with the watercourses and other landscapes comprise an invaluable source of experiences which are vital for the passing on of knowledge concerning the past and present.

Little organisation of recreational activities
All the same, most of Reinheimen is a wilderness with little organisation of recreational activities and this situation must continue if the unique nature with its biological diversity is going to be preserved for future generations. Although the local population hunt and fish, there are few marked trails with staffed tourist lodges or self-service tourist cabins in Reinheimen. The reindeer hunt here is steeped in long traditions, producing a good

quality stock of wild reindeer, and the trout fishing is still a substantial resource, which has been important for some time. From Oppland there are only marked hiking trails from Billingen and Grotli beside Road 15 and the T-marked route from Billingen to the Norwegian Trekking Association's tourist cabin, Torsbu, is estimated to take four hours, without a break. Torsbu's annexe is as a matter of fact a renovated version of the hunting hut built by the legendary J. A. Friis over 100 years ago. The next cabin on the trail is Veltdalshytta or Pyttbua, still within Reinheimen, but more towards the west-country.

An ascent of Gråhø, Reinheimen's highest point at 2,014 metres amsl and the only one over 2,000 metres, provides a real challenge with its great variation in elevation. It is probably easier to reach the top on skis in the late winter or early spring starting from Billingen. However, one should be extra careful as the reindeer must not be disturbed or chased at this time of year. Skiing in the spring (15 April

to 1 June) in the birth grounds is one of the great conflicts between protection of the wild reindeer herd and recreational activity. It is in this very period that the reindeer need to be left in peace.

Starting from Grotli Mountain Lodge a four hour walk will take you on an even ascent via the lakes Kjerringtjønne and Viksvatn to the nearest tourist cabin, Danskehytta, a no-service cabin without provisions. The following day you can choose between two staffed lodges, Reindalsseter or Kaldhusseter. With five or six days at your disposal a longer round trip can be planned from Grotli and down to Billingen. There are several possibilities for starting a hike on the west side of Reinheimen, from Road 63 between Valldal and Åndalsnes, as well as Tafjord.

Jotunheimen National Park
The kingdom of the giants

The Jotunheimen National Park is the most mountainous landscape Norway can offer, as no other place has more summits over 2,000 metres and glaciers than here, and it includes Norway's highest mountain, Galdhøpiggen at 2,469 metres amsl.

There is probably no other mountain trail more obligatory for a Norwegian than Besseggen. On a bright summer day it resembles Oslo's main thoroughfare, Karl Johan, as almost 40,000 people walk this famous route every year. Well, it is after all something quite exceptional.

Gjendesheim Mountain Lodge in the east of the Jotunheimen is the starting point for this walk and most people choose to join the boat "M/S Gjende" which takes them over the Gjende Lake to Memurubu where they can start their climb. The trip down the Gjende Lake is an attraction in itself as this 18 kilometre long mountain lake is generally considered to be Norway's prettiest, something no-one disputes as the motorboat chugs along with a backdrop of fertile green slopes and snow-clad peaks.

There is an even climb from Memurubu, the steeper slopes being quickly conquered, and the walk continues in gently undulating terrain with the beautiful Gjende Lake far below to the right. The climax of the tour is around half way when you arrive at the narrow ridge called "Bandet" which divides the Bessvatn Lake from the sheer drop to Gjende Lake. You can lie down on the edge and study the tourist boat patrolling the lake 400 metres below, or you can look up at Besseggen where the rocky slopes are teeming with people almost like an anthill in warm spring sunshine.

The higher you climb, the more glorious the view, and now you can see with your own eyes what everyone talks about, the difference in colour of the water of Bessvatn Lake in the north and Gjende Lake in the south. While Gjende's

Many people consider the panorama from the mountain Surtningssui as the most magnificent in Jotunheimen. This is a view to the west. Photo: Tom Schandy.

Besseggen is Jotunheimen's most well-known walking trail. From the top there is a fantastic view over Jotunheimen with the lakes Gjende to the left and Bessvatn to the right. Photo: Tom Schandy.

confirmed at Gjende Lake and Russvatn Lake where there are traces of settlements from 3000 BC. Today Jotunheimen is perhaps the most popular national park for mountain trekking with more marked trails here than in any other mountain district, as well as tourist cabins, either staffed, no-service or self-service, which provide ample accommodation. The Norwegian Trekking Association is one of the main operators in the Jotunheimen but there are also a number of private cabins. There is a wide range of tours both summer and winter, either in easy terrain or tougher surroundings on the way to the summits, or on roped treks over glaciers. In fact, something for everyone whether a novice or an experienced summit rambler.

green colour is due to the particles of slam from glacial rivers, Bessvatn Lake is not fed by glaciers and the water is therefore clear and blue.

To the very top at 2,469 metres

At 2,469 metres Galdhøpiggen is Norway's and Northern Europe's highest mountain and there are two starting points for a climb to the top: the tourist cabins Spiterstulen and Juvasshytta. To be explicit, the route from Spiterstulen is the hardest and the top is a long way off when you start the climb which takes you through 1,500 metres of elevation. On the other hand, from Juvasshytta which lies at 1,850 metres amsl, there are only 600 metres of elevation to the top, but severing the cabin from the summit is the Styggebre Glacier which is beautiful to look at but dangerous to walk on because of possible crevasses. To cross this glacier you must join a guided tour and not attempt to walk on it alone.

The panorama from the top of Norway's highest mountain is marvellous and no other place in the country can boast such a crown of summits exceeding 2,000 metres. The view covers approximately 35,000 square kilometres and it is claimed that on a clear day one can gaze over a ninth of Norway lying south of Trondheim.

To the east there is another mountain, Glittertind, whose actual top as a rule measures higher than Galdhøpiggen, but it is a question of ice and not rock which makes Galdhøpiggen the highest point of land in Norway. And not only in Norway. It is the highest point between Greenland and West Siberia, a distance of 188 degrees of longitude or 10,000 kilometres. Galdhøpiggen is also the highest mountain north of the Carpathian Mountains and this comprises 48 degrees of latitude or over half the distance from the North Pole to the Equator.

Wild mountain scenery

Depending on how one defines a 2,000 metre summit, between 80 and 90 per cent of the 300 summits of this description in Norway are in the Jotunheimen. The wildest mountain scenery is in Hurrungane on the western edge with its knife blade ridges, dizzying cirques and pointed mountains and here alone are 24 summits over 2,000 metres, Store Skagastølstind at 2,405 metres amsl, is Norway's third highest mountain. Norway's seventh highest mountain is Surtningssui at 2,368 metres amsl and is well worth a visit. Starting from Memurubu in the centre of the national park the walk takes an estimated five hours up and three hours down, and although the climb engulfs many metres of elevation you will not need climbing equipment or glacier experience.

Popular for thousands of years

Jotunheimen has a long history,

Ormtjernkampen
Norway's smallest national park

Norway's smallest national park at barely 9 square kilometres was formally established in the summer of 1968 in Gausdal Municipality in Oppland County. The park's natural environment, with primeval forest and mountain scenery typical of the east of Norway, has kept its unspoiled character.

Giving the park its name, Ormtjernkampen Mountain (1,128 metres amsl) rises steeply beside the Dokkvatn Lake and then stretches southwards in a long hill. A walk to the top can be recommended for its all-round panorama and the fantastic view of the protected area. On the east side of this mountain the terrain is both steep and stony and here one can find the most characteristic primeval forest. In addition to Ormtjernkampen the other high mountains in the park are Snæreskampen and Dokkampen lying at respectively 1,084 and 1,122 metres amsl.

Ordinary species and a curiosity

The vegetation in the national park consists mainly of the usual species which thrive at this altitude on nutrient poor bedrock. No real rarities, but some of the good old friends like harebells, cow-wheat, lily of the valley, whorled Solomon's seal, field gentian, red campion, alpine cinquefoil and alpine bartsia. On the open, sunny localities in Omrtjernkampen National Park a distinctive, rare flower grows and deserves to be mentioned. It is the bearded bellflower which is a relative of the harebell and quite a curiosity. The abundant white hairs on the inside of these hanging, blue bells have given the flower its name and apart from growing in a few places in the neighbouring municipalities, the mysterious bearded bellflower does not grow anywhere else in Norway or Scandinavia, the closest occurrences being in the Alps and Carpathian Mountains.

Primeval forest interior in Ormtjernkampen National Park. Photo: Tom Schandy.

The Ormtjernsetra mountain farms are a good starting point for exploring this small national park. Photo: Tom Schandy.

❧ FACTS ❧

Ormtjernkampen National Park comprises an area of mountain and forest in Gausdal Municipality in Oppland County. At 9 square kilometres it is Norway's smallest national park.

Attractions:
· The Ormtjernkampen Mountain (1,128 metres amsl)
· Primeval forest
· Bearded bellflower
· Birds of prey

Maps:
Touring map "Jotunheimens for-gård (Jotunheimen's Forecourt) " 1: 100 000, and "Velkommen til (Welcome to) Gausdal Vestfjell" 1: 50 000.

Access:
Gausdal's national park lies right beside the road linking Holsbru Café and Liomseter in Gausdal Vestfjell, west of Dokkvatn Lake. The best access in the summer is to follow Vestfjellveien (Road 204) and then turn down a side road towards Ormtjernsetra, about one kilometre west of Holsbru. At Holsbru Café remember to borrow (for a small fee) the key to the bar across the privately owned side road.

Biological diversity

The bird life in the national park consists of a number of species typically occurring in conifer forests. These include the trusting Siberian jay and the three-toed woodpecker, easily recognised by its yellow crown. This woodpecker nearly always makes its home in old-growth conifer forest where it finds food under the bark of dead or dying spruces. If you spot rows of small holes in the bark of a spruce you know that the three-toed woodpecker has been drinking the nutritious resin straight from the tree. Old woodpecker nesting holes are of untold value for other birds such as tits and the common red-start who make these their homes. Ormtjernkampen's diversity and various biotopes provides opportunities to see a northern goshawk in the old-growth forest, a rough-legged buzzard soaring in blue summer sky or a merlin streaking past in its lightning attempts to catch small birds. Waders such as the common snipe, greenshank and redshank have their haunts in the park's damper areas, while the golden plover feels more at home on the drier territory over the tree line.

One-flowered wintergreen thrives in the old-growth forest.
Photo: Tom Schandy.

Recreational values

Although lovers of the outdoors can stroll in the silence of Ormtjern-kampen National Park's unspoiled countryside all year round, it is easier to do so in the summer months. If you visit the primeval forest areas in the park you should do as the poet Theodor Caspari recommended: "creep among the low-lying mosses". Those who like walking and studying nature can explore a moss-covered fallen tree trunk which is swarming with life, including a number of lichen and fungus species as well as insects and other minute creatures, because this area of outstanding nature is in ecological balance. "The hillside forests fall when the autumn storms rage. New forests grow from the seeds that constantly fall", (Haakon Lie, Forest Manager)

Plans for expansion

The Norwegian Parliament would like to expand the protected area to include neighbouring areas also worthy of conservation. Mapping of the flora, vegetation and nature types has therefore been carried out recently in the area under consideration which totals approximately 1,564 square kilometres in the municipalities of Gausdal, Etnedal, Nordre Land, Nord-Aurdal, Øystre Slidre, Nor-Fron and Sør-Fron. Characteristic of the area is the dome-shaped mountain ridges and the large number of marshlands. Only the future can reveal the size of the expansion of Ormtjernkampen National Park, but at least the natural values of the area will be thoroughly documented in the ensuing report.

21

Vassfaret
Vast forests and glittering lakes

This side valley off Hedal Valley in Valdres is known for its numerous conservation areas, bears, vacated wilderness farms, good fishing, vast watercourses and not least Mikkjel Fønhus. These were the realms of this famous author of the wilds.

Vassfaret, steeped in legend, lies on the border between Hallingdal and Valdres and the counties of Buskerud and Oppland. Human activity here dates back to the Black Death in 1349 and there were permanent settlements from the middle of the 1700's until 1921. People have lived in altogether 10 different settlements and 20 to 30 summer mountain dairy farms have been in operation. Today houses only remain on the old smallholdings at Bjørke, Amundheimen, Vassfarplassen (Mikkelsplassen) and Olsonheimen, while Aurdalssetrene and Hansesprang are the most well-known mountain dairy farms where the houses still stand. The existing rafting dams are proof that the valley sustained forestry and timber rafting for over 300 years. The watercourse is also recognised for its good fishing, something exploited by both the inhabitants in this wild valley and the village people nearby. Today one can buy a fishing licence and try one's luck in the many deep pools and lakes throughout the valley.

Large areas of protected landscape

Where then does this side valley off Hedal Valley begin? If we follow the watercourse, the lakes Hangen and Teinevannene in the border area towards Nes Municipality in Buskerud County are the uppermost sources. Otherwise the local inhabitants consider that Vassfaret starts at the big lake called Strøen, continues down the Strøelv River to Suluvann Lake and further into the two Grunntjern Tarns down to Nevlingen Lake. The old mill standing beside Grunntjernsfoss Waterfall is a voice from the past, and this is approximately where the valley changes direction and veers from north-south to east-west. Stretching from Nevlingen Lake via Skrukkefylla and the more than four kilometres long Aurdalsfjord Lake, the valley floor is so gentle that the river hardly gains any speed before the last kilometres down to Hedal Valley. Vassfaret proper is altogether 25 to 30 kilometres long and the county boundary between Buskerud and Oppland follows the watercourse all the way down to the Aurdal Dam.

The author and nature-lover Mikkjel Fønhus wrote in 1971, "*Vassfaret is one of the most typical forest and mountain districts*

Nevlingen Lake lies in the heart of Vassfaret. Photo: Tom Schandy.

Panorama from Vassfarfjella in Flå looking towards the Vassfardal Valley and the Aurdalsfjord Lake. Photo: Tom Helgesen.

we have in Eastern Norway". His eternal hope was that Vassfaret would be made one of Norway's national parks. But he hoped in vain. However in 1985 a protected area of approximately 26,000 hectares (65,000 acres) was established, though mainly as a landscape protection area where ordinary forestry including clear-felling and road-building were allowed. The building of holiday cabins is not

allowed inside the limits of the conservation area and the watercourse is protected against development of hydro-electric power. As this is a side valley off a side valley there has been very little development here with no large cabin parks or downhill ski slopes, and the valley's distinctive original atmosphere makes it different to most of the other valleys in Eastern Norway.

The Vassfaret and Vidalen Landscape Protection Area comprises approximately 20,000 hectares (50,000 acres) while the size of the Indre Vassfaret Landscape Protection Area is approximately 4,200 hectares (10,500 acres). In connection with the conservation plans for these areas of nature a separate cultural conservation plan has been made for around 800 hectares (2,000 acres) of forest in the Indre Vassfaret Landscape Protection Area. In the spring the forestry is carried out in the old way using horses and timber floating and the release of the timber into the watercourse attracts a lot of people. The purpose of this is to preserve and recreate some of the environment from that era, at the same time as knowledge concerning previous working methods is passed on to new generations.

A total of 9 nature reserves have been established in Vassfaret and apart from Bringen, where the main purpose is to preserve the old-growth conifer forest that resembles a primeval forest, all the reserves are established to look after the areas where the bears have their winter lairs. Unfortunately the protection probably came too late as the bear counts in the beginning of the 1990's revealed that the last entirely Norwegian bear breed was extinct. All the same in 2005 it was documented that there were at least two different bears in this area. Perhaps in a few years time yet another bear cub will squint at the spring sunshine from a lair in the higher slopes of the conifer forest.

A recreational paradise in all seasons

In the winter Vassfaret is fantastic for skiing even though there are no

prepared ski trails and in the summer the long lakes invite exploration by kayak or canoe. Paths lead down to the valley from several places along its length and cycling is possible from Veneli in Flå and Hedal Valley in Sør-Aurdal.

Even though the protection of Vassfaret is not quite what the nature conservationists hoped for, the countryside is still magnificent and diverse with forests, mountains, lakes, rivers and marshland. If in the autumn you look across from Aurdalsfjord Lake at the settlement at Bjørke, or from the high mountain farm at Hansesprang and gaze down into the valley, Mikkjel Fønhus's word are more than applicable: *"One must travel far in this country to find a piece of Norwegian nature equal to this".*

The river between the tarns Øvre and Nedre Grunntjern. Photo: Tom Schandy.

22

Trillemarka-Rollagsfjell
In Theodor Kittelsen's wilderness

Trillemarka and the Rollagsfjell Mountains are sandwiched between the valleys of Sigdal and Numedal in Buskerud and together form Southern Norway's largest area of old-growth forest. Dancing fairies and Kittelsen figures hide behind every bush.

The painter of fairy-tales, Theodor Kittelsen, lived in Lauvlia beside the Soneren Lake in Sigdal. From here he could look right across at the lonely mountain Andersnatten, which took on the shape of a gigantic troll in the hours of dusk. However, behind this familiar landmark there is a forest and mountain region which in its untouched state is even more in keeping with Kittelsen's fantasy world. Among 43 known areas worthy of conservation and exceeding 10 square kilometres, Trillemarka and Rollagsfjell is the largest and most valuable in Southern Norway. It comprises 205 square kilometres of uninterrupted mountain and old-growth forest, Trillemarka being Southern Norway's last more or less intact long valley. Large parts of this region are free of encroachment, that is to say that any technical interference is 1 to 3 kilometres away, and this creates a feeling of being in the middle of a wilderness, unusual for the central areas of Eastern Norway.

Species on the Norwegian red list
Old, twisted pines reach towards the sky and on one of them the yellowy-

Sunrise over Trillemarka. Photo: Tom Schandy.

A walk in Trillemarka's primeval forest imbues a feeling of the wilderness. Photo: Tom Schandy.

green lichen Letharia vulpine, otherwise known as wolf lichen, grows, telling its own special story about the wilds. This lichen which loves old-growth forests contains vulpine acid, a strong poison which attacks the nervous system. As the name suggests this was used in the olden days to kill wolves. In a hollow in the terrain a group of spruces huddle together making a pocket of primeval forest and a habitat for another species of lichen, Usnea longissima also called hanging moss or Methuselah's beard lichen, and could easily be the forerunner to tinsel. These are only 2 of the 72 species found in this area which are on the Norwegian red list. Among the listed birds are the lesser spotted woodpecker, goshawk, stock dove, crane and golden eagle.

However, there are other birds than those which are red-listed, who make a visit to this area a pleasant experience. It is always a delight to meet the trusting Siberian jay when it suddenly appears begging to share your sandwiches. The drumming of the three-toed woodpecker is a welcome sound and if you look carefully at the trees you might find rings of holes where it has pierced the bark for the resin.

Varied walking terrain

Trillemarka offers a variety of different walks with its undulating landscape of hilltops and valleys at varying heights. Vardefjell is just one of the many vantage points and its neighbour a little to the east, Venlifjell, provides a fantastic panorama over the Trilledal Valley, where the lakes lie one after the other, starting in the east with Haslitjern, then Skoddøltjern, Grunntjern, Vindolvann, Danmark, Buvatn and Storvatn.

The Rollagsfjell Mountains to the south are less undulating, with steep rocks jutting upwards and, not least, valuable areas with old-growth forest and threatened species. A climb brings you to the top of Geiteskallen at 886 metres amsl and from the top of Langseterfjell Mountain there is a view over the entire Rollagsfjell Mountains

Trillemarka is at its best when dusk descends and Kittelsen's elves begin to dance, the silence punctuated with the plaintive whistle of the pygmy owl. Then you understand the importance of such areas.

A hiker appreciates the view over Trillemarka. Photo: Tom Schandy.

23

Skarvheimen
Border district between east and west

The colossal mountain mass between Jotunheimen and the Hardangervidda Mountain Plateau is now called Skarvheimen, an area harbouring the gentleness of the eastern Norwegian mountains as well as steep precipices and valleys more akin to the landscape in Western Norway. In the autumn 2006 parts of this area were protected as Hallingskarvet National Park.

Skarvheimen is a constructed name and can cause confusion, but the old mountain names, Hallingskarvet, Reineskarvet, Finse, Bygdin and Tyin are more familiar, and all these areas belong to Skarvheimen. Smaller mountain regions within Skarvheimen have more local names such as Nordfjella, Aurlandsfjella, Hemsedalsfjella and Filefjell.

The mountain tops are remains of a gigantic sliver of rock which in the ancient world was ripped off the northwest edge of Norway and pushed against several regions, one of which was Skarvheimen. External forces have whittled away most of it over the years and only isolations of hard rock types remain.

Name with a double meaning
Of course it was no coincidence to name the area Skarvheimen. Several of the mountain names in the region include 'skarv', such as Reineskarvet (1,788 metres amsl) and Hallingskarvet (1,933 metres amsl). It appears that there are almost 20 other mountain names that include 'skarv', which is a local description of a mountain

Reineskarvet also belongs to Skarvheimen. Photo: Tom Schandy.

which has at least one precipitous side. Furthermore, the local name for the rock ptarmigan is 'skarv', a species which thrives in sterile, inhospitable mountain regions. It has one enemy, the gyrfalcon – a bird often observed in this barren landscape.

It is more fertile under steep rock faces and in valleys mountain valleys where lush oases of botanical jewels find a home, for example around Strandavatn Lake and on the south side of Hallingskarvet. The 400 plant species registered around Finse share the area with reindeer. Collectively called the Nordfjella area for wild reindeer, the winter herds here can number 2,000 animals. There are occurrences of wolverines on Skarvheimen and it is also possible to meet the endangered arctic fox. Arctic foxes constantly visit the mountain lodge, Geiterygghytta, for food, but these animals are apparently tame foxes which after escaping are now reproducing in the wild, at times even underneath the mountain lodge.

Worthy of protection

Hallingskarvet with a total length of 35 kilometres is the most impressive mountain in Skarvheimen and contains the highest summit, Folarskardnuten at 1,933 metres amsl, which is easy to climb by approaching Folarskardet from Raggsteinhytta Mountain Lodge in the north. Hallingskarvet is a relatively large continuous area of nature with few technical encroachments and in order to look after this valuable natural and traditional cultivated landscape Hallingskarvet National Park, measuring 450 square kilometres, was established in the autumn 2006.

The national park embraces the actual Hallingskarv Plateau and the mountain regions westwards to Låghellerhøgdene north-west of Finse. Most of the area is in Buskerud County but the park also penetrates the counties of Hordaland, and Sogn and Fjordane.

Norway's highest lake, Flakavatn at 1,448 metres amsl and 75 metres deep, is in the western region of Hallingskarvet, which also hosts Kyrkjedøra, the knifeedge pass said to be a part of the old Episcopal road when Valdres and Hallingdal came under the Stavanger diocese.

The lords' cabins

In the second half of the 1800's Lord Garvagh and his son of the same name, two Irish noblemen, hunters and anglers, erected several fine stone cabins in Skarvheimen. These two men loved the Norwegian mountains and are said to have built 10 huts in this mountain region. Lordehytta on Folarskardet at 1,620 metres amsl is probably the most famous and still functions as an excellent shelter in the variable weather conditions on Hallingskarvet.

From cabin to cabin

Skarvheimen is an El Dorado for skiers and hikers, who can for example start from Tyin in the north and journey south to Haugastøl or Finse. A detour passes Reineskarvet and ends at Rødungstølen and Bergsjøstølen in Ål, while walkers going westwards will stop at Hallingskeid or nearly down in Aurland (see separate chapter about the Aurlandsdal Valley). The Norwegian Trekking Association and private hostels can offer good food and comfortable beds along these routes. In the summer the red "T"-marks are easy to follow while during the winter it is safest to follow the staked trails.

Lordehytta on Folarskardet (1,620 metres amsl) is probably the most famous of the stone huts which the two Lord Garvagh, senior and junior, built. These two Irish noblemen, hunters and anglers travelled around Skarvheimen in the last half of the 1800's. Photo: Tom Helgesen.

24

Hardangervidda
Northern Europe's largest mountain plateau

The Hardangervidda Mountain Plateau's diversity ranges from wide open plains and rounded hill tops in the east to deep valleys and waterfalls in the west and this is the home of Europe's largest herd of wild reindeer.

This undulating mountain plateau spread between the counties of Buskerud, Hordaland and Telemark gives you a tremendous sensation of freedom, whether you are trying your luck with a fishing rod in the hundreds of trout lakes, or hiking along the "T"-marked trails towards one of the many tourist cabins or lodges run by the Norwegian Trekking Association. Another way to enjoy this outstanding scenery is to canoe or kayak along the long and flat watercourses of the Nordmannslågen River, Sønstevann Lake or Kalhovdfjord Lake. Skiing from cabin to cabin in the winter is very popular, especially at Easter when the accommodation can be quite crowded.

Large national park

The Hardangervidda Mountain Plateau borders to the Bergen Railway in the north, the fjords Eidfjord/Sørfjord in the west, Røldal/ Møsvatn Lake/Vestfjorddal Valley in the south and the Tessungdal Valley/Uvdal/Dagali in the east. In 1981 3,422 square kilometres of the Hardangervidda Mountain Plateau were protected and became Norway's largest national park. Moreover the landscape protection areas Skaupsjø/Hardangerjøkulen (see sepa-

Midsummer and campfire beside Langesjø Lake, one of the flattest parts of the Hardangervidda Mountain Plateau. Hårteigen Mountain in the distance. Photo: Tom Helgesen.

rate chapter on the Hardanger-jøkul Icecap) and Møsvatn Aust-fjell were established.

The plant life on the plateau is extremely varied. The beautiful mountain avens, snow cinquefoil, alpine milk-vetch and northern milk-vetch dominate in the lime-rich belt surrounding the tourist lodges at Hellevassbu, Litlos and Stavali in the west of the plateau, with 140 flowering plants registered around Litlos alone. However it is also quite lush in the limey soil in the east a good example being in the district around Rauhelleren Mountain Lodge.

Old hunting constructions, pit traps and stone built hides for the hunters with bow and arrow tell us that people have hunted wild reindeer here for thousands of years. At present there are 250 known Stone Age settlements on the Hardangervidda Mountain Plateau, the oldest said to be over 8,000 years old. The size of the wild reindeer herd has fluctuated violently, the present target being a winter herd numbering around 10,000 animals. In the spring and early summer the reindeer prefer the west side of the plateau, where they also give birth, but the autumn and winter grazing, because of low snow falls, is usually on the east side towards Numedal and in Tinn and Vinje in Telemark.

Tours and approaches

Such a vast area of nature and the great outdoors is bound to have many access points. Both Haukeli-seter and Kalhovd/Mårbu tourist lodges are good alternatives for an approach from the south, while in the east the lodges at Iming-fjell, Solheimstølen and Seterdalen can be recommended. All the stations along the Bergen Railway

Fjord horses at Hadlaskard with Hårteigen Mountain (1,690 metres amsl) in the background. Photo: Tom Schandy.

offer good starting points from the north, and several places along the Sørfjord (an arm of the Hardangerfjord) provide ideal access from the west. The enormous watercourses, Kinso, Opo, Veig, Kvenna and Dagli are protected although they are outside the national park. The Kinso watercourse can be enjoyed by walking from Kinsarvik and up all the hills to the Stavali Tourist Lodge run by Bergen Turlag (trekking club), passing on the way through the lush and beautiful valley, Husedal. Higher up and along the River Kinso is a series of large spectacular waterfalls which indeed many people consider the finest in Norwegian nature. The trail from Lofthus to Stavali is also steep with abundant places of natural beauty and cultural monuments. The so-called "Monk's staircase" is quite unique and was probably built for packhorses with heavy loads by, according to the legend, the Cistercian monks from the Lyse Monastery in Bergen.

A network of marked summer walking trails and staked winter trails covers almost the entire Har-

dangervidda Mountain Plateau, Norwegian Trekking Association tourist cabins and lodges and privately run accommodation placed at reasonable distances for a day trip. Several of the hiking paths follow old travel routes, so-called tow roads, and they are the oldest thoroughfares between Hardanger and Telemark/Numedal along which wares and animals were transported between east and west for sale. The busiest traffic here was from the middle of the 1600's to the end of the 1800's especially when the Kongsberg Silver Mines were in their days of prosperity.

It is never difficult to find the peace and quiet of solitude on Europe's largest mountain plateau. There is perhaps nothing more magnificent than watching the sun set behind Hårteigen Mountain (1,690 metres amsl) in the west. Hårteigen Mountain is nicknamed the "grey signpost" and is the most distinctive mountain in the whole of the plateau. The tourist cabins, Litlos and Torehytta, are good starting points for a walk to the top of Hårteigen, which is well

worth the effort in fine weather with its splendid panorama over Sandfloeggi, the Hardangerjøkul Icecap, Hallingskarvet and the Gausta Mountain.

25

Blefjell Mountains

Family-friendly range of mountains on the border between Buskerud and Telemark

Bordering the Buskerud and Telemark counties and sporting a mixture of mountain and mountain forest, the beautiful Blefjell Mountains have something for everyone. The massif, Storeble, can offer harsh mountain scenery and desolate regions, while Vesleble is more family-friendly and gently undulating.

Outdoor enthusiasts connect positively to the names Strutåsen, Krøkla, Vasshølet, Gunnulfsbu and Søtdalsseter and Blefjell is the nearest mountain region for a large number of inhabitants in Eastern Norway. Many people associate oranges, cocoa, coffee brewed over a campfire and packed lunch with Easter skiing on Blefjell, this being the most popular time for ski tours crossing the Vesleble range, while Storeble offers more challenges as well as peace and quiet for those who like longer tours.

Winter forest on the Blefjell Mountains with the Storeble Massif as a backdrop. Photo: Tom Schandy.

Two plateaus

Whereas the lower regions of the plateau lie at between 600 and 700 metres amsl, there is quite an elevation in the terrain up to the summits on the Storeble range at 1,300 metres. The highest of these is Bletoppen at 1,342 metres amsl, easily approached from the Kongsberg and District Trekking Association's tourist cabin, Sigridsbu. All the summits on the Storeble range provide a magnificent panorama in fine weather, but remember that these mountains with steep drops in the south and west are dangerous in bad weather. Amazingly enough, the Blefjell Mountain range has its own wild reindeer herd, which numbers around 150 animals in the winter. The reindeer usually keep to the area between the Ble Fjellstue Mountain Lodge in the south and Sørkje Lake in the Rollag Municipality in the north. Animals wandering to and from the Hardangervidda Mountain Plateau can occur, but this is uncertain at the present time due to development and disturbances around important trekking routes.

The Vesleble range is gentler and undulating, speckled in a pattern of marshes and small lakes, a terrain which is ideal for skiing in the winter, something which many people do. 3,000 to 4,000 private cabins as well as a number of tourist companies in the area means crowded ski routes on a fine winter day.

Two cabins run by the trekking association

The Blefjell Mountains are not just snow and skiing despite a network of 185 kilometres of marked trails and a further 50 kilometres of marked summer routes. Kongsberg and District Trekking Association have two splendid tourist cabins available for use all year round, Sigridsbu high and exposed at 1,100 metres amsl at the south end of the Storeble range, and Eriksbu (940 metres amsl) a four-hour march north, nestling beside the Åkli Lakes. Both cabins are no-service (without provisions) but otherwise containing everything a trekker might need – just remember the Norwegian Trekking Association's master key to open the door. The cabins are in fact part of the long distance trail between Kongsberg and the Hardangervidda Mountain Plateau and it is possible to walk for several days either northwards or southwards.

The summer trail between the cabins Sigridsbu and Eriksbu passes two remarkable stones standing beside each other. Called the Stone Brothers the legend tells that these were two brothers working on the summer mountain farm at Gunnulfsbu, who were unfortunate enough to lose their way and were turned to stone while they argued about where they were.

The Blefjell Mountains have several beautiful waterfalls, but none of them compare to the Juvfoss Waterfall in free fall. It can almost seem sinister and dangerous as it cascades over a 30 to 40 metre drop filling the steep mountain sides with white spray. However, due to regulation this waterfall, which runs into the Numedalslågen River in the Flesberg Municipality, is only at its best in the spring thaw and periods of flooding.

A golden eagle has found a dead red fox. Blefjell Mountains in the background. Photo: Tom Schandy.

26

Presterødkilen and Ilene
Internationally important bird localities

The nature reserves Presterødkilen and Ilene in Tønsberg Municipality in Vestfold County are two of the Oslofjord's most significant wetlands. Both reserves are on the Ramsar Convention's List of internationally important wetlands.

Observations of bird species total 234 at Presterødkilen and 253 at Ilene, despite the proximity of the town. Even more impressive is the rarity of some of these species, for example the little bittern, little egret, short-toed eagle and red-footed falcon.

Endangered nature

Presterødkilen just east of Tønsberg is a shallow fjord arm where the low tide reveals vast mudflats. Around its edges grow thick reed beds, while roads, buildings and industry pressurise the outskirts. When the area was preserved in

Presterødkilen is on the Ramsar Convention's list of internationally important wetlands. Photo: Tom Schandy.

1969 Presterødkilen was in the process of being asphyxiated by waste disposal and sewage. One would think that 40 years of conservation would bring the area out of danger, but this is not so. Only recently the Norwegian Highway Authority suggested building a 4-lane carriageway right beside the reserve, and it remains to be seen if this will be carried out.

Innermost in the fjord arm, west of Tønsberg is Ilene, a delta of brackish water dominated by open areas of shallow water with eel-grass and green algae. Extensive coastal meadows, showing signs of grazing and partly overgrown with reeds, surround the mouth of the Aulielv River. The area was preserved by royal decree as long ago as 1947 and gained its present nature conservation status in 1981.

Popular with waders

Together, Presterødkilen and Ilene comprise vital grazing and resting

Bird-watching tower at Ilene. Photo: Tom Schandy.

grounds for swans, geese, ducks and waders, the latter finding the vast mud flats extremely attractive. There are not many places in Norway one can study such a variety

The common shelduck thrives in the shallows like those found at Presterødkilen. Photo: Tom Schandy.

of wader species, ranging from the little stint measuring 14 centimetres to the Eurasian curlew at 60 centimetres, as at these two nature reserves. During the migration period one can observe oystercatchers, common snipes, wood sandpipers, greenshanks, common sandpipers, dunlins, ruffs as well as the northern tundra and taiga species from Siberia such as spotted redshanks, jack snipes, bar-tailed godwits, sanderlings, knots and grey plovers.

The time to observe waders must be chosen with care. They can mostly be seen in the autumn, but be aware that they start flying south quite early. Around the middle of August the reserves are packed with small waders hectically running around on the mudflats looking for food. The best migration period for waders lasts from the end of July to mid September.

The reed beds lining Presterød-

kilen conceal the homes of marshland bird species including the water rail, spotted crake and reed warbler. The latter established itself here in the early 1950's and despite its rather insignificant appearance it sings an exceptional song during the light June nights. If you go for a walk one of these light summer nights you may also hear the nightingale and other rare warblers, like the grasshopper warbler and the marsh warbler.

Getting a complete view over Presterødkilen is not easy but Træleborgodden in the south provides a good vantage point. Due to improved access via the industrial estate, it is possible to reach the north end where a bird-watching tower has recently been erected. This provides the best view of the extensive mud flats at low tide. Ilene also has a bird-watching tower with a panorama over the fjord and the restored crofter's farm, Søndre Holmen, where the Regional Commissioner runs an information centre for nature conservation and environmental protection.

27

The Vestfold Skerries
From the island of Løvøy to the Færder Lighthouse

When it comes to idyllic scenery and outstanding natural beauty the diversity of Vestfold County's skerries is almost equal to that of the south coast of Norway, the nature varying from sheltered bays and soft sandy beaches to exposed islands and white-crested waves.

The Vestfold Skerries stretch from Horten following the coastline south-west to Nevlunghavn. A long line of scenic islands such as Løvøy and Bastøy off Horten, Bolærne at Nøtterøy, Verdens Ende and Store Færder at Tjøme, Østerøy and Vesterøy outside Sandefjord and Svenner Lighthouse south-east of Stavern.

Island gems at Horten

Although the island of Løvøy beside Horten is today connected to the mainland, it still offers exciting nature and culture, being probably best known for the Løvøy Chapel (originally built in the 1200's) and the nearby sacred St. Olav's spring. There is a camping site and several cabins on this island, where the

There are many wonderful rocks and bathing places along the coast of Vestfold County. Photo: Tom Helgesen.

rare, legend-spun mistletoe and perfumed honeysuckle grow.

The island of Bastøy lies a little further south and nearly the entire island has the status of a landscape protection area, with preservation of the plant life and wildlife, or nature reserve and is typified by the unique, unspoiled coastal nature. In reality the Bastøy Jail uses the whole island, but the northern part including the Nordbukta bathing beach is a recreation area and some individual beach zones are open for limited public access. By advance agreement it is possible to take the ferry between Horten and Bastøy Island.

Defences and scenic beauty spots

The old defence works on Østre Bolærne Island are just off Nøtterøy. The commandant's house now functions as a tourist hostel where one can rent accommodation within the "Kystled" organisation which runs a network of tourist hostels and accommodation linked by coastal routes on land and at sea. The Oslofjord also has several linked destinations in this system. For those who do not have their own boat there is a daily boat service from Tønsberg during the school summer holidays from mid June to mid August. It is sheer paradise to lie on the smooth rocks facing out towards a calm Skagerrak Sea on a hot, cloudless sunny day, but Østre Bolærne is more than a beauty spot, it has a rich flora including the rare crested cow-wheat. This member of the figwort family has striking purple-red flowers with a yellow bottom lip and is found only five other places in Norway.

Another exciting island lies in the sea south-east of Tjøme. The lighthouse on Store Færder Island was first lit in the spring of 1697 but although it was moved to the neighbouring island, Lille Færder, a little to the south in 1857, the ruins of the lighthouse on Store Færder can still be seen and these were protected in 1997. The bird station, established on this island in 1973, carries out ringing of the migratory birds in the spring and autumn and more than 200 bird species have been observed here.

Verdens Ende is a protected area for recreation comprising approximately 25 hectares (62.5 acres) on the outermost tip of Tjøme. With its beautiful scenery, smooth rocks, small islands, fishing, good bathing and fantastic view of the sea this is a popular resort. A model of the old seesaw-lighthouse is probably the most photographed motif in the area, preferably with the Færder Lighthouse as a back drop. A long stone breakwater protects Tjøme's largest small boat harbour from wind and weather, and fishing boats often shelter there too. Moutmark recreation area north-west of Verdens Ende offers walks accompanied by a varied flora and abundant bird life.

The islands Østerøy and Vesterøy project like two fingers out of the Sandefjord Municipality. They are popular islands, with cabins and recreation areas and on the outermost point of Østerøy stands the Tønsberg Barrel, a beacon which probably got its name from its large barrel-like appearance from a distance.

Attractive recreation area

South-east of Stavern is Svenner Lighthouse which offers yet another tempting place to put into land along the coast of Vestfold County. Even people without their own boat can visit Svenner by using the boat service from Sta-vern during the tourist season. Numerous common eiders, several colonies of lesser black-backed gulls and herring gulls, great black-backed gulls and mew gulls nest on Svenner in May-June. The bird life on Svenner was protected by royal decree in 1935, and several rare species have been registered in periods when ringing is carried out, one of these finds being the first in Norway of the Bonnelli's warbler.

The outer Oslofjord has Norway's densest concentration of protected and recreational areas and it is important to remember that many of these islands are protected as seabird sanctuaries, which means that it is forbidden to go ashore between 15 April and 15 July. Any disturbances in these colonies can endanger the eggs or young birds if they are left exposed, whether the day is baking hot or freezing cold.

The common tern has caught a fish. A pleasant sight in the Vestfold Skerries. Photo: Tom Schandy.

28

Beech Forests in Larvik
Protected area with woodland park

The last tree to settle in Norway after the Ice Age was the beech, but the country has few beech forests. However in the Larvik district there are two of Norway's finest beech forests, one in the park surrounding Fritzøehus Manor and the other, Larvik's very own Beech Forest, lying between the fjord and the Farrisvann Lake.

The occurrences of beech in Vestfold County originate from natural seeding along the terminal moraine which accumulated after the last Ice Age, approximately 700 AD. Botanical study of pollen grains extracted from marshes has revealed that this forest existed before the time of the Vikings. In order to grow, the exclusive beech needs an average temperature of 11.5 degrees Celsius during June to September and easily drained moraine. The climate and soil in southern Vestfold is perfect for the beech tree which featured on the

The Beech Forest is especially beautiful in May as flowering white wood anemones carpet the forest floor before the leaves come and cast their shadow.
Photo: Øystein Søbye/NN/Samfoto.

town coat of arms for Larvik when it was still a separate municipality.

Beech and rare animals at Fritzøehus Manor

When the Fritzøehus Landscape Protection Area was established in 1980, the one purpose was to protect one of Norway's largest continuous beech forests (there are in fact twice as many trees here as in the neighbouring Beech Forest in Larvik) and the other was to preserve the splendid and varied surrounding nature and traditional cultivated landscape. Fritzøehus Manor and garden were built in the 1860's, the garden being laid out in the English style and it is home to many rare plants and trees such as hickory, Norway spruce and a creeping Korean fir with purple cones. In addition there are old avenues of oak, lime and birch as well as a larch grove.

The park's fauna is quite exceptional and includes grazing fallow deer and mouflon, the latter being a race of sheep that lives wild and is ancestor to Norway's own Old Norwegian Short Tail race. Fences dating originally back to 1920 stop the fallow deer and mouflon from spreading to other areas. Fritzøehus Park totals approximately 163 hectares (408 acres) of protected landscape and is thus safeguarded from encroachments that might change its character, for example, the building of new roads and other building construction. The entrance to the park is through the main manor gates on Road 302, Helgeroaveien. The park is open between 15 April and 1 October and by contacting Treschow-Fritzøe in advance you will be issued with an admission pass and a small information brochure.

Norway's first public park

In 1884 the Beech Forest in Larvik was given to the town's people by Chamberlain Treschow and became Norway's first public recreation area. For over 100 years the Beech Forest has served as a leisure area for Larvik's inhabitants in addition to being used for town festivals and celebrations. The network of footpaths and walks are in use all year round. The people of Larvik love their Beech Forest and on the national day (17 May) it is crammed with people. No wonder the Larvik town song contains the line: *"Where the beech's green canopy spreads on a sunny day in May ..."*.

The Beech Forest is also especially beautiful in May as flowering white wood anemones carpet the forest floor before the trees get their leaves and cast their shadow. A little later follows wood stitchwort, wood-sorrel and the may lily, all three thriving on the quite acidic soil. Some bird species are strongly attracted to beech forest, most typically the wood warbler, chaffinch and hawfinch, the latter although rare in Norway actually nests in the Beech Forest. The bird has an im-

mensely strong beak with a force of 50 kilograms capable of crushing cherry stones and chestnuts. In a mild winter free of snow the ground is littered with beechnuts which attract swarms of brambling to the Beech Forest.

This wonder of nature, one of Norway's most classic beech forest localities, was preserved as a landscape protection area in 1980. These beech forests are the type with an acidic soil (as opposed to a richer forest floor) marked by the abundant growth of wavy hairgrass, and a total area of almost 30 hectares (75 acres) of this type of beech forest is protected. In addition there are 90 burial mounds within this magnificent area of conservation, the eldest being from the time of the Vikings and is therefore over 1,000 years old

A walk in the Beech Forest. Photo: Ove Bergersen/NN/Samfoto.

29 ▸ Mølen
Pebble beaches and rare birds

Mølen lies on the southern edge of Vestfold County and sports Norway's largest pebble beach, old graves of kings, exciting botany and not least, rare birds. Mølen probably holds the Norwegian record for the number of bird species observed.

Large parts of Mølen are covered in gravel, fragments of the huge terminal moraine which can be traced from Finland, through Central Sweden, via Moss and Horten to Mølen, Jomfruland, Tromøya continuing further on land and sea along the coast to Finnmark. This immense gravel ridge arose where powerful masses of ice met the sea and deposited their loads of stones. Freed of the oppressive weight of the ice, the land rose and the terminal moraine climbed out of the sea. While the finer particles and small stones were washed away in the breakers, the large pebbles remained rubbing against each other in the waves and, over thousands of years, Norway's most magnificent and largest pebble beach took form. Winter or summer, it is a fantastic nature experience to stroll along this beach and the sight

Night mood on the pebble beach at Mølen. Photo: Tom Schandy.

of the waves washing over the stones in the sunset is a favourite motif among Norway's nature photographers.

However, the large piles of stones above the beach are the work of humans. These are burial mounds and there are almost 200 of them, the five largest towering 3 metres with a diameter of 30 metres. Although it is claimed that one of the so-called Vestfold Kings, known from Snorre's "Ynglinge-saga", might be buried here, significant finds have only been made in one of these mounds and these are boat rivets in a grave from 30 to 250 years AD.

Strategic position

The bird life on Mølen is unique and there is probably no other place in Norway that can boast more observed species, a total of 320 of which approximately 100 are nesting. During the summer one can observe the rare barred warbler in the low juniper bushes and thorn thickets on the peninsula and this bird has only a few other nesting sites in Norway.

However, during the spring and autumn migrations, Mølen really draws the benefit of its strategic position towards the Skagerrak which directs large numbers of migrating birds to the peninsula. In September to October up to 100,000 birds can pass just in the course of a few morning hours. High pressure areas and wind from the west give the best migration conditions and on such days it is not unusual to observe approximately 100 different bird species.

During this season the dominating species are finches and not least the common wood pigeon which can gather in several tens of thousands, in addition to the

The rare barred warbler nests extremely few places in Norway and one of them is at Mølen. Photo: Leif Rustand/NN/Samfoto.

numerous resting ducks in the area as well as divers, grebes, seabirds, waders and birds of prey. On a good day one can see over 100 common buzzards and rough-legged buzzards in migration. However, most birds do not migrate southwards, but westwards as they try to stay over land as long as possible, following the south coast before they finally turn and cross the sea to Denmark.

Forceful south-westerly winds in the autumn press large numbers of seabirds towards Mølen and one can observe northern gannets, kittiwakes and fulmars and even a rare sooty shearwater. It is in fact the rarer species which have placed Mølen on the ornithological map due to the number of first-occurrence sightings of bird species in Norway, including the black-winged pratincole, red-flanked bluetail, calandra lark, lesser-spotted eagle and willet. The ornithological sta-

tion was established at Mølen in 1976, and since then more than 160,000 birds have been ringed.

Mølen's plant life is also exceptional and you can find rarities such as henbane, an old medicinal plant which was used to cure toothache. In the early summer the rocks and coastal meadows are tinged pink by thousands and thousands of flowering thrift and in the gravel on the outermost point of Mølen you can come upon vast carpets of a low growing plant with blue-green leaves and light blue flowers with a touch of red inside. This is the oyster plant, quite common in the north and rare in the south. Sea kale, garden angelica and sea dodder are other specialities, the latter being a parasite feeding off other plants and a few sea dodder plants can create several kilometres of stems and branches.

You do not have to be a botanist or ornithologist to enjoy Mølen. It is enough to walk in the open landscape or bathe from a lovely sheltered beach. Mølen has something for everyone!

30

Jomfruland
Island jewel off the Telemark coast

There is something special about Jomfruland, this long narrow island outermost in the Kragerø skerries. 65 people have their homes here, five farms are in operation and the nature is unique with luxuriant flora, abundant bird life, sandy beaches and pebbles. It is a tiny piece of Denmark which has weighed anchor in the open sea off the coast of Telemark.

Jomfruland, measuring a length of 7.5 kilometres, is 1 kilometre across at the broadest point and covers an area of 3.3 square kilometres. It is part of the terminal moraine formed during the last Ice Age between 10,000 and 11,000 years ago, stretching from Vestfold to Aust-Agder. Jomfruland consists of a flat ridge with sediments that were pushed together on the ocean floor in front of the inland ice, which explains why the highest point on the island reaches all of 15 metres amsl. There are only a few places with bare bedrock, but on the pebble beach there are rocks from large parts of Southern Norway. These were brought here with the glacier or transported on floating icebergs, and a stroll on the pebble beach can be very rewarding even in unpleasant weather as not only is it exciting to study all the different rocks but also to be at the mercy of the elements out here in the open sea.

Exceptional flora and fauna

However, most people associate Jomfruland with summer, sunshine and bathing, not storms. A favourable climate combined with a special and varied nature provides a special and varied flora and fauna. The white carpets of wood anemones covering the floor of the deciduous forests in May are famous and there are few other places in Norway which can equal this floral magnificence. There are also splendid hazel forests where the local squirrels have a field day in the autumn when the nuts are ripe.

Despite Jomfruland's relatively small size, the bird life is also quite unique with as many as 92 species registered nesting, of which between 40 and 50 nest annually. A total of 300 different bird species have been observed on Jom-

Flowering horse chestnut in a traditional cultivated landscape on Jomfruland. Photo: Svein Grønvold/NN/Samfoto.

Sea holly grows on Jomfruland. It is a rare plant and on the Norwegian red list of endangered species. Photo: Baard Næss/NN/Samfoto.

fruland and in the spring and early summer the thickets and woods are teeming with warblers and other passerine birds. This is one of the barred warbler's westernmost habitats in Europe and the rare greenish warbler nested here for the first time in Norway in 1992. Jomfruland is also the only place in Norway where the splendid yellow-coloured golden oriole visits every year, which explains why the bird station uses this bird in its logo. Jomfruland Bird Station, one of Norway's most active, was established in 1969 and during the major bird migration over the island in the spring and autumn it is the perfect place for ringing, registering and surveying the bird life.

Between 7,000 and 12,000 birds are caught and ringed at the station every year. Some of the birds that are caught here have been ringed in other places in Norway or abroad and by coordinating these finds with the birds caught at Jomfruland the movements of the birds can be mapped. A great many bird species have their natural migration route directly over Jomfruland and the island is the first piece of land they reach in the spring after leaving Denmark, and the last land they see in the autumn. Not only ornithologists and botanists have let themselves be fascinated by Jomfruland. At the tarn, Tårntjenna, the artist Theodor Kittelsen found the motifs for his famous painting "Nøkken" – The Water Sprite.

A lighthouse and a beautiful traditional cultivated landscape

Jomfruland Lighthouse Station was established in 1839 and has two lighthouses, one from 1839 and the other 1938. These are of course two landmarks (respectively 22 and 37 metres high) on this flat island. Apart from the lighthouse which is constructed in cast iron, the rest of the buildings are made of wood and all of them are now protected. The actual lighthouse station was made automatic in 1991 and the people moved out, but the old lighthouse is open to the public for guided tours in the summer season.

In addition to the beautiful and varied nature on Jomfruland there is a splendid traditional cultivated landscape and a lot of exciting history. Jomfruland and Stråholmen, an island lying to the north-east, are included in a national registration of valuable traditional cultivated landscapes and among the five high priority areas in Telemark. There are information boards at the entrance to the protected area in the north of the island. The Telemark County Regional Commissioner's department for the environment has laid out nature and culture footpaths so that people can experience parts of Jomfruland and with a brochure telling you all about the island's fantastic nature and diverse history in your hand you can start your walk either at Tårnbrygga or Øitangen.

Motor traffic and tenting

The island has special rules for motor vehicles. Motor traffic is not allowed in the protected landscape and car driving is strictly regulated on the rest of the island. Only the people who live there are permitted utility driving, while day visitors are definitely not allowed to use their car on the island, al-

though it is permitted to drive to and from overnight accommodation for a small fee (NOK 150,-). A bicycle is the best way to get around and can be recommended. The nature on Jomfruland is extremely vulnerable and tenting is only permitted on the camp site, something which is clearly stated in the management plan for the landscape protection area.

A male common goldcrest, Norway's smallest bird, photographed in connection with ringing at Jomfruland Bird Station. Photo: Baard Næss/NN/Samfoto.

31

Gausta Mountain and Brattefjell-Vindeggen
Landmark and home to wild reindeer

Gausta Mountain is probably Norway's most well-known mountain summit and can be seen from almost the whole of Eastern Norway. The summit at 1,883 metres amsl towers like a pyramid to the north. South-west of the mountain the wilderness areas surrounding Vindeggen (1,516 metres amsl) and Brattefjell (1,541 metres amsl) with its own herd of wild reindeer are inside the landscape protection area.

Viewing Gausta Mountain from the north is a special experience and a popular photo motif no matter the time of year. Its characteristic pyramid-shaped summit and white stripes down the sides is unmistakable, and its profile has also been used to decorate Norwegian stamps. Every year around 30,000 people climb Telemark's highest mountain, often starting from Stavsro (1,173 metres amsl) and

The red light of a November catches Gausta Mountain. Photo: Tom Schandy.

following the red-marked trail reaching the Gaustatoppen Tourist Cabin after one and a half to two hours. On the way up the observant walker will notice stones which have been marked by the wash of waves. It is strange to think that stones lying at such a height have been, in the distant past before the mountain reared almost 2 kilometres into the air, sand on a beach.

Spectacular panorama

Although it is fantastic at the cabin, nothing can compare to the view from the cairn which marks the highest point. A 15 minute walk along a sharp ridge broken up by large boulders brings you to the cairn and at its dizzying height it is not a place for the faint-hearted. 1,600 metres below lie Rjukan and the Vestfjorddal Valley and the view is breathtaking especially in fine weather when over a sixth of Norway's land area can be seen, stretching from Jotunheimen in the north to Østfold County in the south-east and Bohuslän in Sweden. In other words, a clear line of sight for 170 to 180 kilometres. Remember to take enough warm clothes in your rucksack on such a mountain walk as the weather can change abruptly. In fact Gausta Mountain is the place in Eastern Norway with the lowest registered average yearly temperature, only 4.3 degrees Celsius.

Whatever the weather, coffee, waffles and other food is on sale in the Norwegian Trekking Association's over 100 year old stone cabin on the summit. The Gaustatoppen Tourist Cabin with its incredible panorama from 1,850 metres amsl was built in 1893 from natural stones found on the summit, and has recently been

Every year around 30,000 people climb Telemark's highest summit, often along the red-marked trail to the Gaustatoppen Tourist Cabin. Photo: Tom Schandy.

expanded and redecorated inside. This cabin on the skyline is owned by Skien-Telemark Trekking Association and is a meeting place for mountain lovers. It is possible to ski on Gausta Mountain, but not before checking the risk of avalanches and other dangers with people who know the area. However, it must be mentioned that daring speed-skiing enthusiasts have reached awesome speeds of well over 200 kilometres an hour down the Gausta Mountain slopes.

Vast area of nature

Brattefjell-Vindeggen lying south-west of Gausta Mountain is the largest area of nature in Telemark (apart from Hardangervidda Mountain Plateau) without any significant technical encroachment. Therefore in December 2000 a collective area of approximately 382 square kilometres was established as a landscape protection area with preservation of wildlife. The protected area lies in the municipalities of

Hjartdal, Seljord, Tinn and Vinje, that is to say south of Møsvatn Lake, west of Gausta Mountain, north of Hjartdal and east of Rauland.

The purpose behind establishing this protected landscape is to preserve a magnificent and unique natural landscape with unspoiled mountains and mountain forest, safeguard biological diversity including the wild reindeer and abundant plant life and wildlife as well as preserving a valuable traditional cultivated landscape and cultural monuments. The herd of wild reindeer originates from animals which wandered into the area from the Hardangervidda Mountain Plateau at the end of the 1960's. In 2005, 75 animals were killed in the hunting season and the aim is that the winter herd shall total approximately 500 animals. The wild reindeer herd on Brattefjell-Vindeggen is vulnerable and tourists in the area are asked to be careful.

❦ FACTS ❦

Gausta Mountain is considered to be Norway's most distinctive mountain. Situated near Rjukan in the Telemark County. Brattefjell-Vindeggen Landscape Protection Area is the largest area of nature without technical encroachment in Telemark (apart from the Hardangervidda Mountain Plateau).

Attractions:
- Panorama from Gausta Mountain (1,883 metres amsl)
- Gaustatoppen Tourist Cabin
- Wild reindeer in the Brattefjell-Vindeggen Landscape Protection Area

Maps:
Touring map Hardangervidda 1: 100 000 and Rjukan 1614 IV 1: 50 000.

Access:
Drive to the road between Rjukan and Tuddal. Park beside the road at Stavsro or Svineroi. Marked trail to the summit of Gausta Mountain. Skinnarbu beside Road 37 is a good starting point for tours to Brattefjell-Vindeggen.

32

Aust-Agder Skerries
World-class coastline

Norway's south coast, particularly the Aust-Agder Skerries, are synonymous with bathing in the sea, eating fried mackerel, islets, skerries, the cry of the seagulls and a wind from the south. For many people this epitomises summer, sun and holiday in Norway, the whole coastline being an uninterrupted stretch of outstanding natural beauty.

Every year thousands of people are drawn to the south coast of Norway with its fantastic nature and varied coastal landscape featuring low skerries with undulating terrain, bare or forested hills and smooth shoreline rocks divided by narrow necks of water and small inlets. In places the forest reaches right down to the water's edge along a coast dominated by warmth-loving deciduous trees.

This scenic skerry landscape is popular for a number of activities such as walking on springy forest paths under the shady canopy of deciduous forests, bathing on overcrowded sandy beaches or on a desolate islet, fishing from a boat or jetty, and all sorts of boat trips.

Of course the busiest time is the summer, but it is also idyllic here in off peak seasons, for example an autumn stroll beside waves breaking on the beach on a windy day, with the smell of seaweed and salty sea.

The skerry park

Extensive areas of shoreline have been privatised during the last 50 years giving poorer public access to the best stretches of seaside and the authorities have therefore established a Skerry Park. This is part of the Department of the Environment's work to ensure that coastal areas are available to the general public and the work has been granted large sums of money

Few other places have so much boat traffic as the idyllic strait off Lyngør. Photo: Tom Schandy.

in recent years. The Skerry Park now stretches from Grenland to Lindesnes with the aim of preserving the coastal environment and organising outdoor recreational activities in the municipalities concerned.

It should be mentioned that the landowners who agree to join the Skerry Park keep their proprietary rights and can use their properties as before, the point with the park being that the area is also available to the general public and that the possibility exists for the establishment of footpaths, amenities etc. Aust-Agder is the county containing the largest number of safeguarded recreational areas and skerry parks, with most of the islands and islets in Aust-Agder's marine areas belonging to the Skerry Park.

Idylls one after the other

The poet from the south coast of Norway, Gabriel Scott, has called Blindleia the finest jewel in the skerries and indeed it is a well-known attraction for all boaters in these waters. Blindleia is the beautiful inshore route from Gamle Hellesund in Høvåg to Lillesand, one of Norway's most scenic stretches of coastal water and sheltered from wind and rough sea.

Another idyllic place on the south coast of Norway, directly south of Grimstad, is Homborsund Lighthouse, which is open and staffed during the entire Norwegian school holidays from around the middle of June to the middle of August, and by booking in advance it is possible to stay overnight there. The easiest way to reach Homborsund is with your own boat, but for those without it is possible to order a taxi boat from either Lillesand or Grimstad.

Further north in the approach to Arendal, the Arendal and Oppland Trekking Association provides overnight accommodation in two closed down lighthouses at Store Torungen and Lille Torungen Light-house Stations, sharing the responsibility for running them with the society called Friends of Lille Torungen. The facilities on these two islands are often hired out to school classes, private people, companies, societies and other groups.

A pothole at Risør makes a splendid bathing pool. Photo: Tom Schandy.

Lyngør, just off Tvedestrand and bordering on to the Skerry Park, was elected as Europe's best preserved village a few years ago and it is quite a special sensation to stroll around its low white-painted houses. Many people refer to Lyngør as Scandinavia's Venice as the majority of houses on each side of the narrow neck of water are built right on the water's edge. The scenery surrounding the numerous bathing places from smooth rocks in clear, salty water is nothing other than magnificent. There are no roads on Lyngør but it is connected to the mainland by a small local boat service or taxi boat operating from the mainland at Gjeving.

Summer, sun and the south coast sounds idyllic, but there is a lot of wildlife here which does not appreciate the interference from humans and noisy boat motors. Aust-Agder County coastline has around 30 seabird sanctuaries which do not tolerate disturbance at certain times of the year. It is therefore forbidden to go ashore, or move about otherwise in the protected areas from and including

15 April to and including 15 July, and for the remainder of the year all traffic must occur with caution so that the plant life and wildlife suffers the least amount of damage and disturbance.

Jellyfish also belong to Norway's south coast. Not as popular as they are colourful and decorative, as well as the red and yellow stinging variety they also come in shades of blue. Photo: Tom Schandy.

The Islands of Tromøy and Tromlingene
Idyllic skerry scenery and beauty spot

The varied and exciting skerry scenery off Norway's south coast comprises holms, rocks, islets and islands. The area's largest island, Tromøy, lies just north-east of Arendal and together with the much smaller neighbouring island, Tromlingene, they form two spots of natural scenic beauty along the coast of Agder County.

In 1964 nightingales were registered nesting on Tromøy – the first time in Norway. Photo: Pål Hermansen/NN/Samfoto.

Inlets and water nearly separate the special landscape of the south-east of Tromøy from the rest of the island. Terminal moraine ("Ra" in Norwegian) which formed the coast line and headlands has given its name to the extensive Raet Landscape Protection Area established in 2000. Altogether this totals approximately 2,160 hectares (5,400 acres) of which 1,840 hectares (4,600 acres) are sea. The boundary of the preserved area stretches from Jerkholmen in the west and over to Tromlingene in the east spanning around 15 kilometres. The purpose behind protection is to preserve the unique natural and traditional cultivated landscape with its numerous qualities.

The waves break on kilometres of pebble beach where scoured smooth rocks add variation to this exposed coastal landscape. Several levels of elevated shoreline in the slopes rising from the sea tell their interesting geological history from the Quaternary Age. These are traces of land elevation dating back 10,000 years when the terminal moraine rose out of the sea. This sandy soil is therefore dominated by heather and pine forests, the trees of which, in their exposed maritime position, have assumed interesting and amusing shapes. Although the elements have twisted and bent the trees this forest in fact does a good job at protecting the other vegetation.

Reed beds and nesting nightingales

The largest island off the south coast of Norway also has several areas of shallow water and small tarns with special vegetation and an abundant bird life. At Skottjern, a tarn inside the Raet area right below Tromøy Church, one of the country's tallest reed beds grows with plants reaching over 3 metres high. Over 100 bird species have been registered in this area and in 1964 this was the site of nightingales nesting in Norway for the first time. Hovekilen, an inlet west of Hove, is extremely significant as a habitat for swans, ducks, geese, grebes and waders. The vegetation combined with the mild and good climate creates an abundant insect life and several insect species have been found here for the first time in Norway.

Plants, insects and birds are not alone in liking Tromøy. In the summer the island is teeming with people enjoying bathing, fishing or just relaxing at the seaside. Hoveodden, Spornes, Botsfjorden and Alvekilen offer popular bathing and recreational areas.

Tromlingene

Tromlingene lies only five to ten minutes by boat to the north-east of Tromøy. This is a 2 kilometre-long island where only a narrow elevated shoreline connects the north and south parts and this is the first place where the terminal moraine rose out of the sea south of Jomfruland (see separate chapter). Almost all of Tromlingene is dominated by loose stone and sand originating from this moraine and several levels of elevated shoreline can be studied. Although no trees grow on the island nearly 200 plant species and approximately 130 bird species have been registered including 30 different species of waders.

There are old burial mounds on both Tromlingene and Tromøy and according to experts these date back to the Bronze Age, the time of human migration and the early Iron Age. In other words they are between 4,000 and 1,000 years old. Furthermore, there is said to be evidence of Stone Age dwellings on Tromøy that are much older than the above mentioned burial mounds. All in all this tells us that for different reasons people have been attracted to these beautiful islands for thousands of years.

Early morning on the pebble beach on Tromøy. Photo: Tom Schandy.

FACTS

Tromøy is the largest island off Norway's south coast and lies directly north-east of Arendal, with a bridge connecting it to the mainland. Tromlingene (part of the Skerry Park) is a 2 kilometre-long island right beside Tromøy. Both islands belong to the Arendal Municipality.

Attractions:
· Elevated shoreline on Tromlingene
· Ancient burial mounds
· Pebble beach on Tromøy

Map:
1611 I Tromøy 1: 50 000.

Access:
Follow Road 409 to Tromøy. Boat transport is necessary to reach Tromlingene.

34

Setesdal Vesthei-Ryfylkeheiene
Undulating mountain plateaus and wide mountain summits

The counties of Telemark, Hordaland, Rogaland, Vest-Agder and Aust-Agder all meet here along with the Langfjell range of mountains which ends in these regions bordering Southern and Western Norway. This is also the home of Europe's southernmost herd of wild reindeer.

To the north Ryfylkeheiene connects up with the Hardangervidda Mountain Plateau at Haukeliseter, in the south it merges with Frafjordheiene and Bjerkreimsheiene, while it has gradually become a part of Setesdalsheiene in the east, the mountain and moor landscape west of the Setesdal Valley being called Vestheiene. The southern boundary is somewhat vague, but many people claim that it is at Ljosland/Knaben. The majority of this area of outstanding natural beauty is divided between the counties of Rogaland, Vest-Agder and Aust-Agder.

Since World War II the landscape in this area of nature and recreation has changed tremendously. Major hydro-electricpower development at, for example Ulla-Førre, Sira-Kvina and Røldal-Suldal, has resulted in extensive road building, power lines and enormous water reservoirs, one of these being the great Blåsjø Reservoir, a man-made lake and when full of water it is, surprisingly enough, Norway's seventh largest lake.

Vast protected areas
Despite the many encroachments on the countryside, this area can still offer plenty of beautiful and unspoiled nature. In 2000 the Setesdal Vesthei-Ryfylkeheiene Landscape Protection Area was established in the central part of the moor and, situated in the three counties Rogaland, Vest-Agder and Aust-Agder, it totals 2,347 square kilometres. In addition five other landscape protection areas were established at Kvanndalen, Hovden, Dyraheio, Lusaheia and Vormedalsheia, all of them connected to the major area. Totally several million hectares/acres are preserved for the future against watercourse regulation, private holiday cabin development and road building. Next to the Hardangervidda Mountain Plateau, this is Norway's largest area of nature conservation.

The purpose of the Setesdal Vesthei-Ryfylkeheiene Landscape Protection Area is to preserve an uninterrupted, characteristic and beautiful area of nature with unspoiled mountains, moors and mountain forest with its special plant life and wildlife, the summer mountain dairy farms, grazing landscape and cultural monuments. No less important is the preservation of an uninterrupted mountain region which is the habitat for the southernmost herd of wild reindeer in Europe. The reindeer have probably been here for about 8,000 years and remains from Stone Age settlements in the area tell us that reindeer and fish were important food sources for our ancestors. Old cultural monuments stem from the system of trapping used in Vestheiene and Ryfylkeheine and comprise leading fences, stone built hides for the hunters with bow and arrows, and pit traps. From 1820 to 1978 domesticated reindeer were also kept in Setesdalsheiene, but now there are only wild reindeer numbering between 1,500 and 2,000 animals.

Botanical gems
The variation in the landscape and nature in Vestheiene and Ryfylkeheiene makes it difficult to characterise. Whereas towards the north it is undulating with several large mountains and valleys, at Rjuven, a prominent mountain massif south of Dyraheio, the greyish moor landscape with gentle mountains begins. The species of bedrock in the east and south do

This is the habitat of the southernmost herd of wild reindeer in Europe. Photo: Kjell Helle Olsen.

The Taumevatn Lake is a popular destination both summer and winter. Photo: Odd Inge Worsøe.

not support a very varied plant life, but towards the west where there are areas of slate there is more lushness and diversity, the most interesting area botanically being the Vormedalsheia and Dyraheio Landscape Protection Area. Mountain avens, snow cinquefoil, Scottish wormwood and Scandinavian primrose all thrive on the slate in this area which is their southern limit in Norway. Another rarity is the livelong saxifrage, resembling the more well-known maiden saxifrage, it is smaller and has a stiffer stalk. Its key habitat in Northern Europe is in Ryfylkeheiene, only occurring otherwise in two small isolated places in Northern Norway.

Plenty of paths and cabins

There is a well-developed network of Norwegian Trekking Association cabins in these mountain regions, connected by marked paths of various lengths and degree of difficulty. Kristiansand and Oppland Trekking Association and the Stavanger Trekking Association are responsible for marking the routes and maintaining these cabins. A 10-12 day hike southwards from Haukeliseter, following the trails from cabin to cabin will end at Ljosland in Åseral in Vest-Agder County. The cabins are either staffed, self-service with provisions or no-service (without provisions) and it is vital to remember the Norwegian Trekking Association master key.

A large network of Norwegian Trekking Association cabins has been developed in these mountain regions, here at Stranddalshytta. Photo: Kjell Helle Olsen.

35

► **Skjernøy-Ryvingen**
Idyllic skerry landscapes in Vest-Agder

On the southernmost tip of Norway off the coast at Mandal there are magnificent skerries. Two of the largest of these jewels are Skjernøy and Ryvingen. The former is an island which has been connected to the mainland by bridge for 40 years, whereas Ryvingen is an old lighthouse station away out to sea.

The area between islands of Skjernøy and Ryvingen is one of the south coast's finest skerries with a diverse nature ranging from low islets of smooth rock to undulating and lush islands nearer Skjernøy and the mainland. Until the connection to the mainland was established in 1964, Skjernøy was in danger of losing its population but now there are more than 300 inhabitants on this scenic island, making it Norway's southernmost residential area. The most outlying islands are as far south as it is possible to be in Norway, the outermost skerry, Pysen, being in fact more than two and a half kilometres further south than Lindesnes, thus making it Norway's southernmost point.

Boat traffic through the idyllic Skjernøy Sound. Photo: Tom Schandy.

Abundant bird life and a wolf

The southern part of the idyllic island Skjernøy is a recreational area containing paths and walks starting from the hamlet Farestrand. Heath carpets the slightly undulating terrain, and small trees grow where they have found shelter from the wind. Near rocks and bushes the observant walker will spot climbing corydalis, a rare plant with small yellowy-white flowers and tendrils which it uses

to clamber up towards the light. Despite the hard coastal weather the flora is surprisingly abundant and for anyone interested in botany, a walk in the oak forest in the spring will reveal masses of wood anemones, primroses and lesser celandines. The rare orchid, narrow-leaved helleborine, can be found in the south-facing slopes and indeed even the early purple

orchid thrives on Skernøy.

The view out over the open sea is fantastic with the islands Ryvingen in the south-west and Store Vengesholmen in the south, the latter being a seabird sanctuary teeming with life. Around 4,000 nesting pairs of lesser black-backed gulls have been registered in good years. Even if you have your own boat it is forbidden to set ashore

at the seabird sanctuary from 15 April to 15 July, but a good pair of binoculars will enable you to watch the birds from Skjernøy.

Unbelievably, a wolf killed a roe deer on Skjernøy in 2003 even though this is the most southernmost tip of Norway. This large predator swam almost 200 metres and went ashore under the bridge between the mainland and the

The south coast's finest skerries lie between Skjernøy and Ryvingen. Photo: Tom Schandy.

island, but this is a rare occurrence as apparently 150 years have passed since the last time a wolf appeared on Skjernøy.

Large protected area

The Øksøy-Ryvingen Landscape Protection Area was established in the spring of 2005, preserving the outer skerries between Øksøy Lighthouse in the east to Ryvingen Lighthouse in the west, a total area of 100 square kilometres divided between 86 square kilometres of sea and 14 square kilometres of land. This is one of the few large coastal areas which is protected according to the Nature Conservancy Law for Southern Norway. The nature includes seashore, coastal meadows and several types of coastal heaths. This is

the fisherman farmer's traditional landscape and dates back 4,000 years, although it is now sadly in strong decline. Fortunately the sheep grazing on several of these islands today will help to stop this landscape from becoming overgrown and disappearing altogether.

Norway's southernmost lighthouse

Ryvingen Lighthouse Station was established in 1867, but was vacated in 2002 after being made automatic. Norway's southernmost lighthouse lies south of Skjernøy and is a part of Mandal Municipality. In 1897 the old lighthouse building was replaced with a tower of 22.5 metres in cast iron and equipped with a rapidly blinking lens.

Today the lighthouse station comprises a keeper's house, machine house, shed, road, boathouse and landing stage as well as the sites of old houses and remains of German activity. The

FACTS

Skjernøy at 6 square kilometres is Mandal's largest island and is connected by bridge to the mainland. Situated in Vest-Agder County. Ryvingen is an old lighthouse station in the open sea south of Skjernøy.

Attractions:
· Ryvingen Lighthouse
· Skjernøy's recreational areas
· Landscape Protection Area
· Øksøy-Ryvingen

Maps:
1411 II Mandal and 1410 Ryvingen 1: 50 000.

Access:
Turn off Road E 39 at Mandal and drive directly south. After a few kilometres one reaches the bridge over to Skjernøy. There is also a bus service from Mandal to Skjernøy. One needs boat transport to reach Ryvingen Lighthouse.

landscape has clear traces of being cultivated and the island is still used for grazing sheep. All these elements make the island environmentally valuable and this can possibly explain why Ryvingen is set aside for agriculture, nature and recreation with important nature conservancy and recreational interest in municipality planning for Mandal. Ryvingen Lighthouse Station is now protected and the association called Ryvingens Venner – Friends of Ryvingen – collaborate with Mandal Municipality, the Norwegian Coastal Administration and the local County Council regarding the running of the lighthouse. It is possible to make a day visit and overnight stop at the lighthouse both summer and winter, but no refreshments are on sale.

Ryvingen Lighthouse Station, the southernmost in Norway, was established in 1867. Photo: Kai Hakvåg.

Lista Peninsula
Unique countryside on the South Coast

The Lista Peninsula in Vest-Agder County has a unique entirety of nature which is both rare and worthy of protection. Nature reserves and landscape protection areas lie one after the other, Lista being considered definitely the most valuable area of nature on the whole of the south coast.

Few other places in Norway can boast the same density of nature reserves and nature worthy of protection as this peninsula in Farsund Municipality. The variations are vast from the Lista Beaches Landscape Protection Area of endless sandy and pebble beaches to the extremely nutrient rich lake, Slevdalsvann.

Lista is perhaps most famous for its variety of beautiful beaches consisting of sand and sand dunes, pebble shores and steep smooth rocky coastline exposed to the open sea. The sand dunes provide an ideal habitat for plants which are otherwise rare in Norway, such as sea holly, marsh gentian and grey hair grass.

In order to preserve the unique plant and bird life, parts of the beaches are protected as areas of plant and/or bird conservation. Large areas of the beaches at Lista together with a number of shallow lakes comprise the Lista Wetlands which have been awarded European status as a Ramsar region, that is to say wetlands internationally worthy of conservation.

Extremely rich bird life

Lista with its abundant bird life ranks as one of Norway's most outstanding bird localities. Lista Lighthouse also houses Lista Bird Station where continual observation of the birds and ringing is carried out. Until 2004, ornithologists had registered 347 species, which proves there is enough to do for the full-time crew at the station, its geographical location on Norway's south-west tip attracting large numbers of migrating birds in the spring and autumn. Many of

Lista is considered the most valuable area of nature along the south coast of Norway. Lista Lighthouse towers over the terrain. Photo: Tom Schandy.

The bar-tailed godwit comes from Siberia, but rests at Lista during the autumn migration. Photo: Tom Schandy.

these are of course ducks and waders, but also other bird groups are well represented. Lista is also famous for its observations of extremely rare birds bringing enthusiasts from far and near, eager to tick yet another satisfactory sighting off their lists of rarities. Species belonging to the Far East, the Mediterranean or North America have appeared on the scene, including Pallas's sandgrouse, great spotted cuckoo, needle-tailed swift, rosy starling and booted warbler as well as Pacific golden plover, semipalmated sandpiper and long-billed dowitcher.

Ornithologists also work at the newly established Slevdalsvann Lake Nature Reserve, an extremely nutrient rich, reed-filled lake with an unbelievable combination of species not found anywhere else in the country. At this lake alone 230 species have been observed, many of them quite rare nesting birds. In June one can often hear the spotted crake with

its song reminiscent of a dripping tap, and the water rail with its famous call resembling a squealing pig. The marsh harrier nested here for the first time in 1988 and annually since 1995. This is in fact the only annual Norwegian nesting locality for this species which is normally found beside the vast

wetland lakes in Sweden. An invasion of the rather special bearded tit from Sweden in 1992, has led to it nesting here since with a total of three nesting pairs annually, making the nature reserve one of two regular localities for this species in Norway. The density of singing sedge warblers probably exceeds any other locality in the country, between 200 to 250 singing males have been counted in the early summer.

All the species mentioned above are typical swamp dwellers that conceal themselves in the reeds and thick swamp vegetation and 21 of the nesting species are on the Bern Convention List of rare species that need special management. The area is considered to be the most important migration and winter locality for a number of wetland species, not least the spotted crake and the water rail.

Encroachments have left their mark

Although a unique locality today, Lista has been even better. Since the middle of the 1800's drainage

From the beach at Lista. Photo: Tom Schandy.

and new cultivation has reduced the area of open water, swamp and marsh. Four of seven lakes are nearly completely emptied and the wetlands today consist of only 10 per cent of the surface of the flat Lista area as opposed to 25 per cent 150 years ago. This means that the nesting locality for a number of species has been reduced, and the southern subspecies of dunlin, a bird classified as critically endangered in Norway, stopped nesting here during the 1980's.

It has therefore been crucial to safeguard the remaining areas against further deterioration, and this has been achieved. The nature offers excitement for bird watchers and nature lovers alike, with sandy beaches to stroll along and explore. The landscape of sand dunes is in fact not unlike the west coast of Jylland in Denmark.

FACTS

The Lista Peninsula, with unique nature and a number of nature reserves and landscape protection areas southernmost in Vest-Agder County.

Attractions:
· Sandy beaches and pebble shores
· Bird life
· Lista Bird Station
· Slevdalsvann Lake
· Lista Lighthouse

Maps:
1311 III Hidra and 1311 III Farsund 1: 50 000.

Access:
Easy to access by car. Turn off Road E39 at Lyngdal, approx. 30 kilometres west of Mandal. 35 kilometres to Lista Lighthouse.

37

Jæren
A piece of Danish Norway

Jæren is a piece of Denmark which has attached itself to Norway. Although the landscape is as flat as a pancake and mostly ploughed, there are several lakes abundant in bird life and 70 kilometres of coastline dotted with the most fantastic sandy beaches and sand dunes in the country. The scenery is in fact quite unique in Norway.

Jæren is extremely flat, bearing strong evidence of agricultural exploitation since the early part of the Younger Stone Age 6,000 years ago, when the vast hardwood forests were transformed to open pasture by burning and grazing. Since then and right up to the 1900's Jæren was dominated by heath and marsh interspersed with small, green patches of farmland. Over the last hundred years

With the country's most magnificent sandy beaches, the landscape at Jæren is quite unique for Norway. This is the Brusanden Beach. Photo: Tom Schandy.

marshes have been drained, tilled and fertilised for cultivated grazing and Jæren has become gradually greener. This development is almost complete and the few, small remains from the previous Jæren landscape are crucial for the biological diversity which is hugely significant both nationally and internationally.

The loveliest sandy beaches in Norway

Jæren's beaches, reaching from Ogna in the south to Randaberg in the north, are mostly preserved as landscape protection areas taking care of a unique nature and traditional cultivated landscape. Norway's most beautiful sandy beaches and sand dunes adorn the coast along with pebble shores and cliffs and although the majority of shoreline is a narrow strip it widens to 200 metres in places. Within the landscape protection area eight bird sanctuaries, nine areas of plant protection and four protected geological sites have more comprehensive conservation.

The beaches are extremely popular for recreation with an estimated annual 500,000 visitors, who can gaze at the sea in storm or calm, study plants, watch the birds and generally enjoy themselves in surroundings comparable to the continent. The 5 kilometre long beach, Orresanden, is the longest in Norway and it is a pity that the temperature of the water does not always match the quality of the seashore.

Many of the sand dunes have formed following the planting of marram grass to protect the agricultural interests in the interior from shifting sand. This sharp-bladed grass has an extensive root system which binds the sand and this gradually builds up to a dune. However, the life of a sand dune is at the mercy of the waves and wind which can undermine the sand exposing the roots of the marram grass, which dies back leaving open areas where the sand can slip out and blow away. Although traffic from walkers also wears away the marram grass dunes, the most unique and vulnerable areas with regard to plant life are the rear sand dunes and dune meadows. Extensive recreational activity pressurises other vulnerable natural values, especially by its disturbance of the bird life.

Wallowing in seaweed and sea tangle

Seaweed and sea tangle are washed ashore providing tempting habitats for insects and small animal life, which again attracts myriads of waders that can literally wallow in food. Here it is possible to spot most of the waders confirmed observed in Norway and many species are long distance travellers from the Arctic stopping at Jæren to fill their tanks on a route that earns the name "The Bird Migration Motorway". Large flocks of knot and sanderling arrive from Greenland and Siberia. The sanderling sprints at high speed along the beach picking up insects as it runs with the waves constantly on its heels.

At Revtangen, Jæren's westernmost tongue of land, the Revtangen Bird Station (Stavanger Museum) works with catching and ringing birds. Over 300 species have been confirmed observed in the station's area of operation, and from 1917 to 1997 more than four million birds have been ringed, 60,000 of which have been recovered. Revtangen has therefore been of great significance in the research of birds' migratory habits.

There are a number of lakes on Jæren that abound in bird life. Orrevann Lake, directly inland from Revtangen, is extremely popular for winter residents, as well as being a resting place for birds in migration and a nesting area for a large number of bird species. Other rich bird localities are found at the lakes Frøylandsvann, Horpestadvann and Grudavann, all nutritious and surrounded by cultivated land. Frøylandsvann Lake is home to vendace (or lake herring) which is otherwise found in Mjøsa and Lågen. All of Jæren's lakes are to a lesser or greater extent lowered as a result of a project to lower the level of the lakes in order to retrieve more land for agriculture, and in fact some lakes have been emptied completely.

The beaches together with these lakes comprise the Jæren Wetland System which is one of the country's most important bird localities,

FACTS

Exciting coastal landscape and nutritious lakes in Rogaland County. The Jæren Landscape Protection Area measures 17 square kilometres on land and approximately 193 square kilometres including the marine area.

Attractions:
· Sandy beaches and sand dunes
· Birds

Maps:
Individual maps in the main map series for Norway 1: 50 000.

Access:
Easy to access along the so-called Nordsjøveien (North Sea Route), Roads 44, 507, 510 and 509. Information Centre for recreation and nature conservation at Orre.

not least as a resting place and winter area for swans, geese and ducks. In addition the number of waders and seabirds often exceeds 20,000 individuals. These wetlands are a Ramsar region, that is to say, an area of great international significance.

From August to September the Jæren beaches are invaded by small, quick sanderlings from the Arctic. Photo: Tom Schandy.

38

Frafjordheiene
From grey mountains to green hardwood forests

Grey mountains, enormous stone screes, majestic waterfalls and lush hardwood forests combine to give diversity to Frafjordheiene, the joint name for the magnificent mountains between the Lysefjord and the Hunnedal Valley in Rogaland.

Frafjordheiene was recommended as a national park, but instead in December 2003 418 square kilometres were preserved as a landscape protection area. This means that the countryside and landscape, lakes and watercourses, cultural monuments and traditional culti-

vated landscape are preserved for future generations as well as the area accommodating nature experiences, outdoor pursuits and extensive farming.

On the other hand motor traffic, building of holiday cabins and development of hydro-electric

power are forbidden. Today Frafjordheiene is more or less untouched by development of hydro-electric power meaning that parts of this region are absolute wilderness. The famous Kjerag Mountain towering 1,000 metres over the Lysefjord is also included in this

protected landscape (see chapter on the Lysefjord), but the rest of Frafjordheiene is more or less unknown to most people.

In Norwegian "hei" describes a highland heath or moor landscape, but Frafjordheiene is far from just this. A series of valleys make

Fidjadal is a central and exciting valley in Frafjordheiene. Photo: Arvid Tjøstheim.

the area exciting and dynamic; in a row to the north-east of Frafjord are Frafjorddal, Fidjadal and Blåstøldal and from Espedal in the west the valleys of Røssdal and Indredal stretch eastwards, meeting at the green, grassy plains beside the no-service tourist cabin, Blåfjellenden.

A dramatically varied walk

The beautiful walk from Blåfjellenden down the Fidjadal Valley takes six to seven hours and spans the varied countryside in Frafjordheiene, starting at the top in the grey stone mountains and gradually descending. After a while you reach Fidjavann Lake where a colossal untidy accumulation of enormous boulders and an old unspoiled birch forest blocks the whole valley. This goes under the name of Huldrehaugen and in fact it dams up the lakes Fidjavann and Månavann.

These boulders probably date back to a mountain avalanche on the north side of the valley, the stones then being shoved into place by huge masses of ice during the Ice Age. In normal conditions the valley's river flows under these boulders, but in the case of floods, the water, not finding enough space under the stones, is forced upwards and this can cause problems for you on your walk.

Further down you pass old grazing grounds where there was once a farm with horses, cattle and sheep, and at the bottom of the valley the Månafoss Waterfall cascades down, its 92 metres making it Rogaland's largest. To stand beside this immense cataract must be one of the climaxes of the tour.

Røssdal Valley farther north is dramatic, with the sparkling clear waters of Røssdalsvann Lake surrounded by perpendicular rock faces in steep alpine formations. This is also home to the gigantic gorge called Fossjuvet – Rogaland's answer to Jutulhogget. The Norwegian Trekking Association's year book on Frafjordheiene describes the gorge as proof of the huge forces at work when the meltwater masses were released, and also recommends a walk along the edge of the gorge to be as splendid as walking at the top of Preikestolen over the Lysefjord.

On the sheltered floor of the Røssdal Valley there are large areas of gloriously green hardwood forests, including ash, lime, hazel, oak, elm, guelder rose, bird cherry and other trees, all contrasting strongly to the grey stone of the mountain and moor above. In several places the forest does in fact resemble a primeval forest with dead and living trees interspaced. Many of the rotten trees attract woodpeckers looking for a place to hack out a nest, which in turn provides nesting places for

tits and owls. The ample precipitation in the area creates ideal conditions for the growth of lichens and mosses.

Excellent network of paths

There is an excellent network of footpaths in Frafjordheiene and the Stavanger Trekking Association has four cabins in the area, the already mentioned Blåfjellenden (no provisions), Sandvatn (no provisions), Langavatn (self-service, with provisions) and Fløyrli (no provisions). Beside the Månafoss Waterfall the Jæren Recreational Council has restored Mån, the old mountain farm, where it is possible to stay overnight. Mån was the first mountain farm to be cleared in the Fidjadal Valley, probably before the Black Death in 1349. There are also a number of excellent rocky overhangs which can provide an overnight shelter.

Månafoss Waterfall cascades 92 metres and is Rogaland's largest.
Photo: Tom Schandy.

39

Lysefjord
A favourite for priests and BASE jumpers

The 45 kilometre Lysefjord in Rogaland County is lined by colossal and starkly dramatic mountains. While Preikestolen (The Pulpit) towering 600 metres over the fjord is undoubtedly a favourite for priests, the BASE jumpers prefer Kjerag with its 1,000 metre free fall.

Ice has sculptured the Lysefjord. As the ice bulldozed its way forward it dragged along gravel and stones lying beneath which scraped the ground away. In places large channels were gouged out some of which filled with meltwater and became deep fjords, as was the case for Lysefjord with its depth of 460 metres. When the ice reached the sea it spread and, losing its strength, it deposited debris which formed a terminal moraine crossing the fjord mouth at a depth of only 13 metres. However, the bedrock lining the fjord has been extremely stable and the gigantic Preikestolen and Kjerag formations are two of Norway's most prominent natural attractions.

Preikestolen

Every year approximately 100,000 tourists from all over the world walk for two hours from the lodge, Preikestolhytta, up to Preikestolen, which proudly bears its name as it resembles a gigantic old-fashioned pulpit hanging 600 metres above the Lysefjord. It began to take shape when the fjord was filled with ice and frost disintegrated the mountain sides. Tentacles of water filled the cracks, turned to ice and prised loose enormous angular blocks which were then transported away on the glacier, leaving Preikestolen's square formation topped with a flat plateau 25 metres square.

Every year approximately 100,000 tourists walk the two-hour tour from Preikestolhytta to Preikestolen. Photo: Tom Schandy.

Tourists lie down and crawl to the edge to gaze with respect into the depths below, across the fjord and the vista of a majestic mountain landscape, but the view is just as impressive a little back from the edge. Some people anxiously observe the enormous crack cutting straight across the plateau, which one day might break the pulpit in two sending a destructive flood wave over the city of Stavanger. It could happen tomorrow or in a thousand years, but according to the geologists the crack has not expanded over recent decades.

Most people are therefore not bothered by this threat and on a warm summer day there are as many people on Preikestolen as there are in the fish market in Bergen.

Kjerag

Kjerag, lying at the head of the Lysefjord, towers 1,000 metres over the water and is part of the Frafjordheiene Landscape Protection Area (see separate chapter). The walk to Kjerag is steeper and takes longer than to Preikestolen and it is well worth the three hours you must allow to get there. If you

The Kjerag Plateau is a paradise for BASE jumpers. Photo: Tom Schandy.

liked Preikestolen you are bound to like Kjerag, one of the biggest nature experiences in the mountains of Norway.

Kjerag sports the Kjerag Bolt, a massive boulder wedged in a huge crevice. It is popular to walk out on to the boulder, but only for people who are not afraid of heights, as underneath there is a sheer drop of almost 1,000 metres.

Only a few hundred metres away from the Kjerag Bolt is the Kjerag Plateau, and this is the place that BASE jumpers love. It might be the most attractive spot for this sport in Norway and even one of the best in the world, due to its free fall of 1,000 metres. It seems quite absurd to watch people throw themselves over the edge, but for BASE jumpers this is the essence of life, to be able to float free in mid air for a few seconds. One of the jumpers has described the trip down as a long, beautiful and liberating descent where the rock face never loses its enormity. However, the free fall only lasts 15 seconds before the para-

chute must be released. Since the first jump by Stein Edvardsen in 1994, 18,000 jumps have been logged over the last decade or so.

The Kjerag Bolt, a massive boulder wedged in a huge crevice. Photo: Tom Schandy.

40

Suldalslågen River
Salmon river and scenic countryside

Suldalslågen is one of the largest rivers in Western Norway and is the realm of giant salmon, some weighing in at over 20 kilograms. The fishing spots line the banks of this beautiful, quiet flowing river in Indre Ryfylke.

The Suldalslågen River starts at Suldalsvann Lake and flows out in the Sandsfjord beside Sand in the Suldal Municipality. On its 22 kilometre journey it has passed through varied nature and traditional cultivated landscapes. However the headwaters of the Suldal Watercourse are found in the valleys of Valldal and Vivassdal at the southernmost reaches of the Hardangervidda National Park, the entire watercourse spanning a total length of approximately 100 kilometres, stretching from the mountains to the fjords.

Quiet flowing river with two waterfalls
In the course of Suldalslågen River's 22 kilometres down to the Sandsfjord the total fall is only 68 metres, producing long stretches of calm flowing water, only broken at Juvet and Sandsfoss where this majestic river meets rapids and large waterfalls. The thundering Sandsfoss Waterfall with a drop of a meagre 4 metres is all the same an impressive and fascinating sight for both tourists and locals when Western Norway's longest and most voluminous river throws itself into a deep pool below the fall.

A river with giant salmon
The river's large volume of water has attracted several hydro-electric power developers, resulting in a number of regulation points along the Suldal Watercourse. This affects the water flow at different times of the year and leads to among other things reduced salmon fishing in Suldalslågen River. Historically the river is famous for its breed of particularly large salmon, the largest on record weighing in at 34 kilograms. Previously one of the three largest salmon rivers in the county with regard to total kilograms of salmon caught, the river is no

Suldalslågen, a voluminous, quiet running river with long calm stretches. Photo: Jarle Lunde.

Canoeing is a popular activity on the Suldalslågen River. Photo: Jarle Lunde.

longer topping the list. All the same, large fish of over 20 kilograms are caught annually and the salmon fishing is still an important resource for several landowners in the municipality. The river is divided up into 31 fishing zones including both private and open licence fishing. The zones are varied and suitable for both fly and spinner.

The Suldalslågen River's breed of large salmon is both nationally and internationally renowned. Lindum is a "genuine" salmon fishing lodge built by the English Lord Sibthorp in 1884. He was so fascinated by the beautiful scenery in Western Norway that he bought the salmon fishing rights along large stretches of the river and the same year 50 local craftsmen erected the salmon fishing lodge with the best timber in Suldal, completing the building after a record three months. The name Lindum originates from Lord Sibthorp's home town Lincoln in England. Lindum has been used for several different activities over the last 120 years including a home for tuberculosis sufferers and an old people's

home, but today it is again back to being a salmon fishing lodge.

The largest salmon at 34 kilograms was caught in 1913 under Sandsfoss Waterfall, taking all of 12 hours to land after the fish had dragged boat and fishermen several kilometres around the fjord. In addition to salmon the Suldalslågen River is popular for fishing sea trout and the so-called "Lågen" trout. Whereas salmon fishing is best in daylight, the chances of hooking a sea trout or Lågen-trout are best in the evening or at night. The Lågen-trout can be fished in the entire river in the summer season, while sea trout has its main run in July and August. The season for fishing river trout starts 1 May, and the salmon and sea trout season opens 15 July and ends 20 September.

Those who do not fish, or get a bite, can study the salmon closely at Sandsfoss Waterfall, approximately 500 metres from the estuary, where web cameras show you the salmon on their way up river. Alternatively it can be particularly exciting to join a guided tour in the river in a survival suit and diver's mask.

The experience of floating down the mighty Suldalslågen River with a chance of seeing wild salmon and trout in their proper element will be something you never forget. This is the only place in Norway offering this type of "salmon safari".

Canoeing and traditional cultivated landscape

Canoe enthusiasts use both Suldalsvann Lake and the Suldalslågen River. A pretty and varied part of the river starting from the dam at Osavad to Foss/Kvamen provides everything from calm runs to foaming rapids. Experiencing the wildlife close at hand can be an intense experience from a seat just above the surface of the water, but keep away from Juvet and Sandsfoss Waterfall as these are too dangerous to paddle.

Over thousands of years glaciers and the river have transported large volumes of moraine creating large valley plains and providing a foothold for a varied cultivated landscape. The combination of river, waterfalls, forested slopes and lush agriculture creates beautiful country-

side, and cultural monuments such as mills, drying houses, churns, waterwheels and old bridges emphasize the natural and cultural value of this wonderful landscape.

41

Søre Bømlo
Natural paradise in the west

On the island municipality Bømlo, located about half way between Bergen and Haugesund, you are never far from the sea and boats and fishing are a natural part of life for most inhabitants. Søre Bømlo has fantastic nature with abundant bird life and plant life.

Søre Bømlo is a paradise for nature lovers. The bedrock consists mainly of greenstone and green slate, both lime-rich sedimentary rocks, and these combined with the mild climate create vital conditions for the rich flora on the island.

Unique plant life

Søre Bømlo is home to many rare plants such as sea spleenwort, hart's tongue fern and brown bog-rush, and Norway's largest occurrence of arnica is found here. Otherwise the lime-rich meadows and old hayfields offer an abundance of flowers including the fragrant orchid and greater butterfly orchid. Also found on the island is a rare combination for Norway,

The island municipality Bømlo with its fantastic scenery is situated approximately half way between Bergen and Haugesund. Photo: Jan Rabben/NN/Samfoto.

The beautiful bell heather brightens up the forest floor on Bømlo. Photo: Jan Rabben/NN/Samfoto.

pine forest with bell heather. The calcareous pine forest supports other trees, for example guelder-rose, holly, glossy buckthorn and yew, and a floral bouquet of primrose, woodruff and lily of the valley.

In order to safeguard these special plant localities several nature reserves have been established. Sagvatnet Nature Reserve totalling 600 hectares (1,500 acres) is a protected area containing Norway's largest and westernmost pine forest localities. Several areas in this region have pine forest and marshland vegetation blending with both rare and typical maritime species.

Skogafjellet Nature Reserve measuring almost 66.7 hectares (166.7 acres) and situated bet-ween Langevåg and Sagvatnet, has a continuous gradient from 0 to 100 metres amsl, passing from rich calcareous pine forest with ivy and holly to a well-established and unique pine forest floored with bell heather.

Seabird sanctuary

The best way to enjoy the countryside on Bømlo is to cycle and, in addition to a flower book, it is a good idea to carry binoculars and a bird book. A good supply of vast areas without interference has resulted in Bømlo having Hordaland's largest density of white-tailed eagle pairs including probably ten nesting pairs within the municipality. There are several species of birds of prey nesting in

this island community and many other birds drop in during the spring and autumn migrations. A number of islets and skerries in the open sea south of Søre Bømlo are preserved as seabird sanctuaries, the collective name of one of these protected areas being nothing less than the Hovsøy, Låtersøy, Melne, Melneklubben, Lyngsøy, Oksøy and Raudholmane Nature Reserve. Gulls, black guillemots and shags thrive out here and Hordaland's only nesting locality for the northern fulmar is in this area. The common eider often nests within the gull colony, the advantage being that the gulls act as bodyguards in the nesting season, chasing away any intruders. At the end of July beginning of

August the male eiders collect in their thousands in this outermost piece of Western Norway to moult. It is absolutely forbidden for people to go ashore on these islands in the nesting season.

Historic island

In addition to the scenic countryside Bømlo is full of history. On Langevåg the so-called "green-stone" people lived. For thousands of years they made tools and weapons from the greenstone from Hespriholmen. Places where the stone was hewn as well as Stone Age settlements are more dense here than any other place in Western Norway.

Snorre Sturlason relates in The King's Saga that Olav Trygvasson permitted the building of a church on Moster when he came to Norway in the year 995, and the old, stone-built Moster Church stands here today as one of Norway's oldest churches. In other words Bømlo is one of the places where Christianity first found a foothold in Norway.

42

Folgefonna Glacier
National park between fjords and mountains

The Folgefonna Glacier looms over the Folgefonna Peninsula, an area of outstanding natural beauty squeezed between fjords and mountains in the county of Hordaland.

The national park occupies a region of fjords and mountains between the fjords Hardangerfjord, Åkrafjord and Sørfjord. The Folgefonna Glacier is divided into three smaller plateau glaciers with the prefixes Northern, Central and Southern, the latter at 179 square kilometres being Norway's third largest glacier as well as one of the few wilderness-like areas left in Hordaland. With the glacier placed centrally, Folgefonna National Park at 545.2 square kilometres is more than double the size of the entire glacial area. The national park in fact contains vast areas of nature with no icecap, particularly in the west and south of Southern (Søndre) Folgefonna.

Magnificent and varied nature

This national park reflects a wonderful part of Norway, featuring fjords, mountains, large and small lakes, rivers, and river valleys with splendid landscapes of diverse and luxuriant nature. The four landscape protection areas, Ænesdal Valley, Bondhusdal Valley, Hattebergsdal Valley and Buer provide beautiful and distinctive watercourse scenery,

Autumn beside the Folgefonna Glacier. Photo: Stig Tronvold/NN/Samfoto.

and where the mountain terrain ends abruptly at the edge of the fjord, rivers coloured by glacial water tumble wildly down towards the sea.

The valley of Bondhusdal is full of cultural history. An old cart road dating back to the 1800's leads from the village of Sunndal along this pretty valley floor and was previously called the Ice Road as it was built to transport ice from the Bondhusbre Glacier to England, long before the deepfreeze was invented. However, the long distance meant that a lot of the ice melted before it reached its destination. All the same, this road has served as a touring route for over 100 years and a path called Keiserstien leaves it and swings majestically up through the slopes of hardwood forest to the mountain farm, Gardshammarstølen, and on up to the edge of the glacier. The path was made in the 1800's for tourist traffic which arrived by cruise ships sailing up the fjords, some of the tourists even being transported over the glacier by horse and sleigh.

On the opposite side of the glacier, directly west of Odda, is the Buer Landscape Protection Area, one of the district's biggest tourist attractions, especially in the summer, with the Buerelv River cascading down the Buerdal Valley. After a 6 kilometre drive from Odda to the end of the road, it takes only one hour to walk into the edge of the Buerbre Glacier, surrounded by dramatic and fascinating scenery.

Any mention of tourist attractions in Kvinnherad and Hardanger must include the Rosendal Barony, Norway's only barony, lying just outside the national park boundaries. The castle dating back to the 1600's and its marvellous surround-

Moon over the Buerbre Glacier. Photo: Stig Tronvold/NN/Samfoto.

ing rose garden in the park provide a place of natural and cultural beauty which is absolutely worth a visit.

Paradise for tours

This magnificent countryside ranging from fjords to glaciers has provided many people with fantastic experiences, one of the classics being to ski over the Folgefonna Glacier in the spring, finally descending to the glorious sight of flowering fruit trees by the fjord. As well as ski tours it is possible to take part in glacier trekking courses and organised tours over the glacier in the summer. Many people make longer trips that include overnight stays, but this should only be done in the company of competent glacier folk. At an elevation of nearly 1,700 metres amsl it is vital to remember that weather conditions can change rapidly at all times of the year, but in fine weather the panoramas from the

top are wonderful, covering large parts of the Hardangervidda Mountain Plateau, the Hårteigen Mountain, the Hardangerjøkul Icecap in the east and north, and the coastal mountain ranges, the Marstein Lighthouse and the North Sea to the west. One of the most fantastic and scenically rewarding tours, although long, goes from Sunndal via Breidablikk to Fonnabu and Tokheim to Holmaskjær.

Bergen Turlag (trekking club) has three cabins and Haugesund Trekking Association has one cabin in the Folgefonna National Park. Fonnabu, Holmaskjær and Saubrehytta are self-service tourist cabins (with provisions), while Breidablikk is a no-service cabin (no provisions). For the sake of safety these cabins are open all year round.

43 ▶ **Herdla**
A special island

Herdla is the northernmost island in the municipality of Askøy north of Bergen. The nature on the island is quite different from the rest of the municipality and Herdla is also very special for the whole county. The interesting geology and unique bird life on the island resulted in the establishment of the Herdla Nature Reserve over 20 years ago.

The scenery and nature on Herdla, not to mention the fantastic panorama over the sea towards Øygarden in the west, fascinates the visitor. The island is completely flat and therefore quite different to its rockier and more undulating neighbours. Enormous volumes of moraine were deposited on Herdla at the end of the last Ice Age over 10,000 years ago, so this is the outermost limit of the advancement of the ice during the terminal moraine period. The moraine deposits can clearly be seen on the south-west side of the island where there is a splendid pebble shore and a sandy beach with appurtenant coastal vegetation. This type of moraine coast formation is quite unusual for Norway.

Rich in bird life

In addition to the Quaternary geo-

Herdla is a picturesque island in the very north of Askøy Municipality. Photo: Helge Sunde/Samfoto.

The oystercatcher thrives on Herdla's beaches. Photo: Tom Schandy.

<svg>FACTS</svg>

Herdla is an island of 2 square kilometres in the northernmost part of Askøy Municipality in Hordaland. Parts of the area comprise a nature reserve.

Attractions:
· Herdla Nature Reserve with its bird life
· Moraine coast formation
· Herdla Museum
· Herdla Manor

Map:
1116 III Herdla 1: 50 000.

Access:
Follow Road 562 over Askøy Bridge all the way to the north of Askøy and to Herdla.

logy, the bird life on this northernmost tip of the Askøy Municipality is quite unique. A total of 224 different bird species have been observed on Herdla, where the mild, western climate ensures a rich bird life all year round. However, the area is first and foremost significant as a resting place for waders in the autumn migration and as a grazing area for ducks in the winter, the shallow seas north of Herdla, called Herdaflaket, being the most important area for these birds. There are numerous common eiders, the winter record being around 2,300 individuals. This biotope is also important for species of diving ducks with velvet scoters, black scoters and long-tailed ducks being relatively common in the winter season.

The shallow seas and sandy beaches make Herdla special. The beaches attract many different species of waders, and large quantities of dunlins, little stints, ringed plovers, common snipes and knots can be observed, as well as fewer numbers of curlew sandpipers, Temminck's stints, sanderlings, purple sandpipers and turnstones. Large waders also thrive here and the golden plover, ruff, northern lapwing, oystercatcher, curlew, bar-tailed godwit, grey plover and redshank can be ticked off on the ornithologists' lists of species.

Protected area and golf course
Herdlavalen, the vital resting area for waders in the county, is also important nationally because the distance to similar localities is relatively large. Herdla Nature Reserve, with adjoining areas for preservation of bird life, covers approximately 1.3 square kilometres, of which approximately 0.5 square kilometres are on land. The area for preservation of bird life covers around 3.15 square kilometres, of which around 0.5 square kilometres are on land.

In fact the nature reserve contributes to making Herdla an important tourist destination, and to enable the public to experience a little of the rich bird life, two observation houses have been erected at Prestvika and Urdneset. From 15 April to 30 September it is forbidden to traffic a demarcated area between Prestvika and Urdneset. The purposes behind conservation is to preserve a distinctive and highly productive wetland, to protect an especially abundant and varied bird life, interesting and valuable geological features and to protect all plant life and wildlife that are otherwise naturally connected to the area. The area for protection of bird life includes stretches of shallow sea between the islands Store Agnøy and Herdla, surrounding Lammøy Island, the islets of Kvitholmane and parts of Herdla.

The northern tip of Herdla is not only picturesque, but has a lot of fertile soil. Herdla Manor, a royal manor at the time of Harold the Fair-haired, is considered in a national sense to be quite a large manor, and is also Herdla's biggest farm. Besides ordinary farming operations, the farm includes a golf course and the golf club is perhaps the only one in Norway to have a bird in its logo. This is the northern lapwing, a well-known and well-liked bird in Herdla's cultivated landscape.

If you are ever on this fascinating island, the Herdla Museum is absolutely worth a visit. Opened in 1995, it catalogues the history of the island spanning culture, nature and World War II and the exhibitions range from the Ice Age to the present day. Central, fixed exhibitions concern Herdla's origins, the Herdla Bird Sanctuary, Herdla Church and World War II.

44

Vøringsfoss Waterfall
A thundering torrent

The Vøringsfoss Waterfall's 182 metre sheer drop makes it Norway's most visited nature-based tourist attraction. Annually around 620,000 people from all over the world gaze with awe at the foaming torrents thundering down to Eidfjord in Hardanger.

This impressive waterfall in Western Norway has been photographed by millions of cameras over the last 100 years, but it has not always been so crowded here. Until 1821 only the inhabitants of Eidfjord knew about this tremendous waterfall. More often than not it was scholars and "discoverers" who made the scenic attractions in Norway famous, and this was also the case with Vøringsfoss.

"Discovered" by Professor Hansteen

Professor Christopher Hansteen, the director for Norway's Geographic Surveying Authority travelled over the Hardangervidda Mountain Plateau in the summer of 1821 to carry out some astronomy observations. He was impressed by all the waterfalls he saw on his trip, but his two travelling companions, who were

Annually around 620,000 people from all over the world gaze with awe at the foaming torrents thundering down the Vøringsfoss Waterfall. Photo: Bård Løken/NN/Samfoto.

local people, were not as overwhelmed and promised to show the professor a proper waterfall if he accompanied them to Eidfjord. Hansteen was sceptical as they boasted that the waterfall was 1,400 metres high, and in addition he was worried they might rob him and throw him in the waterfall. However, his curiosity won and he joined them, saw the tremendous waterfall, and was not robbed. By using a stone and his pocket watch he measured the fall to be 280 metres, a lot less than he had been told, but the voluminous force of the water impressed him, although time has revealed that the professor was wrong in his measurements by 100 metres. On his return home he wrote a descriptive article about Vøringsfoss Waterfall in the journal "Budstikken", and the scenic falls in Eidfjord became known all over the country.

The perpendicular mountain sides and the raging waterfall are a unique experience in Norwegian nature. The name Vøring comes from the word Vyrd which means proud or handsome, and all visitors agree that this is a very appropriate name. The waterfall is created by the Bjoreia River throwing itself over a ledge on the edge of the Hardangervidda Mountain Plateau, after first having passed through the Sysendal Valley. Incredibly enough Vøringsfoss Waterfall is regulated and the great Sysen Dam in Sysendal Valley tames the falls all winter. However during the tourist season 12 cubics of water per second are released which is more than a normal summer could provide. However, during the snow melting in the spring, Vøringsfoss Waterfall does not manage to reach its former glory.

Tourist route down Måbødal Valley

The route down the Måbødal Valley is nearly as impressive as the waterfall above. This is a "young" valley and before the Ice Age, it sloped gently towards the west coast. After pressure from the ice, the valley was raised and the river found new strength and formed a narrow cleft. With such dramatic nature it is no wonder that Road 7 between Halne on the Hardangervidda Mountain Plateau and Tokagjelet west of Norheimsund has been made a tourist route. The 7

The Vøringsfoss Waterfall's 182 metre drop is quite a sight. Photo: Sigmund Krøvel-Velle/Samfoto.

kilometres through Måbødal Valley are almost a road museum in itself where Road 7 passes through four tunnels with stopping places, vantage points and information boards telling the story about this important thoroughfare between east and west. The old roads are now walking and cycling paths which twist their way up the mountain side in a series of 124 bends and 1,300 steps. From June to September the Troll Train operates taking passengers up and down the valley.

There is also a path at the bottom which goes almost up to the waterfall. It is difficult to describe the sensation of standing under these sheer drops of rock looking up at the waterfall as spray showers your face. Dare devils climb the frozen falls in the winter, but this is not an activity for the majority of tourists.

❧ FACTS ❧

Vøringsfoss is Norway's most famous waterfall. Situated on the edge of the Hardangervidda Mountain Plateau, it has a drop of 182 metres down to the Måbødal Valley in Eidfjord in Hordaland County.

Attractions:
· Waterfall and majestic scenery
· The old roads through the Måbødal Valley

Map:
1415 IV Eidfjord 1: 50 000.

Access:
Road 7 over the Hardangervidda Mountain Plateau. Wonderful view of the waterfall at Fossli Hotel. A dizzier view from Fossetromme beside Road 7. A tourist path to the foot of the falls starts at the uppermost opening of the Måbødal Tunnel on Road 7.

45

Hardangerjøkul Icecap
Majestic and beautiful

The Hardangerjøkul Icecap, Norway's sixth largest glacier, has been called an ice-covered dome and for travellers on the train to Bergen, cyclists on Rallarvegen Road and hikers on the Hardangervidda Mountain Plateau, it has been a famous landmark and guide. Every year hundreds of skiers celebrate Norway's national day, 17 May, on this glacier just south of Finse.

As a plateau glacier, the Hardangerjøkul Icecap is Norway's second largest. It roughly straddles the watershed between Eastern and Western Norway, sticking several short arms out around its edges, the largest of these being Rembesdalskåki in the west and the Midtdalsbre Glacier in the east. Although at 70 square kilometres it is not the country's largest glacier, it scores top marks for being famous, the main reason for this being the opening of the Bergen Railway in 1909, making the glacier more accessible. The large population in Eastern Norway flocked to Finse on the new train connection especially at Easter for the skiing, and in 1910 the Norwegian State Railway had to put on extra trains, even having to utilise sleeping cars for many years in order to accommodate the eager skiers.

Glacier course
In 1958 the Norwegian Trekking Association chose to arrange their

Every year thousands of people celebrate Norway's national day, 17 May, on the top of the Hardangerjøkul Icecap. Photo: Helge Sunde/NN/Samfoto.

The cabin Jøkulhytta on the top of the Hardangerjøkul Icecap has a marvellous view, which includes Hallingskarvet. Photo: Tom Schandy.

was a new enormous flood. Following this a new tunnel was blown out 50 metres under the old and it seems that Nedre Demmevann Lake has finally been tamed.

Glacier research and a protected area

The Norwegian Polar Institute has carried out mass balance measurements on Rembesdalskåki since 1963 (Norwegian Water Resources and Energy Directorate since 1985). There are also records and research material from before this date. During the "Little Ice Age" in the 1700's the glacier arm was 2 kilometres longer than it is today. Despite incredible snowfalls of 5 metres on the Hardangerjøkul Icecap, Rembesdalskåki is in retreat. Large snowfalls are of no use if the long and hot summers melt it away faster than it can accumulate.

North of the Hardangervidda National Park, the protected landscape, Skaupsjøen/Hardangerjøkulen (the Hardangerjøkul Icecap), stretches all the way up to Finse-

vann Lake. The total area of 551 square kilometres includes the Hardangerjøkul Icecap and is of great value for recreational activities. Not only does the protected area contain one of the few localities where the arctic fox breeds, but it is also a vital link for the reindeer in the two wild reindeer regions, the Hardangervidda Mountain Plateau and the Nordfjell Mountains.

first glacier course on the Hardangerjøkul Icecap and it was a success. Since then thousands of people have tried out crampons and ice axes on the glacier's beautiful blue ice field, Blåisen. Roped together they have walked over the highest point at 1,860 metres amsl and begun the western descent towards the cabin Demmevasshytta and the Rembedsalskåki glacier arm.

The glacier trekking courses have to a great extent been centred around the Norwegian Trekking Association's cabin, Demmevasshytta, which originally started as two workmen's barracks used during the damming up of Demmevann Lake at the end of the 1800's. Demmevasshytta was manned until 1942 but changes in the glacier made it difficult to reach the cabin after World War II. However, in the first half of the 1960's the trekking association started a glacier group who took over and restored the cabin, giving it a new lease of life. It has the association's standard lock, but it is

recommended to contact the association before one sets out to walk there.

Airfield and natural catastrophes

It must be mentioned that the Germans during the war unsuccessfully tried to establish a take-off and landing strip on the Hardangerjøkul Icecap. The first plane that landed crashed in a crevasse when it tried to take off again.

Many people are perhaps surprised that Demmevann Lake was dammed as early as the 1800's. The reason was not to extract hydro-electric power but to hinder natural catastrophes resulting from Nedre Demmevann Lake's tendency to cause floods in the Simadal Valley. The glacier arm, Rembesdalskåki, continually dammed up the water which became so voluminous that it finally lifted the glacier and flowed uncontrollably down into the valley. This happened several times and a tunnel was constructed to make a new outlet, which functioned well for many years until 1937, when there

The red light of dawn on the Hardangerjøkul Icecap, Norway's second largest plateau glacier. Photo: Tom Schandy.

46

Aurlandsdal Valley
Wild and exciting

Western Norway is full of exciting and fantastic countryside and the Aurlandsdal Valley is no exception. The path through this wild valley offers spectacular scenery and it seems incredible that people have managed to live all year round on several of the farms here.

The Aurlandsdal Valley is one of Norway most spectacular natural wonders. This is a view towards the old settlement at Sinjarheim. Photo: Svein Grønvold/NN/Samfoto.

After visiting this wild and thrilling valley in Western Norway, the owner of the Aftenposten newspaper, Amandus Schibsted, wrote the following in one of the issues: *"I have now walked through the Aurlandsdal Valley and it exceeds anything else that our country has to offer in the way of wild scenery"*. He was not alone with being impressed by this route. The artist, Johannes Flintoe walked it in 1819, which resulted in among other things the painting called "Bjønnestigvarden" now hanging in the National Gallery. At the end of the 1800's tourism increased here and in 1894 the Norwegian Trekking Association gave the farm Øvstebø economic support so that they could offer hikers in the valley a place to stay. A year later the association's own tourist cabin, Steinbergdalshytta, was completed (it was later sold in 1961 to the person who managed it). Through the years the footpath through Aurlandsdal Valley has become one of Norway's most popular and most discussed walking routes.

Old settlements

Long before the tourists found this valley stretching from Hol in Buskerud to Aurland in Sogn and Fjor-dane, it was an important tho-roughfare as it was the fastest route between east and west for the people who lived here. At the beginning of the 1900's there were people living both at Stran-davatn Lake in Hol and several pla-ces in the Aurlandsdal Valley, the most incredible of these settle-ments being Sinjarheim which was probably cleared as long ago as the time of the Vikings. Sinjar-heim, in the middle of this deso-late and inaccessible valley, was

---

❧ FACTS ❧

The Aurlandsdal Valley, wild, west-country scenery in Sogn and Fjordane where one of Norway's most spectacular hiking trails passes between Øvstebø and Vassbygdi.

Attractions:
- The waterfalls
- The old settlements at Sinjar-heim and Almen
- Path carved out of rocky ledges
- The grotto/pothole "Vetlahel-vete" to the west of the path

Map:
Touring map Aurlandsdal Valley 1:50 000.

Access:
Bus or car on Road 50 between Hol and Aurland.

Milking goats at Sinjarheim. Photo: Svein Grønvold/NN/Samfoto.

inhabited for hundreds of years right up until 1921, although it was still used as a summer mountain dairy farm until 1964, when this activity also ceased. Since then the Society for the Preservation of Norwegian Ancient Monuments has made an all-out effort to save the farm which is now a school for agriculture and horticulture in Aurland. Students come here to learn traditional mountain dairy farming, so do not be surprised if you are offered fresh goats' cheese on your hike through the valley.

Exciting hiking trail
The hiking trail in the valley starts at Øvstebø (also known as Østerbø) and goes through emerald green, west-country scenery with foaming waterfalls everywhere you look. The path passes precipices, steep slopes, rocky ledges and rope bridges. By the time you reach Vassbygdi you have walked 14 kilometres, but most people use up to seven and eight hours on this spectacular trail not only because the terrain is difficult but also there is so

much to look at. With a drop in height of 750 metres it is easier to walk from top to bottom, but many hikers do in fact choose to go in the opposite direction. A bus service between Hol and Aurland can take you back to your starting point. There is a four hour walk from Øvstebø to the privately run tourist cabin, Steinbergdalshytta, and continuing from here it takes three hours to reach Geiterygghytta, a tourist cabin run by the Norwegian Trekking Association.

In the 1970's there was extensive hydro-electric power development in the Aurland Watercourse which resulted in an all-year-round road linking Hol and Aurland. Fortunately the Aurlandsdal Valley was hardly affected and only a short stretch of the road can be seen from the path down in the valley. The most noticeable interference is a somewhat reduced flow of water in the summer, but the tour through the Aurlandsdal Valley is still a must for any hiker who likes exciting, lush and wild scenery.

Flåmsdal Valley
Magnificent scenery

47

Descending the Flåmsdal Valley in Sogn and Fjordane on a sunny summer's day is a revelation of beauty. Bright green valley sides, foaming waterfalls and a fantastic traditional cultivated landscape make this an international tourist attraction.

The Flåmsdal Valley is a typical example of a U-shaped valley with many small hanging valleys running into it. The main valley itself slices deep down in the mountain massif reaching from the Aurlandsfjord to Myrdal Station on the Bergen Railway. Building a railway line in this terrain is an impressive piece of engineering and Flåm Railway is one of Norway's most popular attractions

Kjosfoss in the Flåmsdal Valley is one of Norway's most photographed waterfalls. Photo: Tom Schandy.

and one of the world's most spectacular stretches of railway track. When completed in 1940 the Norway State Railway's calculations, based on passenger traffic in 1915, estimated a possible 22,000 passengers a year. In 2006 over 500,000 tourists travelled on the Flåm Railway which is not surprising considering the wonderful scenery, especially in the Flåmsdal Valley.

Popular cycling route

It is not necessary to see this natural beauty spot in Sogn by train. After the arrival of off-road bikes with sturdy tyres some years ago, the traffic along the so-called Rallarveg (navvies' road) has almost exploded. Originally built between Haugastøl and Voss as a supply road during the construction of the Bergen Railway from 1895 to 1909, it has a detour to Flåm via Myrdal and when people today talk about cycling the Rallarveg they are often referring to the route between Haugastøl and Flåm. Altogether this covers a distance of approximately 80 kilometres with at times quite poor road surface and most people, therefore, choose to divide the trip into several stages with overnight stays at, for example, Finse or Hallingskeid. The whole tour is a gigantic nature experience and the cream on the cake is the last stretch from Myrdal down to Flåm. A lot of cyclists get off and walk the 21 bends down the valley side from Myrdal, so that they can concentrate on absorbing the beautiful and lush scenery in the Flåmsdal Valley instead of struggling to keep the bike on the bumpy road.

If you want to study the flora and really experience the nature in the Flåmsdal Valley close at

The Flåmsdal Valley is a high-class international tourist attraction. Photo: Tom Schandy.

hand, there are many walking trails in the area. Another popular activity in recent years is canoeing in the fjord beside Flåm which also brings you close to nature in this glorious west-country landscape. The Nærøyfjord was made a protected landscape in 2002 (see separate chapter on Nærøyfjord) and the area is listed as a UNESCO World Heritage Site. Parts of the Flåmsdal Valley are included in this landscape protection area.

Abundant flora and impressive waterfalls

The upper part of the Flåm Watercourse in fact contains the richest flora found in the whole of Western Norway. The reason for this is the limestone-rich phyllite bedrock. Over half of all the mountain plants registered in Norway are actually found in this valley. Due to the height variation and large fluc-

tuations in precipitation, all types of vegetation zones are represented in the Flåmsdal Valley. Down beside Flåm there are dry slopes and hazel forests contrasting strongly with the high alpine zone in the mountains. Between these two zones species such as the giant bellflower, alpine sow-thistle, large white buttercup, northern wolfsbane, germander speedwell and touch-me-not balsam thrive.

Cyclists who have not noticed the rich flora have more probably observed the waterfalls in the Flåmsdal Valley. Rjoandefoss with a drop of 390 metres and Kjosfoss beside the Flåm Railway with a drop of altogether 225 metres stretching over 700 metres are the most famous falls. Kårdalsfoss Waterfall down in the valley impresses cyclists crossing the bridge over the river, more because of the ferocity in the tremendous

volume of water than for its relatively modest height. The 300 goats from the goat farm at Kårdal provide another welcome photo motif.

🐚 FACTS 🐚

The Flåmsdal Valley, one of Norway's most picturesque valleys. Situated in Aurland Municipality in Sogn and Fjordane.

Attractions:
· The Flåm Railway
· The waterfalls
· The Rallarveg (the navvies' road) cycling route
· Lush flora

Map:
Touring map for Aurlandsdal Valley 1: 50 000.

Access
Boat or train to Flåm. Road for cars from Road 52 at Aurland all the way to Flåm. Cycling route along Rallarveg.

Every year thousands of boat tourists are literally bewitched by the Nærøyfjord. The steep mountain sides enclosing the narrow fjord arm and the roaring waterfalls make it easy to understand why the Nærøyfjord in Sogn and Fjordane is on the UNESCO list of World Heritage Sites.

There are many people who consider the Nærøyfjord as the narrowest, wildest and most dramatic fjord arm in the world. It is 17 kilometres long and only 250 metres across at the narrowest part, and is a side arm to the Aurlandsfjord which again is a side arm to the world's longest fjord without ice sheet, the Sognefjord. The mountains enclosing the Nærøyfjord reach 1,500 metres per-

A morning mood on the Nærøyfjord. Photo: Tom Schandy.

Foaming water, deep fjords and steep mountains. Nærøyfjord is Western Norway at its best. Photo: Tom Schandy.

pendicularly up from the water creating an atmosphere of magic, and making a boat trip on Nærøyfjord one of the most spectacular nature experiences in Norway. About half way along the two awe-inspiring waterfalls, Odnesfoss and Styvefoss, plunge over the edge of the mountain and close to where the fjord opens out

there is the no less impressive veil of the Lægdafoss Waterfall.

Landscape protection area, and on the World Heritage List

The Nærøyfjord was preserved as a 576 square kilometre landscape protection area in 2002 and is now on the UNESCO World Heritage List along with the Geiranger-

fjord. Large areas of landscape around the Nærøyfjord are unspoiled nature with no technical intervention and the purpose of the landscape protection area is to preserve a beautiful and distinctive countryside and traditional cultivated landscape stretching from the fjord to the mountains. This magnificent scenery formed by glaciers contains a diversity of plant and wildlife. Deer thrive on the steep slopes lining the fjord and above the tree line the wild reindeer make their home, while porpoises and common seals provide wildlife experiences for the tourists on the fjord.

The traditional cultivated landscape of hayfield strips, grazing pastures, summer mountain farms, farms and cultural monuments created by hundreds of years of active farming comprise a substantial part of the landscape. Several small hamlets without roads lie along the edge of the fjord and tell their story of a time when the fjord was vital for transport. On small green patches of pasture the elm and lime trees bear evidence of a particular form for collecting winter fodder, called "styving" which entailed cutting branches and twigs off deciduous trees 2 to 3 metres up the trunk and after years of this practice the trees assume the appearance of candelabra. In addition grass was cut on the small fields between large boulders and under the steep mountain walls during an era based on natural subsistence and moderation.

A trip in this fantastic natural wonder in Western Norway will take most people's breath away. All foreign visitors agree that this is a classic international tourist attraction.

A 17 kilometre long, and extremely narrow, fjord arm off the Sognefjord. The Nærøyfjord, together with Geirangerfjord and Aurlandsfjord, is on the UNESCO List of World Heritage Sites, which includes the world's most significant cultural and natural heritages. Landscape protection area measuring 576 square kilometres.

Attractions:
· The narrow fjord and sheer mountain sides
· Rivers and waterfalls
· Old deserted farms and summer farms high up on the mountain sides

Maps:
Touring map Stølsheim-Nærøyfjord 1: 100 000 and Touring map Nærøyfjord 1: 50 000.

Access:
Road E16 to Gudvangen innermost in the Nærøyfjord. One can drive further along a dead-end road on the west side of the fjord to the village of Bakka. Daily passenger boat service between Gudvangen, Aurland and Flåm all year round and from 1 May to 30 September there is a car ferry running between Gudvangen, Kaupanger and Lærdal.

The Nærøyfjord is a world famous fjord arm in Sogn. Photo: Tom Schandy.

49

Stølsheimen
From fjord to mountain

Stølsheimen has often been called Western Norway in miniature because it has everything from steep mountain ridges, broad valleys, vast marshlands, with lush pasture at the mountain dairy farms and deep fjord arms. The region is framed between the Sognefjord in the north, the Bergen Railway in the south, the Masfjord in the west and Vikafjell Mountains in the east. A majestic and diverse mountain landscape towering over deep fjords and disappearing into distant blue-grey mountains at elevations between 1,200 and 1,300 metres.

The name Stølsheimen is relatively modern being approved by the board of the Bergen Turlag (Bergen Trekking Club) around 1950. It was the opinion of the people in the Norwegian Trekking Association that this district deserved its own collective name and due to the vast number of mountain dairy farms ("støl" in Norwegian) in the district, Stølsheimen became its official name. This area of scenic beauty lies on the border between the counties of Sogn and Fjordane, and Hordaland.

Numerous mountain farms

Bergen Turlag's activity in this area started in the 1930's when it rented a couple of mountain farms. Altogether over 100 mountain farms of various sizes are registered in Stølsheimen. It was quite normal for the farms in the valley to have several mountain farms each, for example, a summer farm on the top of the mountain and a spring farm a little lower down. The journey from the farm to the mountain farm could often be tiring and particularly the farmers around the Sognefjord had a long trip using as much as 10 or 12 hours before they arrived with the livestock.

Today few mountain dairy farms are worked but a lot of the

The autumn sun rises over the old mountain farm building in the foreground. Photo: Helge Sunde/NN/Samfoto.

Bog cotton at Skavlabu, Bergen Turlag's self-service tourist cabin in Stølsheimen. Photo: Helge Sunde/NN/Samfoto.

marked hiking trails follow old cattle paths and thoroughfares. As the mountain farms gradually became abandoned it was necessary to build up a network of tourist cabins to replace the lodging provided by the mountain farms. Worth mentioning is that the world's first self-service cabin, Skjerjevasshytta, was erected in the west of Stølsheimen by Bergen Turlag in 1937, but has been demolished in later years. Bergen Turlag and Voss Utferdslag (trekking club) now have a number of cabins in Stølsheimen, the majority of which are self-service (with provisions), but some of them are no-service cabins (without provisions). The short distances between the cabins make Stølsheimen suitable for families with children.

Lush flora and soapstone

The nature in Stølsheimen is varied. In the east, for example, the bedrock is rich in nutrients and provides an exciting plant life. People interested in botany will find many rare mountain plants thriving on the fertile soil in this region such as the fragrant orchid and white frog orchid, as well as flowering beauties like mountain avens, maiden saxifrage, alpine gentian, rock speedwell and snow cinquefoil.

The majestic summit, Kvitanosi, at 1,434 metres amsl lies to the north-west of the cabin, Volahytta, which is owned by Voss Utferdslag. In fine weather the panorama from the summit is magnificent and should not be missed. Further to the north and only a couple of days' walking is the cabin, Selhamar, which with 50 beds is Bergen Turlag's largest cabin in Stølsheimen. The region around the cabin offers exciting walking destinations and good fishing in the lakes. Approximately 2 kilometres to the north-east is Gryteberget Mountain, its name deriving from an extremely old soapstone locality. This stone is not only easy to form but is also fireproof and the cooking pots (gryter) from this area were much sought after. Soapstone cooking pots were used as long ago as the Bronze Age.

Protected area

The Stølsheimen Landscape Protection Area measures 373 square kilometres and its purpose is to preserve this varied, distinctive and beautiful west-country mountain and fjord landscape, which includes cultural monuments, traditional cultivated landscape and a natural environment with little technical interference.

The fact that this protected landscape stretches from the high mountains down to the pebbles on the shore of the Finnafjord makes it very interesting. The Finnafjord is the only fjord arm belonging to the main Sognefjord that does not have a motor road. The traditional cultivated landscape together with the farm buildings at Finden, plays an important part in the environment at the fjord. The area is valuable for outdoor pursuits, particularly walking and boating. This is a habitat for the golden eagle, white-tailed eagle and white-backed woodpecker, all three being on the Norwegian red list for endangered and vulnerable species.

The herd of wild reindeer in Stølsheimen are really descendents from the domestic herd of reindeer managed by Voss Tamreinlag, which was later disbanded and the herd was left to survive on its own. This has resulted in a herd of approximately 600 animals where hunting is permitted.

Skiers on the trail from Dyrkollbotn to Skavlabu in Stølsheimen. Photo: Helge Sunde/NN/Samfoto.

50

The Skerries at Askvoll and Solund
Island jumping on Norway's westernmost coast

The municipalities of Askvoll and Solund are located in the Sogn and Fjordane County and comprise innumerable islands. Norway's westernmost permanent settlements are found on Bulandet and Værlandet while Utvær has the country's westernmost lighthouse. These islands offer wonderful skerry scenery with screaming seabirds and rare plants.

Whereas Værlandet and Bulandet in the Askvoll Municipality were once two separate island communities, they are now joined by six bridges, enabling easier access for travellers wanting to experience this coastal nature. The new road connecting the islands is rightly called "Nordsjøporten" – The Gateway to the North Sea, and to the capricious weather it brings; one day smooth and calm and the next near gale. Perhaps there is a reason why one of the island communities is called Værlandet – "vær" is Norwegian for weather.

Bulandet-Værlandet
It is important to emphasize that we are not talking about just two islands but more an "ocean" of them and it is said that the communities of Bulandet and Værlandet together comprise as many islands as there are days in the year. They are quite different, Bulandet being flat while Værlandet consists of a number of knolls.

Sunset over an area of natural scenic beauty in the far west of Sogn and Fjordane. Photo: Tom Schandy.

Small, picturesque harbours nestle in narrow straits and bays with red-painted wooden houses and Bulandet has in fact been called the Venice of Norway, which perhaps further describes how idyllic it is. The community offers good cycling and many marked walking trails guide you through this open landscape. An area on the south-west part of Værlandet is protected as the Sørværet Nature Reserve which is a popular winter locality for divers, grebes, cormorants and ducks and it is not unusual to see 400 to 500 cormorants sitting on their resting places. Deer and otters also inhabit the islands.

Bulandet has a first class and exciting plant life including the tiny spring squill flower which grows prolifically on some of the grassy slopes. It is only around 10 centimetres high, but can colour the ground blue in the beginning of June. The plant is extremely rare, only growing a few other places in Western Norway, one being on Gåsvær in Solund, and as it needs a winter temperature above zero it can only survive out here in the open sea.

Værlandet and Bulandet are only the start of a fantastic stretch of coastline. Right beside Værlandet is the island of Alden with its 481 metre high mountain and this, from the correct angle, resembles a horse. This has earned it the name "The Norwegian Horse" and can offer a tour providing a panorama over the skerries in Ytre Sogn as well as towards the mainland.

Solund with Norway's westernmost lighthouse

Solund lies south of Askvoll and is Norway's westernmost municipality. The nature here is characterised by the intense sculptured rock landscape built up of a colourful conglomerate. In June the red thrift flower blooms on islets and skerries while the rocky slopes and heaths are decorated with bell heather and heather during late summer.

Comprising many small islands and skerries, Utvær lies at the outer limits of Solund Municipality. It has Norway's westernmost lighthouse and the small island of Steinsøya is as far as Norway

reaches in the west. Utvær was once a throbbing fishing society with 100 inhabitants but with automation of the lighthouse, the island group has been transformed into a charming holiday resort. Beneath the lighthouse in the narrow bay Utværsvågen there are rows of handsome seaside warehouses, and a prepared trail "Nordsjøløypa" – North Sea Trail – around the island is accompanied by the overwhelming sight of the vast and immense ocean.

If you want to spend some days out here there is accommodation in the old school house which functions as a Norwegian Trekking Association no-service tourist cabin, with no provisions. However, as it is not possible to buy anything in this outpost, you have to take all you need of food and drink from the mainland. The islands surrounding the lighthouse are protected as bird sanctuaries and it is forbidden to go ashore on them. The shag nests here along with many other seabird species, more west than any bird on the mainland. There are several seabird sanctuaries along this coast-

The rare spring squill needs winter temperatures above zero and it only survives out here in the open sea. Photo: Tom Schandy.

line, where it is also prohibited to go ashore, but with a pair of binoculars you can enjoy the bird life. If you have taken a fishing rod you are guaranteed some fantastic days out here in the far western reaches of Norway.

❧ FACTS ❧

The municipalities of Askvoll and Solund including the beautiful coastal gems, the islands of Værlandet, Bulandet, Alden and Utvær. Situated westernmost in the county of Sogn and Fjordane.

Attractions:
· Bird life with numerous shags
· The rare plant, spring squill
· Coastal communities
· Utvær Lighthouse
· The shifting weather

Maps:
1017 I Bulandet and 1017 II Utvær 1: 50 000.

Access:
Ferry from Fure or Askvoll several times a day to Bulandet and Værlandet. A passenger boat goes from Hardbakke to Utvær every Wednesday in the tourist season.

Utvær, outermost in the Solund Municipality, has Norway's westernmost lighthouse. Photo: Tom Schandy.

51

Utladal Valley
Valley of waterfalls

Immense scenery, including one of Europe's deepest valleys, Northern Europe's tallest free-fall cataract and old abandoned farms, makes the Utladal Valley and the Vettisfoss Waterfall natural wonders of international calibre.

The Utladal Valley is a gigantic gash in the Jotunheimen Mountains and a piece of Norwegian nature really worth experiencing. To walk in through this deep valley from Hjelle, with thundering waterfalls all around makes an indelible impression. The gravel road in was built on a voluntary basis by the people in the village and was completed in 1977, making access to the lower parts of the valley considerably easier. The waterfalls lining your walk spill over from hanging valleys, so named because they open out half way up the valley sides of the main valley. Each hanging valley has its own waterfall, the first being Hjellefoss, the most beautiful being Avdalsfoss and Vettisfoss, the largest, not only in the Utladal Valley but in fact it is one of Northern Europe's tallest, un-regulated cataracts.

A classic

275 metres free fall and a total height of 370 metres make Vettisfoss a classic among Norway's waterfalls. In 1818 the Utladal Valley was visited by the vicar of Lærdal, Ulrik Bøyesen, who was the first to describe this mighty waterfall in the Utladal Valley, and wrote after his visit: "*Not a drop of this quite perpendicular waterfall touches the rock face*".

Timber felled in the lush pine forests above at Vettismorki was previously thrown over the waterfall during the winter when snow and ice at the bottom cushioned the timber's fall, which would have otherwise been crushed to matchsticks in the force of the water. Today many of the pine trees, some of which are extremely old, have been badly damaged by the fluorine effluent from the aluminium works in Årdal. All the same Vettismorki is a splendid place with a charming mountain farm cluster of old buildings and a magnificent view right across the Utladal Valley towards the Stølsmaradal Valley and the summits of Ringstindene in Hurrungane.

The three to four hour walk from Hjelle to the bottom of Vettisfoss and back is a spectacular experience for nature and outdoor enthusiasts. Other large waterfalls in the valley are Høljafoss, Stølsmaradalsfoss, Fleskedalsfoss, Skoddedalsfoss, Midtmaradalsfoss, Maradalsfoss, Uradalsfoss and Skogadalsfoss, some of them being difficult to reach while others can be appreciated at a distance. The Utladal Valley is the valley of waterfalls.

Protected nature

At the same time as the Jotunheimen National Park was established in 1980 (see separate chapter on Jotunheimen), the Utladal Valley

It is still possible to stay overnight at the Vetti Farm in the Utladal Valley. Photo: Tom Helgesen.

Landscape Protection Area came into being and included the Utladal Valley and the mountain region from Tyin in the east to Hurrungane in the west. The purpose of this protected landscape, totalling 314 square kilometres, is to preserve a wild and wonderful countryside with its natural environment and cultural monuments which connect up to the Jotunheimen National Park. In 1984 the entire Utla Watercourse above the tributary of the Avdalselv River was permanently protected against hydro-electric power development. Work with protection of the area had in fact been in progress since 1924 when the Norwegian Trekking Association and the Norwegian Society for Conservation of Nature managed to preserve the Vettisfoss Waterfall.

The values found in the traditional cultivated landscape around the old settlements were vital criteria for conservation. This type of landscape is in the process of becoming overgrown and therefore four parts of the total area have been selected for management: Hjelle, Skåri, Avdal Valley and Vetti. In the course of three to four summer months most of the pasture at these farms will be grazed and cut, while many of the buildings, already restored, will be properly maintained. In addition, the old thoroughfares will be preserved and maintained on a yearly basis.

Vettisfoss in the Utladal Valley with its free fall of 275 metres is considered Northern Europe's tallest waterfall.
Photo: Tom Schandy.

❧ FACTS ❧

The Utladal Valley, wild and wonderful, approximately 20 kilometres long reaching north-east of Øvre Årdal in Sogn and Fjordane. Divides Hurrungane and the Tyin Mountains in Jotunheimen.

Attractions:
- Wild valley
- The waterfalls including Vettisfoss Waterfall
- Traditional cultivated landscape

Maps:
Touring map Jotunheimen West or Touring map Årdal 1: 50 000.

Access:
Car or bus via Road 53 to Øvre Årdal. Then 7 kilometres by road, a public thoroughfare, through the Utladal Valley. Follow a walking trail/tractor track to Vetti and from here there is a path to the bottom of Vettisfoss Waterfall. Allow four hours to the waterfall and back.

52

Drægnismorki-Yttrismorki
Forests of huge trees in Indre Sogn

Sogn and Fjordane as a Norwegian county is not really known for its large areas of forests, but in the region from Drægnismorki to Yttrismorki in Indre Sogn there are some really huge trees. In these steep slopes both coniferous and deciduous forests contain trees with unusually enormous dimensions. In addition parts of the region contain a traditional cultivated landscape with valuable qualities.

Gigantic pine trees grow in the area from Drægnismorki to Yttrismorki in Indre Sogn. Photo: Helge Gundersen.

Fortun is situated beyond the Lustrafjord in Indre Sogn and the valley which reaches north towards Nørdstedalsseter is called the Fortundal Valley. On the west side of this valley are Drægnismorki og Yttrismorki. Productive forest of good quality grows on these steep valley slopes beneath the tree line, but few of these forests are protected in connection with the conservation of conifer forests in Norway. The forest at Drægnismorki-Yttrismorki is clearly worthy of protection.

Varied biotopes

The forest area totals approximately 1,000 hectares (2,500 acres). It is bordered in the north by the mountain summit, Bjørkanosi and in the south and west it reaches almost to the summit Hjerseggnosi. Towards the floor of the valley in the east a natural boundary is created by the farms in the village while the forest line is the limit in the west. Sections of the valley side are extremely steep and the forest lies at an elevation between 40 and 850 metres, a variation which also results in a diversity of biotopes particularly when these alternate

A bed of moss with wood sorrel on an extremely old ash.
Photo Bård Bredesen/Naturarkivet.

between nutrient-rich phyllite in the bedrock and some granite-like augen gneiss. Of course the depth of the soil also varies as do the conditions of light and shadow.

All this means that Drægnismorki-Yttrismorki has many forest types including bilberry with a good portion of aspen and birch, berry/heather with a lot of cowberry, some lichen/pine forest,

low-growing herb and grass forest, calcareous pine forest and grey alder/wych elm forest. Felling has been carried out previously, but the centre section contains a forest with pines of exceptional dimensions and timber mass even in national terms. Two people linking hands do not manage to embrace the trunks of some of these giants, some of which are

up to 25 metres high. Concerning deciduous trees there are enormous aspens at Ospesete and in addition occurrences of wych elm, small-leaved lime, hazel and silver birch of tremendous proportions.

North of the farms at Yttri there is an old "styving" orchard with several hundred giant wych elms. "Styving" was a method of collecting fodder where the tops of the trees were cut off and the leaves used to feed livestock, and this was carried out here until after World War II. There is a bewitching air about this forest which is also biologically extremely valuable as, along with several old mountain dairy farms and cattle tracks, it gives Drægnismorki-Yttrismorki an identity which reveals the interaction between nature and culture. The streams were used as ice-slides for the timber during the winter as it was not possible to use horses to transport it in these sheer slopes with little snow cover.

Red listed species

Vascular plants are especially numerous in three types of nature in the area: Mountain vegetation connected to talus slopes and stream beds, limestone dependent species in calcareous pine forest and nutrient dependent species in grey alder/wych elm forest. Plants of interest are great meadowgrass, sweet-scented bedstraw, touch-me-not balsam, ground cedar and not least the great-spurred violet, a plant which only occurs otherwise in Western Norway at Sunndal in Møre and Romsdal.

All the same perhaps the most distinctive plant life is the fungus flora especially in the calcareous pine forest and the grey alder forests used for grazing around

Yttri. Under overhanging rocks, tremendous stone screes spread, with sources of limestone-rich water streaming from their lower edges, making an El Dorado for ground growing fungi. Some of these have few previous occurrences in Western Norway while others are only found here, which is why Drægnismorki-Yttrismorki has been the arena for international fungi congresses.

The red listed bird species registered here are the lesser-spotted woodpecker, white-backed woodpecker and northern goshawk. The white-backed wood-pecker is dependent on old-growth deciduous forest to survive and Western Norway is the species' last bastion in Europe. It is a very special experience to go for a walk in these regions where the huge pine giants grow against a backdrop of towering snow clad mountain peaks in Hurrungane in West Jotunheimen.

53 ▸ Jostedalsbre Glacier
Europe's largest mainland glacier

Perhaps it is the contrasts of the Jostedalsbre Glacier which fascinate most, ranging from lush villages and bright blue fjords in innermost Sogn to the ice-cold glacier and snow-covered summits at 2,000 metres on the glacier plateau.

Once functioning as a barrier between Western and Eastern Norway, the glacier is today a firstclass natural tourist attraction both for residents of east and west as well as thousands of tourists. Not only does this majestic glacier impress when viewed at a distance, with its arms reaching down into many of the valleys in Western Norway, but it can also impress at close contact if you join one of the many guided tours across it.

National park since 1991
The Jostedalsbre Glacier is an important part of typically magnificent and beautiful Norwegian nature, and as a significant part of Norway's national heritage the Jostedalsbre Glacier National Park was protected in 1991. Approximately half of the protected 1,300 square kilometres is covered by glacier of which the uninterrupted Jostedalsbre Glacier proper measures 473 square kilometres.

However, many people also include all the glaciers between Indre Sogn and Nordfjord in this calculation, which increases the total area to 815 square kilometres.

The entire national park, spanning a wide variety of nature, is in Sogn and Fjordane County where lush hardwood forests in the lowlands merge with high lying glaciers and mountains. The Jostedalsbre Glacier, the largest on the European mainland, has an uninterrupted length of 60 kilometres and is 10-15 kilometres across at the widest point. The glacier cap is encircled by U-shaped valleys, moraines, shiny smooth mountain sides, glacial river plains, talus slopes and screes which have been formed by ice and water from time immemorial, providing a landscape which is still changing. It is not only vitally important to protect the glacier, but also the glacial rivers and moraines and not least the traditional cultivated landscape in the mountain farm valleys where the farms, mountain farms and birch orchards are proof that people have subsisted near the glacier for many centuries. Whereas agriculture is still very much alive in the villages surrounding the national park, operation of the mountain dairy farms has only

Foaming river from the Briksdalsbre Glacier in Stryn. Photo: Tom Schandy.

survived in a few places due to modern farming methods taking over.

Large differences

Glaciers are formed when the excessive snow from winter is larger than that which melts in the summer. As opposed to snow drifts, glaciers are a moving build up of snow and ice over many years. While it can be cold, cloudy and windy on the glacier, it can be warm, sunny and windless in the valley. There can be frost and snowfalls on the glacier all year round, with an amazing 6 to 8 metres of snow a year. The pressure of the ever increasing snow transforms the layers underneath gradually to ice, which in turn slides down the glacier like a plastic mass.

The huge variety of nature over a relatively short distance is due to great variations in the local climate, differences in elevation and the influence of the glaciers. Lush hardwood forests of elm and lime flourish in the lower regions along with warmth-loving plants such as the broad-leaved helleborine orchid and the spring pea flower, while 1,500 metres elevation there is alpine vegetation such as the glacier buttercup and wild azalea.

Popular for tours

Incredible as it might sound today, the Jostedalsbre Glacier was previously a thoroughfare and road for livestock from valleys and fjords in the west to Indre Sogn, cattle and horses being driven over the glacier for sale at markets in Eastern Norway.

The areas surrounding the Jostedalsbre Glacier has long traditions of being attractive for tours, especially on the actual glacier and to the summits. In the spring the tour which crosses the length of the glacier, preferably with a detour to the top of the highest summit, Lodalskåpa (2,083 metres amsl) in Luster/Stryn is very popular, as well as Brenibba (2,018 metres amsl) in Luster. Remember that without the necessary knowledge and glacier equipment, a tour on the glacier is extremely dangerous!

The old thoroughfares between the valleys surrounding the glacier provide interesting walks, for example through Oldeskaret and Supphelleskaret. The most renowned tourist destinations on the Jostedalsbre Glacier are the glacier arms in the Briksdal Valley, at Fjærland and the Nigardsbre Glacier, where it is possible to join an exciting guided tour on to the glacier ice. There are also paths leading up to the glacier in the valleys of Kjenndal and Austerdal. Accommodation is provided in the form of camping sites, hostels and tourist lodges in the valleys outside the national park, as well as the Norwegian Trekking Association tourist cabins around the glacier and only a few hours' hike from the main roads.

A roped line of trekkers move towards the Jostedalsbre Glacier's highest point, Lodalskåpa (2,083 metres amsl) in Luster/Stryn. Photo: Tom Helgesen.

Ålfotbre Glacier
Spectacular scenery

A remarkable mountain terrain formed in terraces and with abundant fossil finds. The Ålfotbre Glacier is Norway's westernmost glacier, its surrounding areas making it quite unique where it lies between the Hyefjord, Nordfjord, Road 614 and Road 615 in the far west of Sogn and Fjordane.

The terrain surrounding Ålfotbre Glacier is extraordinary, many of the mountains resembling domi-

noes, some of which are standing upright while others look as though they have been toppled.

The reason for this is the Devon Age sediments of sand and stone dating back 360-400 million years

which were washed into valleys and basins between the enormous mountains in the Caledo-

Maritind, a pole-shaped summit nestling close to and to the right of the western end of the Saga Mountain, which is a fantastic destination for a walk on foot or skis. Photo: Alvar Melvær.

The view west from the Ålfotbre Glacier. The two striking summits are Keipen to the left and Plagen/Saga to the right. Photo: Alvar Melvær.

Future conservation area
The Ålfotbre Glacier Landscape Protection Area measuring 230 square kilometres will soon be resolved by the government, the Department of the Environment's recommendation being: *"This will be the only large protected area in Norway on Devon Age bedrock, with extremely characteristic mountain formation and abundant finds of fossils. The district contains some of the western-most wilderness-like areas in Norway as well as being Norway's westernmost region for glaciers. It is representative for the outer coastal mountain regions in Sogn and Fjordane with heavy precipitation. There is a large variation in the nature types within a limited area, ranging from warmth-dependent deciduous forest at the coast to glaciers and summits. Several Norwegian red-listed species have been found here as well as several rare cultural monuments from the Stone Age, Bronze Age and Iron Age."*

nian range. Today this comprises hard and nutrient-poor conglomerates and grey-green sandstone. These barren mountains slant making deep depressions and the remarkable shelf formations produce a distinctive landscape. Not less remarkable are the long narrow lakes which lie one after the other each on its own shelf.

It is also possible to find fossils of plants, fish and invertebrates in this area as well as petrified sand beds with wave marks. What were once river beds and the ocean floor has ended up high in the mountains, the softer rocks having eroded much faster during land elevation. A result of this is Gjegnen, Norway's highest mountain peak west of the Jostedalsbre Glacier.

Areas with heavy precipitation
Gjegnalundsbre Glacier and Ålfotbre Glacier are the two largest glaciers in this district, their summits reaching 1,400 to 1,500 metres amsl, topped by Blånibba (Gjegnen) the highest at 1,670 metres amsl. All the same it does rather

go against nature to have glaciers so far west, but there is an explanation in the precipitation measurements taken here and in the surrounding area. In a normal winter up to 5 metres of snow can fall as well as an equal quantity of rain, making altogether 10 metres of water. Record precipitation has been registered in this area, for example 206 millimetres during one day and night in January 1992. The usual depth of snow on the glacier in April is 8 metres, but in 1973 it was measured at 12 metres. As a comparison, the normal depth of snow in the Jotunheimen Mountains is between 2 and 3 metres.

The Norwegian Trekking Association's work
Of course, the tremendous amount of precipitation combined with elevation variations has tempted the electricity companies to carry out development of hydro-electric power, but there are still some unspoiled areas. The special topography unfortunately restricts access

to the area, most people being satisfied with viewing these fantastic mountains from a distance. However, for those who are experienced in using map and compass and like challenges, the area around the Ålfotbre Glacier has a lot to offer. The Sogn and Fjordane Turlag (trekking club) has marked trails and built some rather spectacular tourist cabins around the glacier. Gjegnabu, clinging to a rocky crag on the east side of the Gjegnalundsbre Glacier, can be accessed from Hope on Road 615, but be prepared for an elevation difference of 1,100 metres over a 4 kilometres stretch – in other words, the terrain is steep!

On the west side of the Ålfotbre Glacier the trekking club has erected Blåbrebu which can be reached after an approximately four hour walk from the Grøndal Valley, the reward for this strenuous route being wonderful countryside and a magnificent panorama over some of Western Norway's most characteristic nature.

⚒ FACTS ⚒

The Ålfotbre Glacier (17 square kilometres), the Gjengnalundsbre Glacier (12 square kilometres) and bordering mountain regions are located between the Hyefjord, Nordfjord, Roads 614 and 615 in the far west of Sogn and Fjordane.

Attractions:
· Norway's westernmost glacier
· Extremely distinctive landscape formation and extraordinary geology with fossil finds.
· Unusually heavy precipitation.

Map:
Touring map Ålfotbre Glacier 1: 80 000.

Access:
Detour from Road 614 and 615.

55 ▶ Stadlandet
Unsheltered natural beauty spot

From the map the outermost part of Stadlandet, furthest in the north-west of Sogn and Fjordane, almost resembles a dragon's head formed by the characteristic peaks Signalen, Mosekleivhornet, Kjerringa and Stålet. This exposed landscape with vertical rock walls dropping straight into the ocean is reminiscent of the Faeroes.

This is a relatively rare type of nature for Norway, where the mountain plateau's elevation brut- ally meets the sea, but here in Ytre Nordfjord, of which Stadlan- det is a part, this landscape of exposed mountain plateaus end- ing abruptly at the coast is quite normal. The summit called Kjerringa at just under 500 metres amsl is at the outermost edge of Stadlandet, and the travel business has christ-

The sun breaks through at Stad. Photo: Tom Schandy.

Although Stad is known for its storms, the farms here manage to cling on to land. Photo: Tom Schandy.

ened this vantage point the West Cape, which they advertise as having the worst weather and the best view!

Hard weather conditions and splendid hiking terrain

Although the weather can be rough here, fortunately for the visitor it changes quite often, making the chances of enjoying the view from West Cape quite possible, even though it may look hopeless at the start. In clear weather the feared Stad Ocean rolls like a wavy carpet stretching westwards and the view inland is equally fantastic revealing among others Hornelen, the Sunnmøre Alps and the Ålfotbre Glacier. Furthermore Selje has a splendid walking terrain with several marked trails. It is an exceptional experience to go for a mountain walk on the Stad Peninsula as the ocean panorama accompanies you all the way even though you are in the mountains. The touring map for the municipalities Selje and Vågsøy are of great value,

recommending more than 80 different walks.

The area off Stad holds the record in Norway for the number of hurricanes and storms, and it is therefore not surprising that this piece of ocean has been feared by mariners for hundreds of years. In the short distance from Sildegapet in the south to Ervika in the north no less than 58 shipwrecks have been located. For centuries there has been heavy boat traffic along the Norwegian coast and if the weather was too bad, the boats were pulled up on shore either north or south of Stad. The lowest point of the peninsula is called Dragseidet the name deriving from the practice of dragging the boats overland if the wait for fine weather became too long.

Idyllic sandy beaches and ancient monastery ruins

This special natural jewel includes several small, idyllic sandy beaches which attract residents and tourists on fine days. One of these beaches is at Ervika and another at Hoddevik, both on the west side of Stad. The wind blows in on the beautiful beaches in Selje Municipality making them a magnet for surfers from home and abroad.

To the east of Stad is another exciting tourist destination, Tungevågen. This shallow, saltwater, round fjord with narrow inlet is an important bird locality especially in the autumn and winter when many wetland bird species stay here. 55 wetland species are registered, the largest numbers concerning long-tailed ducks, common eiders, black scoters, velvet scoters, red-breasted mergansers, common goldeneyes and cormorants.

After travelling so far west, you should visit the island of Selja. This was one of the first three dioceses in Norway and a religious centre in the Middle Ages.

A short boat trip from the centre of Selje Village takes you to the ruins of Selje Monastery which are easily accessible. A network of paths leads you on a historic stroll around this small island of natural and cultural interest where you follow in the footsteps of pilgrims who went ashore here over a thousand years ago.

*This area of natural beauty also has fabulous sandy beaches.
Photo: Tom Schandy.*

56

Geiranger

World-class area of natural beauty

The Geirangerfjord along with the village of Geiranger in Møre and Romsdal County are definitely international tourist attractions, impressing the almost 500,000 yearly visitors with a combination of precipitous mountain sides, a narrow fjord, cascading waterfalls and a lush traditional cultivated landscape.

The Geirangerfjord situated in Sunnmøre is a fjord arm sticking out of the Storfjord east of Hellesylt. Its 15 kilometres are perhaps best viewed from the deck of the ferry boat between Hellesylt and Geiranger, or with the Coastal Liner Express' (Hurtigruta) daily arrivals during the summer. After passing scenery of sheer mountain walls with foaming waterfalls tumbling down into the narrow fjord, the boats arrive at the village of Geiranger which nestles at the waters edge at the head of the fjord arm. A couple of years ago, the fjords in Western Norway were elected as the world's most magnificent natural attraction by the National Geographic Magazine, and the Geirangerfjord together with the Nærøyfjord in the county of Sogn and Fjordane were included in the UNESCO World

View over the Geirangerfjord from the farm Skageflå. Photo: Tom Schandy.

Heritage List in the summer in 2005, with the description Western Norway Fjord Landscape.

Waterfalls and amazing settlements

Since 1869 when the first tourist ship glided into the Geirangerfjord, tourists have been impressed by the scenery. Today one can also hire a small boat or kayak in Geiranger Village to experience the majesty of these surroundings from the calm waters of the fjord, while on all sides the roaring waterfalls called De Syv Søstre (The Seven Sisters), Friaren (The Suitor) and Brudesløret (The Bride's Veil) drop straight down to the water below, and are some of the fjord's biggest attractions.

Beside the Friaren Waterfall nestles the farm Skageflå, one of many incredible settlements along the steep slopes of the Geirangefjord, along with the elevated Blomberg and Knivsflå which are only accessible by boat and footpath where they cling on to small ledges several hundred metres above sea level. These dwellings have been abandoned for years, but many of the buildings are maintained, some being used as holiday homes.

Roads with a dizzy view

Equally as spectacular as the fjord road is Road 63, the road over the mountain range, Strynefjell, lined with glistening snow and views of glacier arms even in the height of summer. The Nibbeveien Road (toll road) to the summit, Dalsnibba (1,476 metres amsl), leaves Road 63 at the Djupvasshytta Mountain Lodge and winds its way through eleven narrow bends to the top of the plateau, the reward being a fantastic panora-

The view from Flydalsjuvet is one of the post popular postcard pictures from Geiranger. Photo: Arne Aasheim.

ma over the surrounding mountain ranges, the valley and the Geirangerfjord. This road, completed in 1939, is open from June to September when Dalsnibba's accessibility makes it one of Norway's biggest summer tourist attractions.

The last 38 bends in Road 63, the Geiranger Road, eat up the elevation down to Geiranger and the fjord, with fantastic views all the way, the most famous being from Flydalsjuvet and the one which appears on the postcards. The waterfall called Storseterfoss is another interesting attraction for the tourists and can be reached by turning off the main road at Hole and following the approximately 1 kilometre of road to Vesterås Farm. From here it takes around

one hour to walk to the waterfall.

Opposite Geiranger the equally impressive road called Ørneveien has a vantage point providing a view over the fjord. This road is the gateway to Geiranger for people travelling from Ålesund or Åndalsnes via the road over Trollstigen. There are plans to develop this road and give it the status of a National Tourist Route.

Landscape Protection Area

The establishment of the Geiranger-Herdal Valley Landscape Protection Area at 500 square kilometres was resolved in 2004, the resolution being a prerequisite for inclusion on UNESCO's prestigious World Heritage List. The purpose of protection is to preserve the distinctive and beautiful fjord and

mountain landscape with its rich and varied plant life and wildlife. Geiranger-Herdal Valley contains important traditional cultivated landscapes where fjord farms, summer mountain dairy farms and cultural monuments comprise a substantial part of the character of the landscape. The protected area stretches from the Geirangerfjord and Dalsnibba in the south with the eastern boundary following the mountains towards the Tafjord in the north. To the west almost the entire Synnylvsfjord is included except for the innermost part at Hellesylt.

❧ FACTS ❧

The Geirangerfjord is situated in Sunnmøre in the county of Møre and Romsdal, its length of 15 kilometres, an arm of the Storfjord, ends at the village of Geiranger. Together with the Nærøyfjord, Geirangerfjord is on UNESCO's World Heritage List which includes the world's most significant natural and cultural heritages. Geiranger-Herdal Valley Landscape Protection Area measures 500 square kilometres.

Attractions:
- The narrow fjord with its steep sides
- Old abandoned farms and summer mountain farms high up on the mountain sides
- The village of Geiranger
- The Seven Sisters Waterfall (De Syv Søstre)
- The Storseterfoss Waterfall
- Dalsnibba Summit (1,476 metres amsl)

Map:
Touring map for the Tafjordfjell Mountains 1: 50 000.

Access:
Road 63 between Langevatn Lake and Valldal. Car ferry between Hellesylt and Geiranger. Daily arrivals by the Coastal Liner Express (Hurtigruta) during the summer.

57

Sunnmøre Alps
Wild mountains in the west

They appear, on each side of the Hjørundfjord, the Sunnmøre Alps, a row of peaks and a natural wonder in Møre and Romsdal County, not only an amazing sight from the fjord but also fantastic to climb either on foot or skis.

The summits in the Sunnmøre Alps are fantastic to climb either on foot or on skis. Photo: Gunnar Wangen.

"The wildest alpine valley I ever saw was not in the Alps, it was the valley of Norangsdal at Sunnmøre, Norway." The Englishman, William C. Slingsby, was obviously fascinated by these alpine summits as something quite apart, even though he was an expert mountain climber and lover of the outdoors with experience of beautiful scenery both in Norway and abroad.

Dramatic nature

The Storfjord projects eastwards inland south of Ålesund, and directly southwards from here is the Hjørundjord with the Norangsfjord as a small arm towards the east again. At the end of this fjord is Øye where the Road 655 continues on through the Norangsdal Valley towards Tryggestad. Mr. Slingsby was not the only one to be impressed by the magnificent scenery in this part of Sunnmøre; many motorists stop to admire the natural and cultural gems along the road in the Norangsdal Valley.

Any tour which starts at the shoreline and ends in the Sunnmøre Alps' scenery of jagged summits will never be forgotten and in fact several of the peaks are accessible without the use of climbing ropes and crampons. The Ålesund-Sunnmøre Trekking Association has four cabins in the area the most well-known being Patchellhytta. The Englishman, Cecil Watson Patchell, whose monument stands beside Road 655, was almost an annual visitor to Sunnmøre from the turn of the last century until World War II, and he is the local trekking association's second honourable member. He built the cabin Patchellhytta between the peaks Smørskredtind and Slogen and later presented it to the association. The cabin, now rebuilt, lies at the foot of Slogen, Smørskredtind and Brekketindane and provides a paradise for those who love these giddy heights.

On the west side of the Hjørundfjord the Ålesund Skiing Club has its own cabin, where the Ålesund-Sunnmøre Trekking Association has a utility agreement for a no-service department with ten beds. This cabin, Standalhytta, was in the early 1900's the major skiing destination for the people of Ålesund who came to Store Standal by boat directly from their home town. The summits, Kolåstind, Sætretindane, Sølvkallen and Fingeren are Standalhyttas nearest neighbours while further north the Molladal Valley nestles with its spectacular needles and pinnacles, some of them named after such climbing pioneers as Randers, Mohn and Slingsby.

Natural and cultural gem

The Union Øye Hotel at the head of the Norangsfjord is one of the country's most special and historically interesting hotels where royalty, artists and mountaineers have stayed. In 1990 the building was restored to its former state, where it snuggles under the Slogen summit.

Slogen (1,564 metres amsl) is one of Norway's and even, according to some, one of Europe's most glorious mountain tops, with its noble, elegant and perfect summit formation. At a distance it looks impossible to climb Slogen, but in fact a steep, marked footpath goes through the birch forest right above the hotel and after two to three hours of steep climbing you are on the top and can enjoy one of Norway's most spectacular views. If you do not have a head for heights, however, you will be better off walking to the cabin Patchellhytta, which along with Urke are alternative starting points for a tour to Slogen.

Incredibly, Slogen and other peaks in the Sunnmøre Alps are visited by skiers in the winter and spring, although it must be emphasized that such tours should only be undertaken by experienced mountain people with local knowledge and good equipment. These mountains can be extremely dangerous in bad weather and unfortunately there have been some tragically fatal accidents here.

Of all the summits and pinnacles in the Sunnmøre Alps, Bladet is the most spectacular. Photo: Gunnar Wangen.

58

Runde
Bird island in the sea west of Norway

West of Ålesund and out towards the great ocean lies Runde, Norway's largest bird cliff south of the Arctic Circle. The teeming bird life can be enjoyed from a boat or from land along the cliffs which drop down almost vertically into the sea.

The bird life on Runde can take anyone's breath away and a trip on a tourist boat around the island is a powerful experience. The boat drives close to the sheer rock faces with thousands of screaming black-legged kittiwakes hanging overhead and rocky islets covered with shags, razorbills and common guillemots. There are northern gannets, northern fulmars and flocks of Atlantic puffins struggling into flight. Sometimes a white-tailed eagle or a peregrine falcon shows up, scattering the other birds in panic. If the sea is calm it is possible for the boat to actually drive under the bird cliff into several grottoes, the longest being 120 metres where even here some black-legged kittiwakes have managed to stick their nests to the rock wall.

The boat trip encircles the whole island even passing the place where the famous Runde treasure was found. On a summer's day in

The Atlantic puffin is one of the most characteristic species on the bird cliffs on Runde. Photo: Tom Schandy.

1972 three divers, a Norwegian and two Swedes, found a shipwreck containing 57,000 gold and silver coins. The ship, Akerendam, was from the East Indies and sank in 1725 taking with it 230,000 florins. Approximately 700 kilogram's of coins have been raised of which 30 kilograms were in gold.

On the edge of the cliff

After the boat trip you should walk up the path from Goksøyr on the east side of the island and watch the bird life from the top of the cliff. The path takes you from the shore to the edge of the cliff at 300 metres over the sea passing through nesting colonies of great

Runde is Norway's largest bird cliff south of the Arctic Circle. These are some eager bird watchers. Photo: Tom Schandy.

The magnificent northern gannet in flight. This species nested for the first time in Norway on Runde in 1946. Photo: Tom Schandy.

skuas, a large seabird and near relative of the gulls. This bird defends its eggs and young by diving like a fighter bomber at intruders and only swerving away a few centimetres from its target. Remember to keep to the path to avoid unnecessary disturbance of the great skuas.

The cliff top provides a fantastic panorama of the sea, skerries and bird cliffs. Sheer rock walls dive vertically into the blue sea beneath and the weathered bird cliffs are covered in hundreds and thousands of seabirds. The air swarms with them, probably as many as half a million birds staying at Runde during the summer month. Altogether 220 different species have been observed 70 of which are nesting.

A path descends through the puffin colony to Kaldekloven. The bird cliffs are protected for the preservation of the bird life and although it is forbidden to leave the path, you can closely observe the colourful and amusing Atlantic puffin where it nests under stones or in holes it has dug into the ground.

From another vantage point you can look down on the large colony of northern gannets. This beautiful bird nested here for the first time in Norway in 1946 with four pairs. Since then the numbers have increased to today's 2,000 pairs. Runde was also the first place in Norway where the northern fulmar was found to nest in 1921, the present numbers of this species being over 5,000 pairs. The fulmar, which is a relative of the albatross, has a pipe-like outer nostril and if the bird feels threatened it spits the whole of its stomach contents at the intruder.

Runde with its 300 metre high cliffs and flat plateau is in fact a small piece of a special type of coast, only found otherwise on Stadlandet and Bremangerlandet in Sogn and Fjordane as well as Øst-Finnmark. There are also pleasant walks further in on the island and a path descends to Runde Lighthouse where the Norwegian Trekking Association provides accommodation for overnight stays. If you explore the beach between the villages of Goksøyr and Runde Harbour you will find sandy beaches with bathing possibilities, although the water is cold. In addition there is good sea fishing, exciting plant life including the oyster plant and celery-leaved buttercup, as well as shoreline birds such as oyster catcher, redshank, common eider and Norway's largest duck the common shelduck.

The razorbill also nests on the bird cliffs on Runde. Photo: Tom Schandy.

59

Romsdal Valley and the Trollstigen Road
Rugged peaks and green valleys

Trollveggen, Romsdalshorn and Store Vengjetind are all mountain summits which bring joy to the heart of anyone who loves being in the mountains, and the Romsdal Alps and Trollstigen Road are some of the best Norwegian nature has to offer. It can be difficult and tiring to reach the top of the mountains, but the sight of them can also be enjoyed at a distance from both car and train.

When King Haakon VII officially opened the Trollstigen Road on 31 July 1936 he had no idea what a tremendous tourist attraction this would become, the road having been completed that year after eight years' of construction. Until then Trollstigen had been a narrow pack road and important connection between Sunnmøre and Romsdal, although not without its dangers down the steep mountain side beside the waterfall, Stigfoss.

Tourist attraction

The Trollstigen Road, a well-known attraction and one of Norway's best with its 11 narrow bends winding up the mountain side, draws almost 500,000 visitors every year. The waterfalls, Stigfoss with a fall of 320 metres, and Tverrdalsfoss which has an even higher perpendicular drop, are awe-inspiring sights for the motorists. Nature lovers will also find the Isterdal Valley near Åndalsnes quite fascinating, where the mountains have been given ordinary, royal or clerical names. Karitind (1,356 metres amsl), Dronningen – The Queen – (1,568 metres amsl) Kongen – The King – (1,614 metres amsl) and Bispen – The Bishop – (1,450 metres amsl) guard the travellers on the west side of Road 63, while the Trolltindene peaks dominate towards the east.

Whereas several of the climbing routes from the Romsdal Valley end on the highest point on Trollryggen (1,740 metres amsl), it is also possible to get here from the opposite side without needing climbing skills, the start then being from the road at the top of the Stigfoss Waterfall. The hike there and back takes around six to seven hours, but the view from the top is one of the wildest and most magnificent that can be experienced in Norway, with the perpendicular wall of rock, Trollveggen, dropping 1,000 metres down to the Romsdal Valley. The Trolltindene summits with their rows of pinnacles and spires are

When King Haakon VII officially opened the Trollstigen Road on 31 July 1936 he could never have imagined that around 500,000 tourists a year would visit this tourist attraction. Photo: Tom Schandy.

Romsdalshorn's (1,550 metres amsl) characteristic profile has tempted many mountaineers over the years. This view is from the Vengjedal Valley. Photo: Tom Schandy.

bewitching and many enthusiasts have been tempted to parachute jump off Trollveggen, an activity which has been banned after several fatal accidents.

Salmon fishing in the Rauma River

The Rauma River's outstanding scenic beauty also attracts anglers, with its calmer sections and foaming rapids interchanged with ideal fishing pools. The river banks provide lush stretches of bright green traditional cultivated landscape while forest clad valley sides are framed by mighty mountains on both sides. There are not many rivers surrounded by so much natural beauty.

The Rauma Watercourse is 64 kilometres long, with the main headwater of the river being in Lesjaskogsvann Lake in Oppland County. This lake lies on the watershed between east and west and runs out in the east into the Gudbrandsdalslågen River. The Rauma River has a 42 kilometre salmon stretch and was previously a famous salmon river, its angling history dating back to the 1850's. General William Bromley-Davenport secured the upper Fiva Farm (approximately 10 kilometres above Åndalsnes) as well as a good section of the Rauma River for himself around 1850 and every summer for over 150 years the same family has fished from Fiva House, one of the last English-owned river fishing properties in Norway.

Due to infection from the gyrodactylus parasite, the Rauma River is not the same as it was in its days of glory, even sustaining a salmon fishing ban for a period. Following treatment with rotenone and impressive cultivation, this picturesque river is again open for fishing for both salmon and sea trout.

Romsdalshorn

Romsdalshorn (1,550 metres amsl) on the east side of the Romsdal Valley is one of Norway's most well-known postcard and calendar motifs. Although the height is perhaps not so impressive, the characteristic profile has tempted many mountaineers over the years. The Dane, Carl Hall, thought he was the first man to reach the top in 1881, after several attempts, but he found an old cairn on the top which was probably put there by two farm workers who claimed they were the first on the top in 1828, but no-one believed them. To climb to the top of Romsdalshorn requires mountaineering skills and good equipment and it is possible to enrol in organised tours.

A tour to the foot of the mountain from the rear side can be recommended. The approach is from the beautiful Vengjedal Valley from Isfjorden Village (7 kilometres from Åndalsnes) with parking possibilities just beside the small Hornvann Lake under Romsdalshorn. South-eastwards other awe-inspiring tops jut up including Store Vengjetind (1,852 metres amsl) and Kvanndalstind (1,744 metres amsl) with Torshammeren, all of them classics in the Norwegian mountaineering circles and beautiful to admire at a distance.

60

Eikesdal Valley with Mardalsfoss Waterfall
Exciting valley with tall waterfalls

The surrounding mountains drop almost vertically into the 20 kilometre long Eikesdalsvann Lake, making Eikesdal Valley in Møre and Romsdal an outstanding site of natural beauty. The Mardalsfoss Waterfall lies at the southern end of the lake and when the water is released into the watercourse during the tourist season the waterfall ranks as one of the world's most impressive.

The resolution to exploit Mardalsfoss Waterfall for hydro-electric power was passed in 1970 leading to the so-called Mardøla Protest Action. The demonstrators were carried away by force, thus causing a commotion in the media. However, a compromise was reached whereby 2,000 litres of water per second is released in the tourist season from 20 June to 20 August.

The waterfalls are great attractions
The Mardalsfoss Waterfall is an imposing sight with its two sheer

View over the Eikesdal Valley. Photo: Tom Schandy.

In two glorious cascades the Mardalsfoss Waterfall tumbles down towards Eikesdalsvann Lake. Photo: Bård Løken/NN/Samfoto.

cascades of water, 297 metres and 300 metres respectively, before it tumbles out in to Eikesdalsvann Lake. Despite the hydro-electric power development and the reduced water volume, even in the tourist season, it is still a marvellous attraction. There are many methods of calculating the tallest waterfalls in Norway and the rest of the world as there are various definitions for what constitutes a waterfall, some referring only to free fall, others only to unregulated watercourses and

so on. All the same Mardalsfoss Waterfall is considered in Norway, Europe and the rest of the world to be a large waterfall and on some lists it is ranked as among the world's five tallest.

Northern Europe's largest hazel forest
The Eikesdal Valley is not only known for its waterfalls. Several places on the steep slopes lining Eikesdalsvann Lake lush hazel forests thrive so much so that Eikesdal Valley (Oak Valley) could

well have been called Hazel Valley, as Northern Europe's largest hazel forest is found in the middle of the east side of the lake. The hazel trees are so numerous that both squirrels and people have benefited from this prolific resource. Making barrel hoops from hazel wood was an important product for the farmers in Eikesdal Valley along with collection of hazel nuts providing an extra source of income. One autumn in the 1930's 1,700 kilograms of hazel nuts were picked and sold from the Vike Farms, and this exploitation of the hazel forests continued until the 1950's.

Tough cycle ride
The road built along the east side of the Eikesdalsvann Lake brings you closer to these splendid hazel forests and if you are not afraid of cycling up hill, a tough round trip by bike will take you through glorious countryside. Starting at Eresfjord at sea level the road is flat until the southern end of Eikesdalsvann Lake, but it is a stiff climb to Aursjø Lake which lies at 850 metres (amsl). As compensation, there is freewheeling down to the Litledal Valley and Sunndalsøra back at sea level. No other cycling trip of 100 kilometres will take you through so much dramatic west-country scenery, mostly on gravel roads with relatively little car traffic. Aursjøhytta tourist cabin is run by Kristiansund and Nordmøre Trekking Association and provides accommodation should you need it.

Landscape Protection Area
In connection with the establishment of Dovrefjell-Sunndalsfjell National Park in 2002, an adjacent area of 469.6 square kilometres

surrounding the Eikesdal Valley was established as Eikesdalsvatnet Landscape Protection Area with the purpose of safeguarding this distinctive and beautiful natural landscape which includes areas of traditional cultivated landscape where cultural monuments from trapping, agriculture and grazing are vital elements. At the same time the span from rich deciduous forests on the lowland slopes to the high mountain scenery is preserved, including the last remains of Norway's genetically pristine wild reindeer.

61

Trollheimen and the Innerdal Valley
Varied and beautiful

Everyone who considers Trollheimen to be the pearl of all Norwegian mountains and Innerdal Norway's most picturesque valley might well be biased, but this area bordering the counties of Møre and Romsdal and Sør-Trøndelag definitely deserves the description.

The boundaries of Trollheimen are a matter of debate but they are usually described thus: the Surnadal Valley and Rindal in the north, the Orkdal Valley and the Dovre Railway/Road E6 in the east, the Sunndal Valley and Oppdal in the south and the fjords to the west. The Trollheimen Mountains feature variation and contrast, where the west-country mountainous realm of fjords meet the rolling

The profile of the Innerdalstårn Mountain (1,450 metres amsl) has often been compared to the Matterhorn in Switzerland. Photo: Tom Schandy.

horizons of Eastern Norway and the climate changes from maritime to continental. Alpine peaks and sheltered valleys provide fantastic tours both summer and winter, in scenery which has filled an increasing number of hikers with enthusiasm for more than 100 years.

With the purpose of preserving Trollheimen, this distinctive and beautiful landscape of mountain farm valleys and abundant plant life and wildlife, 1,165 square kilometres was made a landscape protection area in 1987, fortunately including large parts of the central areas. In addition two nature reserves have been established, one at Svartåmoen at 800 hectares (2,000 acres) with primeval forest and one at Minilla in Nerskogen at 187.8 hectares (469.5 acres), a marshland with a special flora and rich bird life.

Norway's Matterhorn

The western side of Trollheimen is the wildest and most magnificent especially the area around the beautiful valley of Innerdal, towered over by its highest summits Trolla (1,850 metres amsl) and Såtbakkollen (1,840 metres amsl). The other well-known mountain tops Blåhø (1,671 metres amsl), Snota (1,668 metres amsl) and Trollhetta (1,614 metres amsl) have a more central location, while the most famous although only 1,450 metres amsl is Innerdalstårnet, which Yngvar Nielsen, a previous foreman of the Norwegian Trekking Association, considered comparable to the Matterhorn in the Swiss Alps. It is in fact possible to climb Innerdalstårnet without climbing equipment, but you need to be in good physical condition, dare to free climb in places and not be afraid of heights, and if it is rain-

Blåsalen, the famous palace of ice in Trollheimen, is an ice grotto under the glacier at Blåhø. When the grotto opens it is possible to go inside. Photo: Tore Wuttudal/NN/Samfoto.

ing and slippery - keep away from Innerdal Valley's rocky pyramid.

The Innerdal Valley and in particular the Skardfjell Mountain is legendary in Norwegian mountaineering circles, this being the mountain in Norway sporting most climbing routes. The Englishman, William C. Slingsby, made the Innerdal Valley famous for mountaineering over 100 years ago, and in 1962 Olaf Innerdal at the cabin Innerdalshytta (400 metres amsl) launched climbing courses, something which the Norwegian Trekking Association has also organised here for many years. The cabin remains in the Innerdal family and it is still possible for visitors to join a climbing course.

Rich hiking traditions

With mountain names such as Trollhetta, Trolla and Trollauget it was not surprising that the Trondhjem Trekking Association should

name the area Trollheimen in the 1880's. This same trekking association is responsible for the hiking routes and cabins in Trollheimen and the Innerdal Valley where there are long hiking traditions. Although the tourist cabin, Trollheimshytta, was inaugurated in 1890 there was very little hiking activity during the first years, whereas today it is actively used by outdoor enthusiasts. Trollheimshytta lies sheltered and inviting in the valley and is one of three cabins used on the popular three-day hiking route in Trollheimen, the other two being Gjevilvasshytta and Jøldalshytta.

Most hikers in this region recognise the Trondhjem Trekking Association cabins for their unique architecture with walls built of huge logs, their large solid fireplaces and furniture reminiscent of old farmhouses, and it is seldom that one sees cabins harmonizing

so well with their surroundings. It is well worth the trip just to experience the cultural atmosphere at these cabins as well as the fantastic and strikingly beautiful scenery on route.

The ice grottoes Blåsalen and Speilsalen are two remarkable phenomena that occasionally reveal themselves to anyone fortunate enough to pass at just the right time. Both ice grottoes lie beside the Blåhø Mountain and are created by movements in the glacier, melting snow and meltwater streams, a combination of conditions which do not occur every year, but it is worth planning your route to pass Blåhø on your way between Trollheimshytta and Gjevilvasshytta in case the ice palace has opened its door and you can view this rare and impressive sight.

62

Hustadvika and the Atlantic Ocean Road
Exposed and splendid

Hustadvika, in Møre and Romsdal, is known for dangerous seas, fantastic underwater nature and its unspoiled character. The 8 kilometre Atlantic Ocean Road, elected in 2005 as the construction of the century in Norway, connects the municipalities Averøy and Eide. It starts north of Hustadvika and gives motorists a fantastic experience.

In this starkly dramatic scenery out towards the Norwegian Sea the weather can vary immensely. The stretch of sea at Hustadvika is considered one of the most dangerous along the Norwegian coast, several ships having been wrecked in these foul waters. A number of people, however, let themselves be challenged by the weather, like surfers who voluntarily ride the foaming waves. The water is said to be only a little colder than in Hawaii, while the nature and the sea are just as beautiful!

The Atlantic Ocean Road in a storm. Photo: Bård Løken/NN/Samfoto.

El Dorado for diving

Divers have found their paradise in this underwater world teeming with life and Hustadvika is compared to below surface El Dorados like the Maldives and the Red Sea. The nature is undisturbed and hardly affected by pollution. Otters, seals and several whale species, including flocks of killer whales can appear in Hustadvika, where the grey seal and European common seal, have their birth grounds. The bird life, abundant with gulls and terns also includes oystercatchers, turnstones, shags, common eiders and greylag geese, to mention some of the nesting species. Flocks of divers, herons, whooper swans, common eiders, velvet scoters, red-breasted merg-ansers and black guillemots are species of aquatic birds which stay over the winter.

The Atlantic Ocean Road

One usually has to put some effort into experiencing areas of great natural beauty by for example, cycling, walking or diving. The Atlantic Ocean Road, winding its way over 12 bridges and stone fillings from islet to islet outermost in the open sea has changed this slightly. You can now drive from one scenic jewel to the other with plenty of easily accessible parking on the way from where you can take a short stroll out to the nearest smooth rocks and fishing places. A little to the west are the shipping lanes over the feared

The Atlantic wolf-fish is part of Hustadvika's exciting underwater nature. Photo: Fredrik Naumann/NN/Samfoto.

Hustadvika with the shipwrecks lying on the ocean floor and during the autumn storms huge waves can flood over the road.

Divers in a kelp forest at Hustadvika. Photo: Fredrik Naumann/NN/Samfoto.

63

Sølendet
Traditional cultivated landscape with orchids

This unique nature reserve in the Røros Municipality is full of beautiful countryside, an incredibly magnificent traditional cultivated landscape where marshes and meadows have been reaped for centuries resulting in a glorious flora, especially a number of orchids.

Sølendet, near Brekken in the Røros Municipality in Sør-Trøndelag, has been farmed for hundreds of years right up until the 1950's. Marshes and meadows cut by scythe provided winter fodder for the domestic animals, firewood was chopped, branches from deciduous trees were collected for fodder through the hard months of early spring and the birch bark was used for roofing. Over the centuries all this has influenced the nature in the area, the plant life gradually adapting to the haymaking and the other "encroachments" and resulting in Sølendet's characteristic landscape.

Lime-rich springs

Sølendet sits on moraine rich in limestone, the high clay content providing a basis for stagnation and creation of marshes, which are also fed by 50 springs of lime-rich groundwater. These springs combined with the haymaking in outlying meadows have resulted in fertile marshland and Sølendet's unique plant life. Established in 1974 and measuring over 300 hectares (750 acres), this nature reserve has registered approximately 270 species of superior plants. Sølendet contains one of Norway's largest areas of uninterrupted fertile marshland (lime-rich

Sølendet is a splendid traditional cultivated landscape containing marshes and meadows used for haymaking over several centuries. Photo: Tore Wuttudal/NN/Samfoto.

The beautiful dark reddish-brown black vanilla orchid has its main habitat in Norway at Sølendet. Photo: Ove Bergersen/NN/Samfoto.

marshland) and this covers around half of the total area of the reserve, the rest being mainly forested meadows and heath.

Within the protected boundary several rare plants grow in large quantities including 12 species of orchids and at least as many orchid hybrids. The fragrant orchid, the flecked marsh orchid, the early marsh orchid and the Lapland orchid all grow in abundance. There can be tens of fragrant orchids per square metre and one year it was estimated that an amazing 4 to 5 million fragrant orchids adorned the reserve. Other orchid beauties thriving in the reserve are the common spotted orchid, heath spotted orchid, frog orchid, white frog orchid, lesser twayblade, common twayblade and last but not least the exclusive black vanilla orchid. This beautiful dark reddish-brown flower with its vanilla perfume has its main habitat in Norway at Sølendet, where a third of its total Norwegian population grows.

Necessity for care management

If these beautiful and rare plants are to survive care management is necessary. The country's farming methods have changed drastically over the last century and with hay no longer being cut in the wild outlying haymaking meadows these are in the process of becoming overgrown throughout the country.

Following the preservation of Sølendet, a lot of work has been put into clearing and hay cutting, as well as restoring the old buildings. The largest activity is the annual hay cutting of approximately 20 to 30 hectares (50 to 75 acres) to maintain the influence of cultivation, which favours species that need light. The intensive areas comprising a tenth of the total 160 hectares (400 acres) under maintenance are cut every third year, while the remainder is cut every tenth year. The rest of the reserve's 200 hectares (500 acres), which were originally used for haymaking, are becoming overgrown. Since 1973 the Science Museum at the Norwegian University of Science and Technology in Trondheim has engaged in a combination of basic and applied research and has made recommendations for the skilled activity and practical management carried out in the reserve, which makes Sølendet a reference area for studies of the traditional cultivated landscape of outlying grazing meadows.

Visitors to this site of scenic beauty in Sør-Trøndelag can choose between two marked nature trails, the longest being 4 kilometres. As well as showing the best of Sølendet the footpaths also help to reduce wear and tear in this vulnerable landscape. In July the marshes come alive with the mauves, reds and violets of thousands of orchids, something which can easily be appreciated from the informative nature trails in the open traditional cultivated landscape, with its panoramic backdrop of Aursunden Lake and the Norwegian and Swedish mountains bordering Kjølen. Annually, on the first Monday in July, Sølendet holds an open day with guided tours given by the researchers from the Science Museum and in the summer months guided tours in the reserve are arranged from the Norwegian and Swedish sides.

Large quantities of fragrant orchids grow within the protected area. One year the total number in the reserve was estimated at an incredible 4 to 5 million. Photo: Ove Bergersen/NN/Samfoto.

❧ FACTS ❧

Sølendet is a nature reserve situated near Brekken in the Røros Municipality in Sør- Trøndelag County. One of Norway's largest uninterrupted areas of fertile (lime-rich) marshland.

Attractions:
- Orchids
- Traditional cultivated landscape with haymaking meadows
- Haymakers' huts and hay sheds

Map:
1720 II Brekken 1: 50 000.

Access:
Sølendet is situated beside Road 705. Turn off Road 30 beside Glåmos or Road 31 at Brekken. Follow the road along the north edge of Aursunden Lake to Mælen. Parking area 700 metres from the main road (signposted). The nature trail into the reserve starts here.

Sylane
Thrilling mountain border district in Trøndelag

As a recreation area Sylane is for some reason better known in Sweden than in Norway. The Swedes have the same relation to this area of natural beauty as Norwegians living in Eastern Norway have to the Jotunheimen Mountains and the Hardangervidda Mountain Plateau. The contours are vast and undulating, but the Syl Massif contains fiercer mountains, deep cirques and sheer rock walls.

These mountains occupy a border region stretching from Trøndelag to the Jämtland Mountains in Sweden. In Norway the municipality proud to share these mountains with Swedish skiers and hikers is Tydal. The Trondhjem Trekking Association, Nord-Trøndelag Trekking Association and The Swedish Tourist Association run a number of tourist cabins in Sylane connecting a network of trails and providing abundant possibilities for round trips. The cabins Nedalshytta, Schulzhytta and Storerikvollen are staffed in the tourist season, while Græslihytta, Kjølihytta, Ramsjøhytta are self-service cabins (with provisions) and all six cabins belong to the Trondhjem Trekking Association. As far as the Norwegian Trekking Association is concerned parts of Skarvan and Roltdal Valley are also included in

Sylane is the mountain range in the border region in Trøndelag stretching towards the Jämtland Mountains in Sweden, the majority of the area being in Tydal Municipality in Norway. Photo: Erlend Haarberg/NN/Samfoto.

A fox's tracks in Sylane. Photo: Erlend Haarberg/NN/Samfoto.

Sylane. In fact Schulzhytta is situated in Skarvan and Roltdalen National Park, while Ramsjøhytta and Græslihytta are just outside.

Old thoroughfare

For centuries these mountainous regions have been used as a thoroughfare and there was an old trading and pilgrimage route from Sweden over Stugudal and along the Nea Watercourse to Trondheim. In 1878 at Gressli in Tydal, Norway's largest find of old coins was made, a total of over 2,000 from the period 1022 to 1069 being uncovered, which ascertains that Tydal was a travel junction or place of passage for trading traffic in the Viking Age and Middle Ages.

These border mountains also witnessed the tragedy of General Armfelt and the Carolingians death march. Severe weather took the Swedish General and his army by surprise on their way home to Sweden at New Year 1719, following King Carl XII's unsuccessful crusade in Norway. Between Tydal in Norway and Handøla in Sweden approximately 1,400 soldiers froze to death, and of the 1,800 who survived most became cripples for the rest of their lives due to frost injuries and primitive amputations. Fortunately today the skiers are better equipped for winter conditions and the routes are marked by large twigs or poles.

Summit ascent and abundant flora

Sylane is a mountain region which both Norwegians and Swedes share and the hiking trails cross the border as a matter of course, the hikers hardly noticing whether they are in one country or the other. Sheltered and idyllic in the birch forest at an elevation of approximately 780 metres amsl, and tucked in under the mighty Syl Massif nestles the tourist cabin Nedalshytta and awaits visiting mountain hikers. The cabin provides a stunning view to Skarddørsfjella and over the Nedal Valley and Nesjø Lake. In the summer the most popular summit ascent is from Nedalshytta to Storsylen (1,762 metres amsl), Sylane's highest point. This is a long tour taking between eight and nine hours there and back and after such a strenuous trip, dinner at the charming Nedalshytta is especially appetising.

These mountains have a lot to offer the hiker. The fishing is good and those interested in plants, birds and wildlife will not be disappointed. The flora at Essandsjø Lake is diverse, with Oeder's lousewort, alpine bartsia, moorking and yellow saxifrage in the marshy areas and orchid species such as the fragrant orchid and white frog orchid in drier places.

Large conservation areas

As early as 1917 the Nedal Valley was protected as a "botanical nature park", so a number of people were already aware of the qualities of the nature in this area. Gradually the hydro-electric power developers won the fight to take over substantial areas, which were then dammed and destroyed. It has now been recommended to safeguard many of the remaining values in Sylane by establishing the Sylane Landscape Protection Area and Sankkjølen Nature Reserve, incorporating totally 191 square kilometres, 167 square kilometres as a landscape protection area and 24 square kilometres as a nature reserve. South of the Syl Massif itself, a recommendation is also being processed for the Skardsfjella-Hyllingsdalen Landscape Protection Area in the Tydal and Røros Municipalities. The total area recommended for protection measures 333.5 square kilometres including four nature reserves in Røros Municipality, and the fate of both of these protected landscapes will be decided by the Norwegian Government in the course of 2007.

65

Gaula and Orkla
A paradise for salmon fishermen

If you mention Gaula and Orkla to salmon fishermen they get this dreamy look in their eyes. These are two of Norway's best salmon rivers and many a large salmon has succumbed to a fly imitation and been landed here.

Alongside Finnmark, Sør-Trøndelag is Norway's most important county for salmon fishing. In fact in 2005 Gaula was Norway's best salmon river with a catch topping 37.5 tons, while Orkla was not far behind in fourth place with 26.4 tons.

The largest river in Central Norway

Gaula is Central Norway's largest river stretching from the high mountains down to the sea. It starts its 145 kilometre journey at Gaulhåvola north of Aursund and ends in Gaulosen, an arm of the Trondheimsfjord. The watershed covers a fifth of Sør-Trøndelag's collective area and is permanently protected from hydro-electric power development. You can fish for salmon in Gaula on a 95 kilometre stretch from its estuary at Melhus to Haltdalen. Whereas the lower regions are calm, further up the river runs fast with small rapids and many pools, the only large rapids being the waterfall, Gaularfoss. When the water volume is large, the salmon have problems pushing up river and collect in shoals in the so-called Gaulfosshølen, one of the best fishing places on the river. The Eggafoss Waterfall at Haltdalen stops the salmon almost completely, even though the waterfall is only 5 metres high. The record fish taken by rod weighed 24 kilograms, while around 1960 a 31 kilogram salmon was taken by casting net.

However, Gaula is more than salmon and salmon fishermen. The huge variation in nature and countryside along the river provides an enormously diverse wildlife, from wild reindeer, bears and arctic foxes to moose and roe deer. Splendid grey alder and bird cherry forests provide habitats for a rich bird life and in three such forests nature reserves have been established (Gammelelva, Hovin and Ytter Skjærsvollslykkja all in the Melhus Municipality). The many lakes and oxbow lakes along the river have rich vegetation and a characteristic fauna of birds, insects and other small animals.

A fly fisherman standing in the Gaula River casts for large salmon one night in June. The best chance of landing a salmon is between sunset and sunrise. Photo: Kjell Erik Moseid/NN/Samfoto.

Furthermore at Gaula's estuary in Gaulosen there is a landscape protection area and two nature reserves with an unusually abundant bird life as well as a coastal meadow and sea-buckthorn forest. However, the area is most typified by the pink-footed goose, a species which nests on Svalbard but spends the winter in Denmark, Germany and Holland. During the spring migration north in April and May more than 1,000 geese can rest in the reserve, while the flocks in the autumn migration can best be observed in September and October.

Orkla

The Orkla River, lying west of Gaula, has its headwater in Orkelsjø Lake in Oppdal County and runs eastwards into Hedmark County before it swings back again to Trøndelag. 174 kilometres later it runs out in the Orkdalsfjord, which is an arm of the Trondheimsfjord.

Orkla has a salmon stretch measuring 70 kilometres, 30-50 metres wide and varying between calmer and faster sections and surrounded by beautiful scenery. The river has often been called "the fishing river for ordinary people", because it is easily accessible and the price is reasonable. Moreover the river is splendid for both fly fishing and worm/spinner fishing, especially when the water flows large. Through the years the

How much does it weigh? Salmon fishers on the Orkla River. Photo: Tom Schandy.

biggest fish ever taken was registered at 25 kilograms, and fish of this size can be taken the first days of the season. The medium-sized salmon usually arrive from the middle of June to the middle of July, while the smaller salmon come in the middle of July, and from then on there is usually a lot of salmon in the entire river.

Salmon fishing is a passion, but one does not need a fishing rod to enjoy a late summer evening walk along the river bank, watching the fishermen in action, listening to some fishy stories with a red sunset backdrop mirrored in the river water. This can make a pleasant break on a journey to or from Trondheim, and who knows, you might even see the biggest salmon ever being landed!

Beautiful Gaula, the best salmon river in Norway in 2005 with a catch of 37.5 tons. Photo: Bård Løken/NN/Samfoto.

❧ FACTS ❧

Gaula and Orkla in Sør-Trøndelag, two of Norway's best salmon rivers. Protected areas at Gaulosen with resting pink-footed geese in the spring and autumn.

Attractions:
- Salmon fishing
- Abundant bird life in the protected areas at Gaulosen
- The landscape

Map:
Touring map in the 1: 50 000 series.

Access:
Easy access. The river Gaula runs alongside Road E6 between Støren and Trondheim as well as along Road 30 between Støren and Ålen. The river Orkla runs alongside Road 700 between Berkåk and Orkanger.

66

Hitra and Frøya
Large islands off the coast of Trøndelag

Hitra and Frøya are two large islands in Sør-Trøndelag. The landscape, strongly influenced by the sea and natural forces, has a surprising diversity of topography, vegetation and wildlife. Hitra's population of deer is the densest occurrence in Northern Europe.

The densest occurrence of deer in Northern Europe lives on Hitra. Photo: Erlend Haarberg/NN/Samfoto.

Hitra is Norway's seventh largest island south of Lofoten. The name derives from the Old Norwegian word Hitr or Hitrar which means divided from the mainland, which is no longer the case as a long underwater tunnel now connects the island with the rest of Sør-Trøndelag. The exposed climate leaves its mark on the scenery on the island's south, west and north coasts which are clad in treeless heath while inland there are pine forests, mountain terrain and enormous marshes. One of the island's characteristic plants is the heath spotted orchid which is found in its thousands and was therefore elected as the municipality's flower in 1999. The municipality is otherwise marked by its coastal area which in addition to Hitra includes several small islands, numbering altogether almost 2,500 islands and skerries.

Havmyran and deer

The interior of Hitra contains the enormous Havmyran Nature Reserve, which has the status of being a Ramsar region, a conservation area of international importance. The vastness of the marshes (40 square kilometres) and their lack of landmarks make it advisable to take a map and compass with you on a hike. The vegetation includes various types of heath and marsh plants, with heather dominating on the heaths, including the typical coastal species, cross-leaved heath. More demanding species such as early marsh orchid, flecked marsh orchid and fragrant orchid also grow here.

All the same it is the bird life which draws most attention, with waders in dominance and the whimbrel as the characteristic species, Havmyran probably being its most important nesting habitat along the Trøndelag coastline. The reserve also provides a home for dunlin, redshank, golden plover, common sandpiper and common snipe.

Another interesting feature for Hitra is its 7,000 lakes and tarns, 1,000 of which contain char and trout, not to mention a salmon river with the characteristic Hitra salmon. The flood river, Lakselva, south of Fillan has its own salmon breed with particularly slender fish.

Hitra is otherwise most renowned for having the densest occurrence of deer in Northern Europe.

Sunset on Frøya. Photo: Dag Røttereng/NN/Samfoto.

There are 163 lakes and tarns with tempting trout fishing and the Hitra deer have also migrated to Frøya, establishing a small herd which can be hunted.

Frøya Municipality consists of 5,400 islets and skerries and offers organised deep-sea fishing trips far out in the ocean. These trips can provide quite a varied experience in that the weather can change from sunshine and summer to rain and gale force winds in the course of just a few hours, accompanied by fantastic displays of light. A normal catch includes cod, saithe and haddock with a possibility of ling, tusk, pollack or mackerel biting. If you have bad experience from fishing in forest lakes, it will be encouraging to know that nearly everyone who holds a deep-sea fishing line catches fish. These trips often visit a small fishing village south-west of Sula called Kya where although there has never been any permanent settlement, it was previously used by up to 500 fishermen during the fishing season.

If you drive the ring road circling the island on a summer's evening you will see several grazing deer as well as roe deer and perhaps even a moose. Since the 1800's the landowners have gleaned extra income by renting out hunting rights, a practice which results in the shooting of between 600 and 900 animals annually. There has been a lot of speculation as to why the Hitra deer are smaller than deer on the mainland. The reason is probably due to the deers' quality forage with high protein content being available over a shorter period on Hitra than on the mainland. When the deer from Hitra were raised domestically they became just as large as other deer.

Frøya and deep-sea fishing

Frøya lying even further out to sea is also connected to the rest of the world by a long underwater tunnel to Hitra. Whereas its neighbour in the south has some pine forest, nearly all the forest on Frøya has disappeared, revealing a gently undulating treeless landscape with a lot of marshland, rocks and water. The dominating and original vegetation comprises Atlantic red-brown coastal raised peat bogs, a so-called purple landscape, with heather, bog rosemary and cross-leaved heath.

The whimbrel is the characteristic bird species in the Havmyran Nature Reserve. Photo: Tom Schandy.

✆ FACTS ✆

Hitra and Frøya, two large islands in Sør-Trøndelag.

Attractions:
- The densest occurrence of deer in Northern Europe
- Heather moor landscape
- Havmyran Nature Reserve
- Deep-sea fishing

Maps:
Individual maps in the main map series for Norway 1: 50 000.

Access:
Easily accessible on Road 714 from Orkanger. Undersea tunnels to both islands. Havmyran is reached by a path from Gryta in the north-west.

67

Froan
Where the ocean churns

Froan, Norway's most isolated group of islands, lies in the churning ocean 40 kilometres west of the Fosen Peninsula in Trøndelag. The abundant wildlife includes seals, cormorants, black guillemots and white-tailed eagles.

Froan derives its name from the Norwegian word "fråde" which means to froth or foam, which is very apt for this windswept group of islands surrounded by the churning ocean, the Frohavet Sea on the inside and the Halten Bank on the outside. Froan consists of several thousand islands, islets and skerries of which only two islands are inhabited, Sørburøy and Sauøy. 50 years ago 400 people lived here but as with other outlying districts in Norway, depopulation is noticeable. Today only 50 people inhabit Sørburøy and one family lives on Sauøy.

Seal reserve
Froan is Norway's largest maritime nature reserve and landscape protection area. On 14 December 1970 a 400 square kilometre area of islands and sea was allocated as a nature reserve where land traffic is prohibited from 1 April to 10 August. Also established at the same time as the nature reserve was an 80 square kilometre landscape protection area where the rules are not so strict. This area is the largest Ramsar region in Norway, that is to say an area incorporated under the Ramsar Convention, which targets preservation of internationally vital wetlands.

Froan is known in particular for its seal species, the common seal which can be observed everywhere in the group of islands all

Froan is a key area for the Norwegian population of grey seals. Photo: Tom Schandy.

Common seal with young in the Froan Nature Reserve. Photo: Tom Schandy.

year round and the grey seal which is mainly seen in the most exposed areas in the autumn. Whereas the common seal gives birth in June, the grey seal does so as late as September-October, on the most exposed rocky islets at the most exposed time of year.

However, the seals are extremely vulnerable during this period and people are forbidden to go near the birth grounds from 10 September to 15 November.

Until the beginning of the 1990's approximately half of the Norwegian grey seal population reproduced at Froan, with almost 300 females arriving from Stad in the South to Lofoten in the North, and an estimated 300 young were born. Today one is unsure of the total population of grey seals in Norway, but in 2002 it was estimated that a total of 340 young were born at Froan, making this group of islands a key area for this species of seal in Norway.

Cormorants, black guillemots and white-tailed eagles

Froan is a paradise for birds, the characteristic species being the black guillemot with its black body, white patch on its wings, black beak and bright red legs. Around 1,000 pairs nest among stones and in rock crevices on these islands and in fact constitute Scandinavia's largest concentration of this species. Species of cormorants are also one of Froan's trade marks, the shag nesting as a rule under stone screes while the great cormorant nests on bare rocky islets out in the ocean. Approximately one sixth of Norway's great cormorant population has Froan as its home.

Due to Froan's isolated position large numbers of ducks come here to moult, that is to say, change their feathers. Ducks change all their flight feathers in one go and cannot fly for about two weeks, but they are relatively safe here where they gather in large flocks. Red-breasted mergansers, common eiders and greylag geese are three species often staying at Froan at this time of year and if you are lucky you might also spot an otter, while the white-tailed eagle sails overhead on his powerful wings, a scene not uncommon among the Froan Islands.

Beautiful Froan is Norway's most isolated group of islands. Photo: Tore Wuttudal/NN/Samfoto.

❧ FACTS ❧

Froan is a group of islands in Trøndelag. Nature reserve of international significance.

Attractions:
· Common seals and grey seals
· Shags and great cormorants
· Black guillemots
· White-tailed eagles
· Isolated coastal community

Map:
Touring map for Froan 1: 50 000.

Access:
You can take the car ferry from Sistranda on Frøya to the islands Gjæsingen, Sørburøy and Sauøy and even possibly to Halten. However there is no need for a car there, so another alternative is to take the Coastal Express from Trondheim (passenger traffic only). You will have to arrange transport with a local boat in order to see the group of islands.

68

Skarvan and Roltdalen National Park
National park with forest and mountains

Skarvan and Roltdalen, one of Norway's newer national parks, is situated in the boundary areas between Nord-Trøndelag and Sør-Trøndelag and spans a wide range of different types of nature from dark unspoiled spruce forests and vast marshes to roaring rivers and summits with an alpine climate.

This national park incorporating 442 square kilometres is situated north-west of Sylane and between Meråker and Selbu. The name Skarvan comes from the summit (1,171 metres amsl) of the same name in the north part of the national park, and Roltdal is the valley where the Roltla River meanders down to the west.

Old-growth forest and mountainous areas

The spruce forest is dense in this national park in Trøndelag, the trees only falling when nature considers it time, and the sheer amount of this old-growth forest, untouched by modern forestry, has created a great number of key biotopes. Skarvan and the Roltdal Valley are botanically rich because of a large diversity of habitats. The mountain regions are popular with the glacier buttercup, alpine rockcress and snow buttercup, while the extremely fertile marshes at lower altitudes attract yellow saxifrage, yellow wood violet and moor-king as well as the flecked marsh orchid and the fragrant orchid. Altogether 300 different flowering plants are registered in the national park.

As regards the bird life, around 125 bird species have been observed including birds of prey such as the golden eagle, osprey, gyrfalcon, eagle owl and snowy owl. Thriving in the abundant marshes and wetlands are velvet scoters,

This site of scenic beauty in the boundary regions between Nord-Trøndelag and Sør-Trøndelag spans a wide range of nature. The Skarvan Summit (1,171 metres amsl) forms the backdrop here. Photo: Torbjørn Moen.

Pine forest in the Roltdal Valley. The Fongen Massif and Fonskaftet Summit tower in the background.
Photo: Jon Arne Sæter /NN/Samfoto.

impression of how vast and varied this national park is. A walk to the south or east from the centrally placed Schulzhytta brings you to the cabins respectively Græsli-hytta and Ramsjøhytta.

The region gives an impression of being undisturbed, but mankind has exploited the area for centuries and summer mountain dairy farms, reindeer keeping, charcoal burning and mining have left their mark, mining comprising two completely different activities. Whereas in the 1700's copper was mined several places including the Roltdal Valley, 500 years ago millstone quarries were in operation, leaving their name to the Kvern (Mill) Mountain as evidence of the tradition. Millstones from Selbu were renowned for their first-class quality and were exported to both Russia and the USA. The path from Schulzhytta to Prestøyhytta passes right beside one of the largest millstone quarries.

black scoters, greater scaups, broad-billed sandpipers, purple sandpipers, ruffs, common cranes and several species of snipe.

The reindeer you meet here are domesticated, the Roltdal Valley providing the spring, summer and autumn grazing for the animals from the Essand reindeer grazing district. Spending the winter in Femundsmarka, these reindeer thrive near the snowdrifts beside the national park's highest mountain, Fongen (1,441 metres amsl). Domestic reindeer graze over the entire national park.

Several tourist cabins run by the Norwegian Trekking Association. Unlike many of the national parks in Norway, Skarvan and Rolt-dalen is easily accessible to the public. The Trondhjem Trekking Association and the Nord- Trønde-lag Trekking Association run several cabins in or just beside the protected area and they also mark hundreds of kilometres of walking trails in the surrounding district, even in winter when large twigs or canes are used to mark the skiing routes between several of the cabins.

The cabin, Schulzhytta, sits in the heart of the protected area and outdoor enthusiasts can eat a delicious three course meal right in the centre of a great national park. It is the only tourist cabin in the park and is staffed at Easter and in the peak season during the summer. Since the 1920's the Trondhjem Trekking Association has had lodging agreements with the summer mountain farms in the Roltdal Valley, initially at Lia-vollen and from 1929 at Stormoen. In 1948 the cabin in the area around Fongen, called Schulzhytta after Carl Schulz the first foreman of Trondhjem Trekking Association, was erected at Stormoen as part of the work to make these regions appealing to mountain tourists.

Prestøyhytta is an approximate five hour march, without stops, in a north-westerly direction from Schulzhytta, and directly north is the cabin Kvitfjellhytta a few kilometres west of the park boundary. These long treks give you an

FACTS

Skarvan and Roltdalen National Park (442 square kilometres) encompasses the boundary regions between Nord-Trøndelag and Sør-Trøndelag.

Attractions:
· Old-growth forest in the Roltdal Valley
· Fongen Massif (1,441 metres amsl), the highest point in the national park
· Cultural monuments from millstone quarrying
· Several old mines

Map:
Touring map for Sylan 1: 100 000.

Access:
Several entrances via Road 705 between Selbu and Tydal or Road E14 through Stjørdal to Meråker.

69

Forra in Nord-Trøndelag
Characteristic watercourse and marshlands

The Forra Marshlands are classified as internationally worthy of protection, the entire Forra Watercourse from the inland lake Feren and down to Hegra being a splendid area of natural beauty with abundant flora, interesting bird life and a lot of unspoiled countryside.

A vast region of forests and mountains is framed between the Stjørdal Valley in the south, the Verdal Valley in the north, the Trondheimsfjord in the west and the Swedish border in the east. Occupying the centre of this region is the Forra Watercourse with a total length of 67 kilometres from the western end of Feren Lake down to the mouth of the Stjørdalselv River. At the eastern end of Feren

Evening mood at Forra. Photo: Torbjørn Moen.

A canoe or kayak can provide practical transport for appreciation of the countryside around the Forra Watercourse. Photo: Jan Arne Sæter/NN/Samfoto.

Lake the Nord-Trøndelag Trekking Association (NTT) runs self-service accommodation at Sulåmo Mountain Farm.

Possibilities for canoeing and kayaking

Apart from the trekking association's trail east of Feren Lake there is little other organised activity in these relatively desolate regions and in fact a canoe or kayak can be a practical means of transport for appreciating the countryside in the Forra Watercourse. From Heglesvollen on the tributary Heståa the paddling is good down to Forra and a 5 kilometre wide marshy basin, where the Forra River has meandered in enormous loops from its outlet at Feren Lake. The narrow strip of forest lining the river makes paddling this stretch a fantastic experience. Remember that Øvre (Upper) Forra is a wonderful trout river where you might be lucky enough to catch your dinner. Forra more or less keeps in a westerly direction after Feren, but at Grytesvola the river swings towards the south and the valley becomes narrower with several waterfalls and rapids making paddling down river to the outlet into the Stjørdalselv River much less hospitable.

Roknesvollen, in the far north of the reserve and only 2 kilometres from the car park, is an actively used 4-H Club summer mountain farm where old and young alike can learn about the cultural history, animals and countryside.

Watercourse and nature reserve

This magnificent and vast marshland in a typical U-shaped valley with all its lakes, tarns, streams and rivers as well as the unspoiled conifer forest has made this landscape interesting for hydro-electric power developers and nature conservationists alike. Hydro-electric power was first considered in the 1920's but not seriously until the spring of 1970. In 1986, following a tug-of-war which lasted many years, the entire Forra Watercourse was permanently protected against hydro-electric power development and in 1990 the government resolved to establish the Øvre Forra Nature Reserve totalling 108 square kilometres. It is one of the largest nature reserves in Norway and safeguards this area of exceptional natural beauty in Trøndelag for future generations. In August 2002 Øvre Forra was declared a Ramsar region and is therefore on the list of internationally important wetlands.

Varied nature

Lush mountain areas, conifer forests, wetlands and a diversity of marshes make the Forra Watercourse a popular area for a number of bird species. Waders are in abundance with golden plovers, common snipes, great snipes, whimbrels and redshanks. It is also possible to observe broad-billed sandpipers, common cranes, grey herons, black-throated divers, red-throated divers, tufted ducks, black scoters and goosanders in the watercourse.

The Forra Watercourse contains two basic types of marsh and several varieties of each, which makes the area extremely interesting botanically. Raised peat bogs receive their nutrition only from the precipitation while groundwater marshes are strongly influenced by the type of bedrock. To the west of the watercourse there is more limestone in the ground and some of the extremely fertile marshes can contain over 100 different vascular plants. Hårskallen in the north-west limits of Forra is also botanically exciting as the false musk orchid and white frog orchid as well as mountain avens, northern milk vetch, kidney vetch and Dahurian willowherb find their home here.

Blåfjella-Skjækerfjella
Primeval forest and high mountains in Nord-Trøndelag

Although relatively unknown, Blåfjella-Skjækerfjella is one of Norway's largest national parks totalling an awesome 1,924 square kilometres. Wolverines, lynxes, bears and wolves pass through this protected area of immense forested valleys and wild mountainous regions.

This vast protected area was established as recently as 2004, which might explain why so few have heard about it. The "old" Gressåmoen National Park which totalled 151 square kilometres was absorbed into Blåfjella-Skjækerfjella National Park resulting in an expansion of over ten times the originally protected area.

The national park is situated in the five municipalities Lierne, Snåsa, Verdal, Grong and Steinkjer, with in fact half of the Snåsa Municipality incorporated into the park. In simple terms the park is boun-

A mountain trekker beside a tarn with dead twisted trees in the Blåfjella-Skjækerfjella National Park. Photo: Jon Arne Sæter/NN/Samfoto.

Blåfjella-Skjækerfjella National Park has varied nature. This is a marsh in the protected area. Photo: Torbjørn Moen.

ded by the Verdal Valley in the south, the Swedish border and Lierne in the east, Grong in the north and towards Snåsa in the west.

The protected area has an unusual shape, starting quite wide in the south in the Skjækerfjell mountain region and then narrowing substantially between the Raudfjell Mountain and the Swedish border, only to spread again towards the area around Blåfjell and the previous Gressåmoen National Park. The landscape varies from immense forested valleys, including some primeval forest, to mountain regions and is home to several vulnerable species of plants and animals.

Conservation with several purposes

Blåfjella-Skjækerfjella National Park targets several purposes concerning conservation as well as having to take a number of different user groups into consideration. First and foremost a large uninterrupted area of relatively unspoiled countryside must be looked after. The biodiversity in the park must be ensured with its natural and varied plant life and wildlife, with the lower lying valleys, Tverdal, Skjækerdal, Seisjødal, Gaundal, Holden (Snåsa) and Gjevsjø comprising particularly important landscapes and nature. In addition the cultural monuments must be safeguarded.

The public should have the opportunity to enjoy the park by means of traditional and simple forms of recreational activity involving little technical interference. Looking after the basic nature within the park is important for the Lapps' culture and subsistence exploitation and it should be possible for them to use the park for keeping reindeer herds. In addition to the Southern Lapps' reindeer herds, there is some agricultural activity and it must be mentioned how wonderful these huge wilds are for traditional outdoor pursuits including hunting and fishing. The lakes higher up have good trout and char fishing, the area otherwise having excellent stock of ptarmigan, black grouse and capercaillie. Nord-Trøndelag Trekking Association maintains trails and tourist cabins of which three are self-service (with provisions), Skjækerdalshytta, Sætertjønnhytta (in the Skjækra Landscape Protection Area) and Holden, and the first two are ideal for a weekend trek. From the car park beside Lustadvann Lake it takes only three hours to walk into Sætertjønnhytta, and a five hour march the next day to Skjækerdalshytta. In addition there is a no-service cabin (no provisions), at Gressåmoen Mountain Farm just outside the national park.

Diverse nature

The landscape features relatively low mountain areas with undulating terrain, the largest mountain massif being in the eastern part of the national park. The highest mountain is Midtiklumpen in the Blåfjell Massif (1,333 metres amsl). A landscape protection area and four nature reserves are also connected to the Blåfjella-Skjækerfjella National Park, where both coastal plants and plants dependent on a continental climate grow. Within the protected area at, for example, Skjækerfjella and Raudfjell Mountain in Snåsa there are several abundant and rather special botanical occurrences, and many of the plants you can find in the park are on the Norwegian red list of vulnerable and endangered species. This also applies to several birds and animals, the park containing one of the few sites in Norway where the arctic fox breeds. The wolverines in Blåfjella-Skjækerfjella belong to the southern part of the entire group which frequents Northern Scandinavia. Apart from these two predators, 26 other mammal species have been registered in the national park, which as well as being an area of extreme natural beauty in Trøndelag, also has a real air of wilderness about it.

FACTS

Blåfjella-Skjækerfjella National Park measures 1,924 square kilometres, is Norway's third largest national park and is located in Nord-Trøndelag County.

Attractions:
- Good hunting and fishing
- Vast areas of unspoiled nature
- 28 species of mammals

Maps:
Individual maps in the main map series for Norway 1: 50 000.

Access:
Road 74, Road 765, Road 763 and the road to Vera on the Swedish border are good starting points. Several minor roads lead off these main roads and into the national park.

71

Lierne

National park and uninterrupted wilderness

The Lierne Municipality in Nord-Trøndelag calls itself the wilderness municipality and quite rightly so. In the west is Blåfjella-Skjækerfjella National Park, in the east the Lierne National Park, and these together with the mountains on the Swedish side of the border form a huge uninterrupted wilderness.

This national park covering 333 square kilometres is north of the Sørli Watercourse, passes over Hestkjølen northwards towards Muru on the border with Sweden and together with the Swedish Nature Reserve in the mountains of Hotagsfjellene, this forms a large uninterrupted wilderness even in Scandinavian terms. The terrain though relatively flat has some steeper and more undulating

Storbursklumpen in the Lierne National Park. Photo: Torbjørn Moen.

Sunset over Lierne. Photo: Torbjørn Moen.

mountains the highest being the summit Hestkjøltoppen at 1,390 metres amsl, which is a curiosity in itself as it embodies the watershed between the Baltic Sea and the Norwegian Sea.

No organized outdoor activities

Quite unlike Blåfjella-Skjækerfjella National Park (see separate chapter) in the west of the municipality, Lierne has no marked trails for summer or winter, no footbridges over rivers swollen by floodwaters in the summer, and the Norwegian Trekking Association has no activities within the national park. With all this in mind it is a good idea to include map, compass and tent in your back pack as well as food and other equipment if you plan to explore this scenic area in Nord-Trøndelag. Despite the vastness of this untouched wilderness of harsh mountains there are other alternatives to pitching a tent. The mountain authorities have some relatively roomy and

well-equipped cabins for hire at reasonable prices just outside the national park boundaries. Nearly all the lakes, rivers and streams contain lively trout, but if you are planning a fishing trip take some mosquito repellent with you as these fellows are just as lively and plentiful.

Of course these tremendous areas of wilderness are ideal for large predators such as wolverines, bears and wolves as well as the smaller arctic fox, all of which need a lot of space for their subsistence. As far as Nord-Trøndelag is concerned, the number of bird species living and thriving in the mountains is quite unique and includes Eurasian dotterels, dunlins, red-necked phalaropes and long-tailed skuas. To illustrate the quality of the wilderness of these regions, two mountain wardens had quite an exceptional experience a couple of years ago as not only did they observe a female bear with three cubs on a slope a

few hundred metres away, but suddenly a golden eagle swooped out of the mist and snatched one of the cubs with its claws and disappeared again.

Rich Quaternary geology and Lapp cultural monuments

The purpose of the Lierne National Park is to safeguard an uninterrupted mountain region with its natural plant life and wildlife. The central areas support a rich mountain fauna while birch forest with tallgrowing perennial plants and willow thickets provide rich biotopes in the transition between mountain and lower regions, where there are also several valuable wetland areas. In terms of Quaternary geology, the landscape of the national park is special for the whole region and the richest in the whole county when it comes to the abundance of Quaternary formations, among others the thick moraine deposits and numerous moraine formations including

Rogen moraine, which is a series of small moraines lying parallel to each other in a ribbed pattern. Lierne is a long way from the coast and the ice moved very little compared to other places in Norway at the end of the Ice Age, the ice more or less sinking down where it was as the climate became warmer.

Even if there are almost no technical encroachments in the national park, there are traces of human activity in the area as the Southern Lapps have lived here for many centuries. Lapp cultural monuments and natural elements such as old settlements, meeting places, burial sites and sacred places are numerous and shall be safeguarded within the national park. It is important for Lapp culture and subsistence exploitation that the basic nature is looked after and it should be possible for the area to be used for keeping reindeer herds in the future.

72

Solem Nature Reserve in Nord-Trøndelag
Coastal rain forest of international value

There is no need to travel to the Amazon to see a mysterious rain forest. The Solem Nature Reserve in Grong Municipality in Nord-Trøndelag is nearer and has a moist coastal rain forest containing many rare fungi and lichens. This nature reserve belonging to the elite of coastal rain forests is of great international value.

Coastal rain forest is a rare habitat and only two to three per cent of the forest in temperate regions can be classified as temperate rain forest. Such forests can be found along the west coast of USA and Canada, along the south coast of Chile, in New Zealand and Australia, Georgia, Turkey, Scotland, Ireland and Trøndelag in Norway.

Heavy precipitation

All rain forests, the Norwegian rain forests included, get a lot of rain and to be called temperate rain forest the annual precipitation must exceed 1,800 millimetres, evenly distributed over the year. The winters in these districts are typically long and wet while the summers are cool and foggy.

Temperate rain forests often occur where there is a network of streams, on marine sediments from the Ice Age, in river valleys, in the spray zone near waterfalls or on north-facing slopes. In other words, in damp regions which never dry up, even in extremely dry summers.

Although Norway has an international responsibility to protect these unique areas, of the 250 temperate rain forests in the whole country only 26 are protected, and these occur from Agdenes in Sør-Trøndelag to Rana in Nordland County.

Of course the rain forests in Trøndelag do not have the diversity of a tropical rain forest, with jaguars, macaws, tapirs and strangling fig plants, but instead support obscure species of lichens, mosses, fungi and insects. Many of the lichen species are so distinctive that a group of 15 species have been given their own name, the Trøndelag Element, in the lichen flora, because the only known occurrence, or main concentration is in Trøndelag.

Threats to these rare species of lichen are tree felling and ditch-

Interior from the coastal rain forest in the Solem Nature Reserve. Photo: Kim Abel/Naturarkivet.

One of two European localities for boreal felt lichen is found in the nature reserve. Photo: Sigve Reiso/Naturarkivet.

environment such as capercaillie, hazel grouse, northern goshawk and some woodpeckers.

Internationally important

One of the peak areas in Norway for this rare type of nature is the Solem Nature Reserve in Grong, protected since 2001. The reserve occupies a large and partly intact system of ravines, the main one formed by a stream which runs through the locality and is fed by many small streams running from branches of the main ravine.

Solem, perhaps the most vital and valuable area of remaining coastal rain forest in Norway, is clearly world-class as it contains one of six localities in Europe for boreal felt lichen. The majority of botanists believed that boreal felt lichen was wiped out in Europe as the last few finds were registered in Grong in 1938 and 1939 but in 1995 two specimens were again found in Nord-Trøndelag, one in Solem and one in Overhalla. Following this a further three occurrences were found in Grong, making a total of five registered localities in Trøndelag, although

unfortunately the lichen has now disappeared from four of these only occurring now in one locality in the form of two or three individuals on a spruce tree. However, in 2005 boreal felt lichen was amazingly found in quite another locality in Norway, Rendalen in Hedmark, thus making a total of two known localities for this species in Europe, other localities on a world basis being on North America's Atlantic coast.

Boreal felt lichen is not the only rare species registered in the reserve as other species on the Norwegian red list grow here, for example, the critically endangered brown shingle lichen, and the vulnerable yellow specklebelly, cartilage lichen and beech crust fungus. As well as the diversity of species found in these coastal rain forests, the whole experience of being inside this green mysterious world with its canopy of fresh leaves makes it worthwhile for the few that visit.

ing, as the resulting changes in the local moisture conditions result in the lichens drying up and dying. Some lichen species already show 90 per cent decline and

urgent conservation of Scandinavia's rain forests is needed.

Besides the lichens, mosses and fungi, there are a number of birds that appreciate this forest

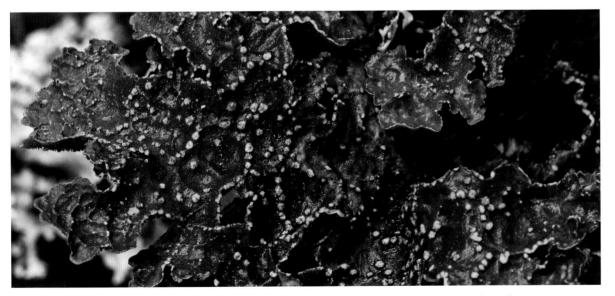

Yellow speckelbelly is one of several vulnerable species of lichen found in the coastal rain forest at Solem. Photo: Sigve Reiso/Naturarkivet.

The world's largest colony of European shags

Out in the sea off the coast of Nord-Trøndelag County is a small group of islands called Sklinna, with among other things the world's largest colony of European shags.

Sklinna, a group of over 30 islands 20 kilometres west of Leka, is the last outpost before the Norwegian Sea. The lighthouse on the island Heimøya was built in 1910 and quite a landmark at a height of 45 metres. Sklinna was previously an important fishing community with permanent residents and up to 500 fishermen during the fishing season. When the lighthouse was made automatic in 2004 the last two residents, the lighthouse keeper and his assistant, left for good.

Sunset and shags

To see the European shags in the sunset on Sklinna is quite a magic experience, there they sit silhouetted against the evening sunlight on the islets and rocks where they will stay the night. The flock is in constant movement, some landing with wings open wide

The lighthouse on Heimøya Island was built in 1910 This picture is taken from the 45 metre high lighthouse. Photo: Tom Schandy.

among their colleagues on the rock while others take off for one last flight before the sun finally sinks in the Atlantic Ocean. The large flocks of shags that choose to lie in the sea can be heard bathing and splashing or taking off with powerful beats of their wings on the surface of the water.

The Sklinna group of islands is today considered to be the world's best habitat for shags, capturing the title from Runde Island in Møre and Romsdal County. Whereas previously 5,000 pairs of shags nested on Runde, these numbers unfortunately decreased drastically and now number less than 2,000 pairs. When researchers first started registering this green-black seabird in these islands off the coast of Trøndelag in the 1980's, there were only approximately 500 nesting pairs, in 2003 they had increased to over 3,000 pairs.

In order to provide shelter from the ocean, a couple of breakwaters have been built where the shags love to make their nests, finding safe places for these large sturdy constructions of seaweed, heather and twigs among the

European shags silhouetted in the sunset. Photo: Tom Schandy.

rough rocks and boulders. However, each couple has to keep a look out for their neighbour who is only too eager to steal nesting material while their backs are turned.

As well as shags, there are many other bird species on the islands, which are considered as containing the only real bird cliffs between Runde in Møre and Romsdal and Lovunden on the Helgeland coast. Colonies of comical Atlantic puffins, nesting black-legged kittiwakes, razorbills, common guillemots and black guillemots make their home here along with greylag geese and common eiders. It is not unusual to see majestic white-tailed eagles circling overhead – there is no shortage of food for them at Sklinna.

Restrictions

Sklinna was made a nature reserve in 2003 and this introduced strict regulations. It is forbidden to go ashore or move about on the island Heimøya, with the largest bird colonies, from 15 April to 31 July, and for the puffin colony this prohibition lasts until 31 August. However, it is permitted to walk along the marked paths in the vicinity of the lighthouse station, as well as drive boats around the islands except for the areas surrounding the vulnerable colonies of great cormorants in the island group. Sklinna is included in the national surveillance programme for seabirds which means that every summer the islands are visited by researchers who study the shags and other seabirds.

The world's largest colony of European shags is found at Sklinna. Here is a solitary individual. Photo: Tom Schandy.

FACTS

Sklinna, group of islands and nature reserve way out in the ocean in Nord-Trøndelag County.

Attractions:
· The world's largest colony of shags
· Lighthouse worthy of conservation

Map:
1625 II Sklinna 1: 50 000.

Access:
Difficult. Most of the islands are protected and it is forbidden to go ashore. Walking on the marked paths near the lighthouse station on the island Heimøya is permitted. Otherwise the islands must be experienced from a boat, but even boat traffic is prohibited near the vulnerable nesting areas for great cormorants.

74

Børgefjell Mountains
The arctic fox's last bastion

The Børgefjell National Park lies on the border between the counties of Nord-Trøndelag and Nordland. While being a huge wilderness with plenty of good fishing lakes and a rich bird life, it is also one of Norway's last bastions for the endangered arctic fox.

The Børgefjell National Park leaves a powerful impression. In the west there are soaring summits, including the 1,699 metre high Kvigtinden, Børgefjell's highest and the bedrock is dominated by dark granite making the landscape seem rather desolate. In the south there are several wild rapids and beautiful waterfalls, while the east can offer rounded mountain tops and extensive heaths.

Børgefjell became Norway's second national park in 1963, only one year after Rondane. In 1971 the park was expanded slightly followed by an enormous expansion in 2003 and it now totals 1,447 square kilometres of pristine wild-erness.

In fact Børgefjell is one of the largest remaining wilderness-like areas in the country, so it is not surprising that the outdoor enthusiast Lars Monsen loves it here. Before he made his expeditions to Alaska and Canada he wrote the book "90 Days Loafing Around in Børgefjell".

There is very little organised recreation activity in these mountains, because in 1932 the Norwegian Trekking Association decided that Børgefjell should be spared the building of tourist cabins and marked trails. A trek in Børgefjell means carrying your own tent, sleeping bag and fishing rod, which will always catch you your dinner in this El Dorado for trout fishing.

Abundance of birds

The Børgefjell landscape, with several fine watercourses and marshes with willow thickets, is very suitable for birds. Especially around the lake Vestre Tiplingan and the lower part of the Simskardelv River in the north of Børgefjell there is a rich bird life includ-

Børgefjell catching the evening light. Photo: Torbjørn Moen.

Børgefjell National Park is one of Norway's last bastions for the endangered arctic fox. Photo: Tom Schandy.

ing a number of duck species and waders, such as the red-breasted merganser, long-tailed duck, greater scaup, black scoter, wood sandpiper, common snipe, redshank, Temminck's stint, common sandpiper, ringed plover and purple sandpiper. Whereas at one time there was a quantity of bean geese and lesser white-fronted geese in Børgefjell, their numbers have declined substantially, the latter having disappeared altogether and today the bean goose is found mainly south of the park. When there are multitudes of small rodents in the mountains the long-tailed skua is quite common, an elegant bird which attacks aggressively if you get too close to its nest.

Otherwise, the Børgefjell Mountains are famous for birds of prey. Again, in the years when there is an abundance of small rodents, the rough-legged buzzard nests,

but the bird which arouses most interest is the noble snowy owl which has been observed nesting here a number of times. This is a nomadic invasion species that travels over great distances in accordance with the occurrences of small rodents. Although 1985 saw an excess of these creatures in Børgefjell and 17 pairs of snowy owls were registered nesting in the national park, there have been no signs of nesting since and the cause of the snowy owl's disappearance from this and most of its other nesting grounds in Norway, is unknown.

The arctic fox, Børgefjell's speciality

Børgefjell's speciality is the arctic fox, as the national park is one of Scandinavia's last bastions for this predator on the brink of extinction. The total Norwegian population is estimated to be approxi-

mately 50 adult individuals and Børgefjell is home to a large proportion of these foxes. 2005 was a good year for the arctic fox with 11 of the 21 Norwegian litters registered in the national park. It was assumed that there were up to 21 adult foxes, and 15 of the 39 arctic foxes born in Norway that year, were born in Børgefjell.

Despite 70 years of protection the arctic fox is still an endangered species, probably due to a combination of several factors, for example, competition from the red fox, change in availability of food, division of the landscape and a warmer climate.

If you spot an arctic fox in the national park, just enjoy the sight and withdraw quietly. State-employed wardens monitor the dens and make sure that the arctic fox is not disturbed unnecessarily.

❧ FACTS ❧

Børgefjell National Park, 1,447 square kilometres, in the counties of Nord-Trøndelag and Nordland.

Attractions:
· Wilderness
· Fishing lakes
· Abundant bird life
· Arctic foxes

Map:
Børgefjell touring map folder 1: 50 000.

Access:
Several access points. If you arrive by train you can get off at Majavann and walk into the national park. The simplest way by car is to drive to Store Namsvatn Lake at Røyrvik and then take the boat across the lake. It is also easy to access from Susendal Valley in the north and from the Stekenjokk Road in Sweden. You can also walk in from Simskaret in Grane. There are a few simple cabins in the park, but basically you will need a tent.

75

Helgeland Coastline
The world's most beautiful skerry coast

It is difficult not to use clichés when describing the Helgeland Coastline, but can there by anything more beautiful? The mythical mountains, including the range called the Seven Sisters (De Syv Søstre), soar skywards in peaks and cones, while 12,000 islands nestle one after the other along the coast.

The Helgeland Coastline stretches from Nord-Trøndelag County in the south to Salten in the north and with 57,000 kilometres of shoreline and 12,000 islands it is entitled to be called the world's most beautiful skerry coast. The coastal road, Road 17, winds its way through this region, over bridges, on ferries, through deep valleys and at the foot of majestic mountains. The Helgeland Coastline offers spectacular experiences in scenery overflowing with mountains and summits, the vast ocean, sheltered coves, beaches, large unspoiled countryside and an extremely abundant flora and fauna. There are innumerable small islands and some large ones and like pearls strung together they adorn a beautiful and exciting coastline. Some of the most famous mountain formations are located along the inshore channels of the Helgeland Coastline and this fairytale realm of islets, skerries and mountains provides some of the most distinctive holiday resorts along Norway's coast.

One of the famous mountain formations on this coast is the Seven Sisters (De Syv Søstre) just beside Sandnessjøen and the Norwegian Trekking Association has prepared marked paths to each summit so that one can walk up unguided. At Brønnøysund we find another characteristic mountain on the Helgeland Coastline, Torghat-

The Coastal Liner Express (Hurtigruta) leaves Brønnøysund. Photo: Tom Schandy.

Norway's largest owl, the eagle owl, thrives in the skerry landscape along the Helgeland Coastline. Photo: Tom Schandy.

ten (258 metres amsl), which is famous for the hole that pierces right through the mountain. The hole, 160 metres long, 35 metres high and 20 metres wide, was created during the Ice Age when ice and water laboriously bored through the loose rocks, while the harder rocks resisted.

Archaeological finds

Archaeological finds, among others at Vega and Træna, indicate that people have lived on the Helgeland Coastline for more than 10,000 years. On the island of Sanna in Træna there are many caves, where the breakers have washed out weaknesses in the rock at a time when the ocean was higher than it is today. Altogether 19 such caves have been found of which Kirkhelleren is the most splendid and famous. It is 45 metres deep, 20 metres wide and 30 metres high and before the Second World War a 3.5 metre thick layer of debris from the Stone Age was excavated. Beneath the cave there are several remains of Stone Age house sites, among them Norway's oldest, "Langhå-gen", approximately 6,000 years old. This is interesting as it proves that several thousand years ago there were sea-going ships that could reach far off the coast. In addition a mass grave has been found with 33 skeletons from the Middle Ages and the legend tells that this is the crew from a Dutch boat which carried the Plague to Norway.

Cackling flocks of geese

In the course of some hectic weeks in the spring, April to May, cackling barnacle geese congregate on the islands along the Helgeland Coastline. They fatten themselves up on the grazing and haymaking meadows before their final journey to the breeding grounds on Svalbard. If you visit Herøy Island just outside Sandnessjøen in the middle of May you will think you have been abandoned in a gigantic goose farm, and they are only some of the 13,000 barnacle geese that take a breather on the Helgeland Coastline.

This skerry scenery also supports large stocks of otters, common seals, grey seals and porpoises, and the common eider are still exploited for their eggs and down. When the Vega Islands were put on the prestigious UNESCO World Heritage List in 2005, the farming of common eiders and the down collecting traditions were heavy arguments in the islands' favour.

"Lundkommardagen" – The day the puffins arrive

The island of Lovunden is in a class of its own concerning the number of birds. It is believed that there are over 200,000 Atlantic puffins on Lovunden, but today the 270 inhabitants are only allowed to enjoy the sight of this amusing bird. However, in the olden days, the puffin provided a welcome additional source of food for the coastal population and the so-called "Lundkommardagen" – the day the puffins arrive – on the 14th April was celebrated with great festivity. This was traditionally the day when huge flocks of puffins returned and equally huge crowds of people welcomed them back. Even today the inhabitants show their appreciation of the puffins' return and continue to celebrate this day.

It is perfectly possible to climb the 619 metre high mountain on the island and the reward is a glorious panorama where one can gaze over the thousands of small islands and skerries and towards the mainland at the infinite mountain ranges.

The domain of the birds of prey

The numerous islands on the Helgeland Coastline provide a domain for the birds of prey. The sight of a white-tailed eagle is inevitable as it hangs over the fjords and mountains, which is not surprising when Nordland County is the home of half of Norway's white-tailed eagles, and Norway has half of North Europe's stock of this bird, which means that the county can boast 25 per cent of the stock within its borders. Norway's largest owl, the eagle owl, also thrives in this skerry scenery, living off the large, fat voles that are numerous on these grassy islands. The eagle owl, white-tailed eagle and willow ptarmigan can tumble around in this nationally romantic scenery, and if you have ever visited the Helgeland Coastline, you will understand how difficult it is to avoid the clichés.

🙠 FACTS 🙢

The Helgeland Coastline stretches from Nord-Trøndelag in the south to Salten in the north.

Attractions:
- Lovunden Island with its puffins
- White-tailed eagles and eagle owls.
- Migrating barnacle geese
- Træna with mountains and archaeology
- Dønnesfjell Mountain with a view over the archipelago
- Torghatten
- The Seven Sisters (De Syv Søstre)

Maps:
Individual maps in the main map series for Norway 1: 50 000.

Access:
The Helgeland Coastline is long and there are many places for accessing it. You can take the car ferry from Stokkvågen on the mainland to Sleneset, Lovunden and Træna islands. All islands have accommodation. Another pleasant trip is to take the ferry to Dønna Island. Here there are several views of the islands to the north. You can also drive south to Herøya Island where the barnacle geese rest. Or you can take the ferry to Vega Island and join a smaller boat trip around the islands.

76

Saltfjell Mountains-Svartisen Icecap
Icecap and marble castle

Boasting Norway's next largest glacier, underground grottoes, formations in marble, steep summits and waterfalls, the area around the Saltfjell Mountains and Svartisen in Nordland County has some wonderful sights, the central part of this region being included in the Saltfjellet-Svartisen National Park.

Together with the surrounding landscape protection areas, this national park is much larger than the whole of Vestfold County and reveals a splendid cross-section of the nature in the Nordland County. Do not be led astray by what you see from the car window as you drive along Road E6, because further inside the national park there are a number of outstanding areas of natural beauty. The trekking association also has a well-developed network of routes on the east side of the park providing good access for most people to explore this fantastic countryside.

Svartisen, divided in two

Svartisen's Icecap totals approximately 370 square kilometres, but today the glacier is divided in two. Whereas during the so-called Little Ice Age in the middle of the 1700's Svartisen was an uninterrupted icecap, the following gradual regression ended in division of the glacier at the Glomdal Val-

The Austerdalsisen, an arm of the Svartisen Icecap which is Norway's next largest glacier. Photo: Tom Schandy.

The marble castle is perhaps the most wonderful geological formation in the area surrounding the Svartisen Icecap. Photo: Bård Løken/NN/Samfoto.

ley around 100 years ago. The ice melt resulted in the formation of several lakes, but because the ice grinds down the rocks, enormous volumes of stones, gravel and slam are continually deposited in these lakes. At Holandsfjord, the Engabre Glacier alone deposits around 18,000 tons in Engabrevann Lake annually, which will eventually lead to the entire lake being filled in. The trekking association has arranged glacier courses on the Engabre Glacier for several years and for many people this is their first taste of walking on a glacier. The rich plant life in the area includes maiden saxifrage,

which thrives close up to the foot of the glacier, and the Svartisen poppy, a subspecies of the arctic poppy, has its only global habitat here, possibly surviving on one of the nunataks during the last Ice Age.

Although the glacier is divided, Vestre Svartisen and Østre Svartisen are still large glaciers in Norwegian terms, Vestre being the country's next largest and Østre fourth largest. Svartisen is quite accessible, with Austerdalsisen, Østisen's largest glacier arm, being visited by thousands of tourists every year. The approach is by driving to the Svartisvann Lake

and taking the boat over the lake or by taking the path on the north side to the glacier face at Austerdalsvann Lake. Remember to keep a safe distance from the glacier as there is a constant danger of avalanches from the glacier face.

Marble castle and grottoes

Much of the bedrock in the Saltfjell Mountains consists of mica slate with tremendous sections of limestone where numerous grottoes have been washed out. Over half of the grottoes registered in Norway are found within this national park, but the most well-known among tourists, the Grønli Grotto at Langvann Lake around 20 kilometres north-west of Mo i Rana, lies just outside the park's southern boundary. The grotto is 1,200 metres long and 100 metres high at the lowest point at the entrance, and is an easily available tourist attraction for its annual volume of 10,000 visitors who can reach it from the road leading to Austerdalsisen.

Marble is transformed limestone, and both these rock types are easily eroded by water, something which has happened in the vein of white-striped marble which goes diagonally over the valley of Glomdal. A journey through this valley is quite an experience with the marble castle at Glomåga, limestone hollows, small caves, underground rivers and extremely lush vegetation and everything is easily accessed by the marked footpath from the parking area where the road ends at the bottom of the Glomdal Valley.

Well-developed network of tourist cabins and routes

Particularly the eastern part of the Saltfjellet-Svartisen National Park

contains a well-developed network of tourist cabins and routes. The trail up the Blakkådal Valley and down to Beiardal Valley crosses the entire park, as does the route from Dunderlandsdal Valley, through Tespdal Valley and further on up Bjøllådal Valley to the cabin Bjøllåvasstua. The first stretch of the trail between Bjøllånes and Krukkistua is relatively long, around eight hours' walking, but further on the trekking association's no-service cabins (without provisions) lie quite close to each other, the reason for this being that Bjøllådal Valley is an old thoroughfare to Øvre Saltdal. The telegraph wires erected in 1867 followed this route and in this connection small stone huts were built to give shelter, these being later replaced by timber cabins all of which have now been renovated.

77

Junkerdal
Rare flora and soaring summits

As well as small glaciers and long rows of mountain summits, Junkerdal National Park in Nordland County can offer an exceptionally lush flora and several botanical rarities. Together with mountain regions in Norway and Sweden, the national park is one of Scandinavia's largest remaining wildernesses.

The Junkerdal Valley is a Mecca for botanists. Together with Knutshø in the Dovre Mountains this valley is one of the earliest classical biological areas in Norway, with the flora especially abundant in the Junkerdalsura Nature Reserve. Otherwise the nature in the national park is varied, containing flat plains, steep rock faces, swirling rapids and sharp mountain peaks, in addition to it being a well-known Lapp district with several cultural monuments.

The protected area is situated between the actual Junkerdal Val-

The Solvågtind Summit (1,559 metres amsl), tall and majestic, even in the blue light of dusk. Photo: Espen Bratlie/NN/Samfoto.

The beautiful and protected orchid, lady's slipper, thrives in the Junkerdal Valley. Photo: Øystein Søbye/NN/Samfoto.

ley in the south and Sulitjelma in the north, bordering with Sweden in the east. Unlike many of the national parks in the north which are difficult to access, Junkerdal has many marked paths and trails and several tourist cabins, huts or Lapp turf huts open for overnight accommodation.

Exciting flora

Junkerdal Valley, a side valley off the Saltdal Valley, is considered among Norwegian botanists to be one of the country's most interesting places. The national park lies in a rain shadow in relation to the Svartisen Icecap producing a hot, dry summer climate, which combined with a favourable type of bedrock, sustains many plant species. Whereas to the south of the deep Junkerdal Valley and the narrow gorge hard and nutrient poor granite dominates the bedrock, the opposite is the case at the north side where the metamorphic sedimentary rocks such as slate, limestone and marble give a fertile soil and an exceptionally luxuriant flora.

As early as the 1820's Vicar Sommerfelt (in Saltdal) studied botany in this greenhouse-like area at the north side of the Junkerdal Valley. Almost at the same time a Swedish vicar and colleague discovered a new plant species for Northern Europe beside Balvann Lake a little to the north of the present day national park. This was the very rare livelong saxifrage, and it was later found in Nordreisa in Troms County and in the Suldal Mountains in Rogaland County, its nearest habitat otherwise in Europe being in the Alps. Several rare types of vegetation in the protected area are heaths of arctic bell heather and mountain avens with arctic rhododendron. Many other plants are only found further north or on other continents and northern single-spike sedge, the Tromsø poppy (a subspecies of the arctic poppy), Ellesmereland whitlow-grass, arctic alpine fleabane, and narrow-leaved arnica are all at their southernmost limits here. Other rare plants worth mentioning are arctic bellflower, woolly everlasting, flame-tipped lousewort and hairy lousewort as well as a number of orchids, perhaps the most beautiful of them all, the lady's slipper orchid, which thrives in the scree slopes in the Junkerdalsura Nature Reserve. In order to protect these rare plant species eastern parts of the area were preserved as long ago as 1928. This was expanded in 1935 and in 2004 the national park was established.

Rich fauna and splendid walks

As well as rare flowers the park can offer long and exciting hiking tours. The so-called Arctic Fennoscandia Route, a marked trail which traverses the park, is linked by several tourist cabins that provide overnight accommodation. The cabin Argaladhytta in the Skaitidal Valley is rumoured to be one of the most comfortable tourist cabins in Norway, and it takes only a couple of hours to walk there from the nearest road. While the centre of the national park surrounding the Balvann Lake is wide and open, in the south west the park's most prominent summit, Solvågtind (1,559 metres amsl) majestically watches over the protected area. Ascent of the summit looks impossible for the average person without climbing equipment, but in fact for the more experienced mountain walker the top of Solvågtind is within reach.

Gyrfalcon, golden eagle, red-throated diver, black-throated diver and long-tailed duck, though occurring in few numbers, are some of the endangered bird species which nest within in the park. The wildlife is diverse due to the abundant vegetation, and the park is also home to the large predators, wolverines and lynxes, while bears pass regularly through and the rare arctic fox, which is on the brink of extinction, probably exists in this district. The national park also has occurrences of the rare diurnal butterflies, the glandon blue and the northern clouded yellow.

Part of a Scandinavian wilderness

Marvellous experiences in nature await those who challenge the wilderness of the Rago National Park. Established to preserve an unspoiled natural environment in Nordland county's mountains bordering on Sweden, the park features wild, magnificent mountains with deep chasms, glaciers, waterfalls and enormous boulders.

With its 162 square kilometres Rago National Park is one of Norway's smallest, but it borders on the Swedish national parks Padjelanta, Sarek and Stora Sjöfallet and totalling collectively 5,700 square kilometres they form the largest conservation area in Europe. Due to its desolate location, this wilderness is mainly left alone without interference from people, and with no nearby roads, there is little human traffic in these regions.

Cold summers

The parking area at Lakshola is the easiest place to approach Rago, by following the path through the Storskogdal Valley to the unlocked cabin, Storskoghytta. There is a small network of marked trails here suitable for mountain hiking and a round trip back to Lakshola will take you past the Litlverivann Lake. The other no-service tourist cabin in the park is Ragohytta, also unlocked and located further east. Between them the cabins provide

From the entrance to Rago National Park. Photo: Trym Ivar Bergsmo/NN/Samfoto.

The national park features a wild, magnificent mountain landscape with deep chasms, glaciers, waterfalls and enormous boulders. Rago borders on large Swedish national parks. Photo: Jon Arne Sæter/NN/Samfoto.

especially along Storskogvann Lake where they have reached tremendous dimensions. Incredibly, forestry was carried out here in the olden days, so long distances and terrain without roads obviously did not deter people from collecting timber for house building.

For a short time during World War I there were experimental operations to take out galena and silver from beside Ragotoppen, the national park's highest summit at 1,312 metres amsl, and even a seven to eight hour walk from the village district did not hinder the workers of that era. The name Rago derives from Lappish and means literally sliding glacier. The area has been used for hunting and trapping for many centuries and the Lapps' domestic reindeer were traditionally driven over Rago on their way from Sweden to the summer grazing in Norway.

only six beds, Storskoghytta two and Ragohytta four, so it is advisable to take a tent if you plan a trek lasting several days.

Rago's mountains are wild and barren with a climate characterised by cold and damp summers. The winter snow still lies late in the summer and as a rule the summits hang in a swirl of fog. Due to the cold summers the typical mountain plants like roseroot (golden root), alpine lady's mantle, yellow wood violet and moorking may even grow down in the forests here. In particular, the south-eastern parts of the protected area are exciting for botany enthusiasts as the bedrock contains nutritious slate and supports more demanding mountain plants such as alpine whitlow-grass, snowbed draba, woolly everlasting and snow buttercup. The protected area can also boast several fine waterfalls, Trolldalsfoss in the north-west and Verifoss, with its steep descent from Litlverivann Lake down to Storskogdal Valley, are probably the ones that impress most.

Originally the national park contained no fish due to the numerous and huge waterfalls in the Storskogelv River. However, between and following the great world wars, trout and char have been released and at present there is a good stock of fish in several of Rago's lakes. Small game hunting and fishing are permitted in the park for those who have licences. There is not a great diversity of mammals, but there are wolverines which live and hunt in these wild mountains and a lynx occasionally passes through, with bears keeping more to the Swedish side of the total protected area. In recent years moose have settled in the lower elevations of Rago National Park.

Human activity in former times

Pine trees have managed to cling on to the poor soil and in some places they are quite numerous,

79

Lofoten-Hinnøya
An alpine world in the middle of the ocean

Lofoten and Hinnøya resemble an alpine world in the middle of the Norwegian Sea. A 190 kilometre long chain of craggy peaks rising straight out of the ocean, distributed between a number of large and small islands. These mountains hide sheltered coves, wonderful sandy beaches and picturesque fishing villages and it is not surprising that tourists from all over the world flock to Lofoten.

Lofoten consists of five large and numerous small islands. Six bridges and underwater tunnels connect the islands, collecting the 25,000 inhabitants into one community. Cod fishing forms the basis for people making their homes in this stretch of open sea and if you want to experience the vitality of these islands, then you should visit in March when the famous Lofoten Fishing for the equally famous Lofoten cod is in full swing.

In at the deep end on the island of Moskenesøy

The ferry transports you directly from Bodø to Moskenes in the outer reaches of Lofoten and drops

There can hardly be any other village in Norway with such a spectacular location as Hamnøy in Lofoten. Photo: Svein Grønvold/NN/Samfoto.

you in at the deep end for your adventure as the attractions line up waiting for you. Not far away is Reine and there cannot be many villages with such a spectacular location. The ocean on the outside, the Kjerkefjord on the inside, red fishermen's huts and alpine summits on all sides. The landscape at Reine has been described as follows: *"Remove the lower 1,000 metres of the Jotunheimen Mountains and place the rest in the sea, then you have the landscape on the tip of Lofoten"*:

It is also possible to hike in this border region sandwiched between the sea and the mountains. Lofoten Turlag's (trekking club) only tourist cabin, Munkebu, is south of Reine and after a two to three hour walk on a marked trail from Sørvågen you have arrived and can appreciate the view of soaring spires and wide cirques.

Island jumping

Starting from Reine you can go island jumping northwards. The next island is Flakstadøy and between Ramberg and Flakstad the road follows the outside edge of Lofoten which means that there are 4 kilometres of uninterrupted view of the midnight sun. The midnight sun lasts for nearly two months, from 27 May to 20 July. Flakstadøy harbours the small idyllic fishing village of Nusfjord, wedged between two high walls of rock.

Following this you arrive at Vestvågøy Island where there are not only mountains but also vast open spaces with traditional cultivated landscape. A visit to Utakleiv and Eggum on the north side is a must, and on the way to Utakleiv you pass Hauklandsstranda which was elected as "Norway's most

magnificent bathing beach" in 2001, despite the water temperature unworthy of the same status.

Further east is Austvågøy Island with its high mountains, wonderful sandy beaches and strong tidal currents with biting saithe. Svolvær and Kabelvåg are on the inside of the island with their splendid harbours for fishing boats. Right behind Svolvær towers the famous Svolværgeita (The Svolvær Goat), a mountain peak with two goat-like horns.

Møysalen National Park

Norway's largest island, Hinnøya, lies in the very east and is separated from Austvågøy Island by the strait of water called Raftsundet. Hinnøya has some of the wildest mountain terrain in Norway and the Møysalen National Park is located on the island. Protected since 2003 it totals only 51.2 square kilometres and is thus the third smallest national park in Nor-

way. One should not be fooled by its size as this park can give you some really tremendous experiences with its alpine formation, lush slopes of deciduous forest and open fjords; there is nothing like it anywhere else in Norway. The no-service tourist cabin, Snytindhytta with its 15 beds can make a fine starting point for a summit ascent on Møysalen Mountain. There is only one marked trail in the national park and a couple of chains assist you to reach the very top of Møysalen which, with its 1,262 metres amsl, is the highest mountain in the whole of Lofoten-Vesterålen.

Møysalen is also a good place to spy for birds of prey. Nesting of the golden eagle, white-tailed eagle, rough-legged buzzard, gyrfalcon, peregrine falcon, common kestrel and merlin has been registered within the park boundaries, and the otter is quite a common sight in the fjord arms.

The moon hangs over the Møysalen National Park on Hinnøya Island. Photo: Trym Ivar Bergsmo/NN/Samfoto.

80

Røst

A gem on the outer edge of Lofoten

Røst lies 100 kilometres from the mainland and 25 kilometres from its nearest "neighbour" in Lofoten. It is a fairytale community with as many islands as days in the year and millions of seabirds.

Most of the inhabitants live on Røstlandet, a 4 kilometre long and 3 kilometre wide island 11 metres amsl at its highest point, thus forming a strong contrast to the bird cliffs in the south west which rise out of the ocean like enormous stone monuments. Røstlandet is in fact a row of small treeless islands and islets joined by breakwaters and roads which create numerous bays and coves perfect as resting and feeding grounds for waders and ducks.

Monumental bird cliffs

South-west of Røstlandet the bird cliffs lie one after the other, the first of which is Vedøya Island where it is permitted to go ashore. The path taking you to the top brings you near razorbills, puffins, shags and black-legged kittiwakes. Moreover you will probably see a

The harbour where the inhabitants of Røst live. Photo: Øystein Søbye/NN/Samfoto.

white-tailed eagle hanging over-head. From the top of the island there is a superb view over the entire Røst Archipelago.

Following Vedøya Island is Storfjellet with its 259 metres amsl making it the highest island in the group. There then follows three conical, marine haystacks, Ellefsnyken, Trenyken with its three characteristic peaks and Hernyken. It is forbidden to go ashore on any of these bird cliffs, but one can come quite close to the bird colonies by boat which provides good opportunities for both observation and photography.

Skomvær is the last outpost towards the Atlantic Ocean, a green and lush island with its proud lighthouse which was erected in 1887. The artist Theodor Kittelsen lived here for two years at the end of the 1800's and it was here he illustrated the famous legend of "The Cormorants on Outer Røst".

Røst is considered Norway's largest bird cliff with several hundred thousand Atlantic puffins nesting. Trenyken in the background. Photo: Tore Wuttudal/NN/Samfoto.

Food shortage

Røst is considered to be Norway's largest bird cliff, but unfortunately shortage of food in the sea has resulted in a dramatic decline in the number of Atlantic puffins. In 1979 there was estimated to be 1.4 million pairs of puffins here, but today the researchers have calculated the stock to only 400,000 pairs. The problems began with the collapse of the atlanto-scandic stock of herring in the 1970's and for many seasons the adult puffins abandoned their chicks because there was insufficient herring fry in the sea.

The common guillemot is another species which has declined even more and in the long term there is a danger that it will disappear completely. In the 1970's 12,000 pairs nested on Røst, but in

2004 the stock was reduced to 200 pairs.

Mysterious European storm petrels and Leach's storm petrels

The mysterious European storm petrel and Leach's storm petrel are less well-known and they are a relation of the albatross. However, the European storm petrel with its 15 centimetres is in fact the smallest seabird in the Atlantic Ocean and the first breeding observation in Norway was on Røst in 1961.

These two species have a very unusual nesting behaviour on Røst in that they first appear in July and leave in November to December. They nest in the autumn and feed their young when the autumn storms howl around the Røst Islands. The reason is that, in order to avoid greedy skuas and large

gulls, they only dare to land when the nights are dark and therefore they do not lay their eggs until August, a while after the season of the midnight sun.

The European storm petrel and Leach's storm petrel have a slow reproduction cycle. They sit on their solitary egg for 40-50 days and the young bird leaves the nest after 60-70 days. Such a long nesting period means that some of the young do not leave the colony until the beginning of December.

As a rule, birds with slow reproduction live a long time and European storm petrels and Leach's storm petrels are no exception: in 1993 a European storm petrel with a ring on its leg was caught on Røst, and this revealed that it was ringed 27 years previously.

81

Tysfjord

Including Norway's national mountain, grottoes and an enormous canyon

The Tysfjord Municipality, far north in the Nordland County, and far south in Ofoten contains the national mountain, Stetind (1,392 metres amsl), the enormous canyon, Hellemojuv and the grottoes at Musken - all natural wonders difficult to match anywhere else in Norway. Large shoals of killer whales cruise around in the autumn, hunting for herring in the network of fjords.

Five fjord arms run out into the Tysfjord, these are: Hellemofjord, Grunnfjord, Mannfjord, Sørfjord and Stefjord. They form a part of the landscape around Tysfjord, originally an ancient highland plain where the rivers gouged out narrow, deep canyons, which were

Stetind (1,392 metres amsl) is almost vertical and a colossal stone monument. Photo: Frode Jensen.

later made deeper and broader by glaciers, finally becoming these fjord arms. Where these meet in the outer wide fjord basin the depth of the water is around 900 metres and with many of the surrounding mountains dropping vertically to the edge of the fjord the scenery can compete with Western Norway for attracting the tourists.

With only 6 kilometres to the Swedish border, Norway is almost at its narrowest at Hellemobotn, there being only a couple of places in Sør-Varanger in Finnmark County where Norway is narrower.

Norway's national mountain

Out of Norway's numerous beautiful and striking mountains, Stetind was elected as the national mountain in 2002 by the listeners to one of the Norwegian broadcasting company's radio programmes. Everyone who has seen Stetind understands why it won this acclaim, with its 1,392 metres amsl and direct ascent without rocky outcrops or ledges. It can be both fascinating and foreboding and resembles a colossal perpendicular monument. The mountaineer, author and philosopher, Peter Wessel Zapffe, once described Stetind as "an anvil for God to hammer on", and the Lapp word for Stetind also means anvil or support. The mountain is also a time-honoured navigation guide for mariners along the coast of Nordland.

In the 1800's there were several attempts to climb Stetind, but even the legendary and competent English mountaineer, William C. Slingsby, had to give up, describing the mountain as "The ugliest mountain I ever saw". However, on 30 June 1910, Ferdinand Schelderup, Carl Wilhelm Rubenson and Alf Bonnevie Bryn finally conquered the giant beside Tysfjord and since then many others have reached the top. Tours are even arranged so that non-climbers can also get to the top of Norway's national mountain, but one should have good physical form and a good head for heights.

The Hellemojuv canyon

The Hellemojuv Canyon, located inside Hellemobotn, is a dramatically impressive gorge several hundred metres deep, up to 500 metres wide and approximately 3.5 kilometres long. The canyon starts steeply about half a kilometre from the outlet of Kuvann Lake and goes right out to Hellemobotnvann Lake. There are no roads in the area so the only transport to this natural wonder is by boat. From Hellemobotn where Norway is at its narrowest there is a hiking trail through Sweden to a cabin called Røysvatnhytta further north and lying along the Arctic Fennoscandia Route, a long day's march of approximately 12 to 14 hours.

From grotto wandering to whale safari

Among Tysfjord's natural wonders are a number of limestone grottoes, the deepest lying at Musken, Råggejavri-Raigi, which descends a total of 575 metres. Wandering through grottoes is quite a close-to-nature experience in a dark and quiet world where there is absolutely no mobile telephone cover.

Tysfjord is also famous for the large concentration of killer whales which collect in the fjord every autumn, and people from all over the world come to see this spectacular sight. Several companies in the area arrange whale safaris giving tourists the chance to see

Tysfjord is also especially famous for the great concentrations of killer whales which arrive in the fjord every autumn. People from all over the world come to see this natural performance. Photo: Asgeir Kvalvik.

complete families of killer whales including males, females and young from the boat.

Nominated on the World Heritage List

Norwegian authorities have recommended nomination of Tysfjord /Hellemobotn for UNESCO's World Heritage List, based on its vital settlement of Lule Lapps combined with magnificent nature and old traditional cultivated landscape sustained without modern technical encroachment. This area provides enormous knowledge and is significant as a baseline reference of the Lule Lapps' identity and culture. Tysfjord is nominated together with the Swedish Lapland district for inclusion on the World Heritage List.

82

Andøya
From sandy beaches to whale safaris

Located northernmost in Vesterålen, Andøya Island has mountains, endless marshlands, long sandy beaches, bird colonies and not least the world's largest toothed whale which dives freely off the edge of the continental shelf outside Andenes.

The 60 kilometre long island of Andøya resembles neither Vesterålen nor Lofoten. The landscape is long and open with wide shorelines and long sandy beaches and the two kilometre long beach at Bleik is considered one of the longest in Norway, lacking only the palms, and 10 to 15 degrees of heat.

Compared to Lofoten, the mountains on Andøya are emerald green and rounded. They are easy to climb and from the top there is a magnificent view of the Norwegian Sea in the west as well as the

Picturesque Andøya Island lies in the north of Vesterålen. Photo: Bård Løken/NN/Samfoto.

islands of Hinnøya, Grytøya, Bjark-
øya and Senja to the east separated by the Andfjord.

Remember to take a fishing rod
with you in the Andøya countryside, because wherever you go
there are idyllic lakes and rivers
full of fish. The best of Nordland
County's salmon rivers, Åelva in
the Roksdal Watercourse, is on the
island where the annual salmon
catch exceeds three tons.

Largest marshland in Northern Europe

Northern Europe's largest marshlands are on Andøya and it is
therefore not surprising that the
marshes have had and still have
great significance for the island's
inhabitants. Peat litter and juicy
golden cloudberries bring a welcome income and in fact at the
beginning of the 1900's 35,000
litres of cloudberries were sold,
something equivalent to the value
of 50 annual wages. No wonder
the people in the north guard their
cloudberry marshes as if they
were gold treasure!

Skogvoll Nature Reserve, located in the north half of Andøya,
includes marshes on the interior of
the island and wetlands along the
coast. There is a broad range of
marsh types and plant species, as
well as ample numbers of ducks
and waders.

Bleiksøya Island, with its 156
metre high cone and approximately 70,000 pairs of Atlantic
puffins, lies off the coast outside
the small village of Bleik. While
there is also a good supply of
black-legged kittiwakes and shags,
the occurrences of razorbills and
common guillemots are more
modest. In addition the northern
fulmar and the European storm
petrel nest on this island.

The sperm whale, the world's largest toothed whale measuring 20 metres and weighing 50 tons, can be observed on a whale safari from Andenes. Photo: Tom Schandy.

Whale safari

Whales are in their element
where the continental shelf stops
and the deep ocean abruptly and
brutally begins. Nowhere else
along the Norwegian coast is the
continental shelf so near than at
Andøya and this makes it ideal for
whale safaris. Although it is possible to spot minke whales and
humpback whales, the safaris
mainly concern the sperm whale,
the world's largest toothed whale
measuring up to 20 metres and
weighing 50 tons. When the whale
relaxes on the surface it regularly
sends up a spout which makes it
easy to spot and the whale safari
boats can get into position before
the next dive. The guides keep a
look out and give the sign just
before so that the tourists are
ready with their cameras and
camcorders, because it is the dive
which is the climax. The whale
arches its back and shoots straight
down into the ocean, while its

enormous tail fin seems for a
moment to stand like a monument in the water. The whale descends to 1,000 metres to search
for squid, its favourite food.

The whale safaris also assist the
research of these mysterious
mammals. The sperm whale's tail
fin is its fingerprint and the shape
differs from individual to individual. By photographing as many tail
fins as possible one can register
these and thus collect information
about the whales' movements,
social life and not least the size of
the stock. In the period 1987 to
2001 approximately 400 different
sperm whales were identified off
Andenes.

Only male whales visit Andøya
and they stay only for the summer, spending their winters
somewhere off the Azores in the
Atlantic Ocean. Here they meet
up with the females who stay in
these warm waters all year round,
mate and become fathers to a

new generation of whales. In the
spring the males return to the
north to feed on squid outside
Andøya, to the joy of the people
of all nationalities taking part in
the whale safaris.

❧ FACTS ❧

Andøya Island located in the north
of Vesterålen in Nordland County.

Attractions:
- Long sandy beaches
- Northern Europe's largest marshland
- Bleiksøya Island with puffins
- Whale safari with sperm whale
- Northern Lights

Maps:
Individual maps in the main map
series for Norway 1: 50 000.

Access:
Easy to reach. Road around the
whole island. Airport at Andenes.
Whale safari with daily departures
from Andenes during the summer
season.

83

Øvre Dividal National Park
The realm of the wolverine

Øvre Dividal National Park, situated in Indre Troms on the border with Sweden, has a varied landscape with pine and birch forests, high mountains, lakes and marshes, abundant plant and bird life, but most of all it is the realm of the wolverine.

The Øvre Dividal National Park lies in an arch around the upper part of the Dividal Valley, with a piece to the west and a piece to the east of the valley. Westwards the national park stretches up and along the Anjavassdal Valley, a large, wide side valley to the Dividal Valley. Although it has a north-west direction, at one time it ran out eastwards, but the ice ploughed its way into Dividal Valley from the west and the water then ran out in that direction.

It is easy to reach the national park by driving the Dividal Valley as far south as possible to the car park at Frihetsli. From here you can either follow a path up and along the Skakterdal Valley which contains some of the wildest and most unspoiled landscape in the area, or you can walk south along the Divielv River to the tourist cabin, Dividalshytta. This cabin and two others in the park, Vuoma-hytta in the west and Dørtahytta in the east are owned by the Nor-

The Northern Lights create an atmosphere of magic during a tour in the national park. Photo: Lars Krempig.

wegian Trekking Association and Troms Turlag (trekking club). They are no-service cabins so you must take all the food you need with you. The marked trail between the cabins is a part of the so-called Arctic Fennoscandia Route which starts in Kautokeino and ends in Kongsvinger.

Primeval forest and wide expanses

Pine forests with a pristine air grow along the deep river gorge in the Dividal Valley. There has been no significant felling here and some of the trees are almost 500 years old. Birch forest grows above the pine forest and gradually merges into wide expanses with gentle valley sides and soft rounded mountain ridges, but far west in the park beside the majestic mountain Njunis (1,713 metres amsl) there are glaciers and summit peaks. The typical bedrocks for much of the area are conglomerate, sandstone and slate and this limestone rich layer of slate almost 80 metres thick with sediment is so pronounced that it has received its own name, the Dividal Group.

This rich bedrock supports an abundant flora including Norway's only rhododendron, the arctic rhododendron, which covers large areas along with alpine arnica, flame-lipped lousewort, hairy lousewort and arctic thrift, all species which do not occur in Southern Norway. White arctic bell heather is also extremely common here and, in total, 315 superior plants have been registered.

Birds and predators

The bird life is also exciting, especially in years with ample numbers of small rodents, when it might be

The Dividal Valley probably has the densest population of wolverine in Northern Europe. Photo: Asgeir Kvalvik.

possible to observe the rare snowy owl as well as the long-tailed skua. The gyrfalcon, a magnificent bird of prey, is also in its element in this harsh terrain and hunts ptarmigan in the mountains. At the lakes and watercourses you can see the common teal, tufted duck and greater scaup while on the marshes there are ruff, redshank, wood sandpiper, Temminck's stint and common snipe.

The Dividal Valley is perhaps best known for its predators. All Norway's largest predators have been observed in the national

park, but whereas wolves are only dispersal animals, lynxes are permanent residents. The Dividal Valley shares its bear stock with Sweden and females with cubs are observed in the valley nearly every year. However, the characteristic animal is the wolverine and there are several dens inside and outside the valley, the area probably having the densest population of wolverine in Northern Europe. The wolverine, Norway's largest species of marten, is a shy animal and difficult to spot and if you visit the area in the early spring the most

you will find is footprints in the snow. The endangered arctic fox also reproduces here when there are plenty of small rodents, the numerous mounds of moraine providing ideal places to make a den.

There is good fishing in the national park with char as the most common while trout has a somewhat limited distribution. Burbot and grayling have come from the Swedish watercourses and although common whitefish and pike do occur, it is seldom.

Sørdalen-Isdalen

South of the Altevann Lake is another area of wilderness, Sørdalen-Isdalen, which has been recommended as a new national park. This is a wild and beautiful region with deep valleys, narrow gorges, glaciers, jagged mountains and good fishing lakes. The bedrock is rich in limestone and marble providing the same abundance of species as in the Dividal Valley. The wolverine also thrives here.

84

Senja in Troms
Pine forest and the Devil's Jaw

The island of Senja in Troms County is a unique area of natural scenic beauty with fjords and rearing mountains on the outside and a rounder, more gentle landscape on the side nearest the mainland. Ånderdalen National Park in the south of the island contains coastal pine forest where the trees have grown particularly thick trunks.

Senja, with its 1,583 square kilometres, is Norway's second largest island, and the beauty spots are never-ending. People from the south of Norway are probably first of all most attracted to the outside of the island where small and far-flung fishing villages cling on to a narrow shoreline beneath high and soaring mountains which rise abruptly 1,000 metres out of the sea.

Crossing the Devil's Jaws

Work is underway to make the entire length of road from Botnhamn in the east to Gryllefjord in the west into a National Tourist Route, and that tells us quite a bit about the quality of the scenery along this stretch of coast. The tourist route winds through this intense countryside, up and down hills, in and out of fjords, and facing the open sea there are wild

Evening mood on a beach at Ersfjord on Senja. Outermost is a glimpse of the Devil's Jaw. One of many idylls on Senja. Photo: Tom Schandy.

Ånderdalen National Park is located in the south-east of Senja. Photo: Erlend Haarberg/NN/Samfoto.

most glorious bird. It was in fact here that the whooper swan was first observed nesting in Troms County, and this was at the beginning of the 1960's. Until then whooper swans had only nested in Øst-Finnmark.

In July you can watch pairs of swans swimming with their young in several of the reed-clad tarns on the island, and there is in fact a nature reserve called Svandalen (Swan Valley) where of course the whooper swans nest. This swan is usually considered to be a shy bird of the wilderness, but on Senja several of the pairs have become used to people and are no longer so afraid. All the same, one should not disturb the whooper swans unnecessarily.

and rugged mountains locally known as the Devil's Jaw.

Some kilometres south of Botnhamn there is a road to Husøy, a very special island which lives up to its name as there are 50-60 houses lying side by side. In recent years this little island has experienced a rush of new inhabitants and house building to the envy of any other outlying district. The fact that the houses on this tiny rocky knoll nearly blow into the sea every winter obviously has no influence on attracting newcomers. Another idyll along the coast is Melfjordvær, where a path takes you up the 100 metre high mountain called Knuten to an absolutely wonderful view over the fjord and all the mountains. The cute hamlet of Ersfjord is in the next bay boasting one kilometre of sandy beach, and surrounding this fjord you can see some of Senja's wildest moun-

tains including the characteristic Okshornan, which could in fact resemble the jaw of the Devil.

Ånderdalen National Park

After first having explored the outer edge, one should take a look at the inner coast and the interior which has a milder climate, more lush vegetation and a gentler landscape with long valleys and splendid watercourses. In fact, not unlike Eastern Norway. There are lakes with trout and char as well as rivers with salmon, sea trout and sea char.

Ånderdalen National Park is located in the south-east of the island and tempts you to visit, and at 125 square kilometres it is one of Norway's smallest national parks. It takes only a couple of hours on a marked path to walk from Kampevoll to Åndervann Lake, which is considered to be the heart of the park. There are

rivers and lakes, sharp mountain peaks, mountain plains and unspoiled birch and pine forests, the latter being especially magnificent here containing low, huge coastal pines with particularly thick trunks. There are magical forests with some giant pines almost 500 years old and so large it takes three people to embrace them.

Marshes with whooper swans

East of the national park, between Vardnesvann Lake and Skoglifjell Mountain there is the Vardnesmyra Nature Reserve with vast marshlands, islets and promontories with pine forest, dazzling lakes and myriads of tiny ponds. This bird marsh is teeming with life all round the clock especially at night in the light of the midnight sun. You can observe curlews, whimbrels, dunlins, common cranes, slavonian grebes and not least whooper swans – Senja's

85

Otertind

Northern Europe's answer to the Matterhorn

The valley Signaldal projects southwards from the Storfjord in Troms County and ends at Treriksrøysa between Finland, Sweden and Norway. This valley cradles glorious and dramatic scenery on all sides, the jewel being the twin summits of Otertind (1,356 metres amsl).

Often called Northern Europe's answer to the Matterhorn, Otertind's twin summits (1,356 metres amsl) tower over the west side of the lush Signaldal Valley. The summits are one of the most photographed motifs at Storfjord and they are best observed from Signalnes which lies approximately 15 kilometres into the Signaldal Valley. Since the two German climbers, Endell and Martin, reached the top of Otertind in 1911, the mountain has had many visitors including the philosopher and mountaineer Peter Wessel Zapffe who was originally from Tromsø.

At a distance Storfjord's Matterhorn seems impregnable, but in fact it is possible to climb Otertind without using climbing equipment, as long as one finds the right channel, and that lies on the south-west side. However, impor-

Northern Lights shining over Otertind. Photo: Bård Løken/NN/Samfoto.

Otertind in a winter setting. Photo: Bård Løken/NN/Samfoto.

tant prerequisites are good physical condition and hiking equipment and it is an advantage to take someone who is familiar with the mountain on such an aerial excursion, as well as evaluating the weather. There are guided tours to Otertind and the panorama is needless to say absolutely fantastic surveying the Storfjord, the Lyng Mountains and deep into Sweden.

Culture and nature

Signaldal is a valley of outstanding natural beauty in its own right. People from several valleys in the south of Norway settled under the majestic mountains encompassing this valley in the middle of the 1800's, which explains the combination found here today of a valley culture and unique nature. The hut at Signalnes is the first dwelling these outsiders erected, a building with a centrally located corridor, the oldest part of the house being constructed with axed timber and using a special cogging joint structure with chinking and daubing at the corners. The central corridor and the newest part of the house are built with timber cut on a gate saw. The hut at Signalnes is not normally open to visitors but is a splendid sight with Otertind as a backdrop.

Besides the famous Otertind, there is plenty of other striking scenery in the region. The luxuriant Signaldal Valley is lined by towering majestic mountains; Mannfjell (1,552 metres amsl), Markusfjell (1,541 metres amsl), Polvartind (1,272 metres amsl) and Vassdalstind (1,467 metres amsl). The Mannfjell Mountain, named after the remarkable stone formation which resembles a person, can be climbed from several angles, the easiest being from the Sørdal Valley in the Kitdal Valley.

Treriksrøysa in Troms County

Two places in Norway bear the name Treriksrøysa, one in Pasvik and the other innermost in the Stordal Valley, a side valley off Signaldal Valley and is an alternative hiking destination for those who do not like tackling the highest alpine peaks. There is a cart track from Rognli Farm in Signaldal Valley which follows the Paraselv River in Parasdal Valley and after a three to four hour walk along a marked path you arrive at Troms Turlag's no-service tourist cabin called Gappohytta. The following day a four hour march brings you to the next cabin, Goldahytta, which is also no-service (without provisions), and after a further three hours you are at Treriksrøysa, which is the name of the place where the border between Norway, Sweden and Finland meet. The actual spot is marked by a large stone monument in the middle of a stony lake and a system of footbridges help you walk out to it. This lake is in fact the head of the Stordalselv River which runs down into Signaldal Valley.

Treriksrøysa is a popular tourist destination and in Finland there is organised boat transport to Kilpisjärvi during the summer which takes approximately 30 minutes, leaving a 20 minute walk to the monument. The walking route called "Grensesømmen", literally "the border seam", follows the border between Norway and Sweden, alternating countries as it goes and is the Norwegian Trekking Association's way of marking the centenary celebrations for the dissolution of the union with Sweden, as well as the Recreation Year 2005. The Norwegian Trekking Association and the Swedish Tourist Association collaborate on this uninterrupted trail along the border from Svinesund to Treriksrøysa in Troms County.

86

Lyng Alps
Glaciers and mountain summits in Troms County

Little visited and quite inaccessible, but perhaps the most beautiful scenery in Norway, the Lyng Alps in Troms County are underrated. The mountain range covering this peninsula has 140 glaciers and a row of craggy peaks that can take the breath away from any mountain enthusiast, even the most blasé, and it certainly deserves more visitors.

Nearly 90 kilometres stretch from Nordkjosbotn innermost in the Balsfjord in the south to Lyngstuva in the north. Except where the Kjosenfjord and Lyngseidet nearly divide it in two, this peninsula comprises a 15-20 kilometre-wide belt of uninterrupted craggy spires and approximately 140 glaciers, as well as abrupt precipices, wild inlets and deep valleys. The Lyng Alps do not shame their name and

The Lyng Alps mirrored in the fjord. Photo: Bård Løken/NN/Samfoto.

Evening light illuminates the Lyng Alps. Photo: Tom Schandy.

in 2004 they received their own landscape protection area.

Little organised recreational activity

The Lyng Alps have been compared to Lofoten in the neighbouring county of Nordland, except that they soar a further 1,000 metres into the sky. Many of the mountains in the north of Norway impress because they generally rise vertically out of the sea's surface to a possible 1,800 metres elevation. The tallest in Troms, Jiek'kevarri (1,833 metres amsl), is located between the Sørfjord and Lyngenfjord and similar to most other summits, scaling it demands experienced mountaineers with the right equipment, skills and local knowledge.

With hardly any marked trails and no private holiday cabins, the nearest one comes to organised recreation is Troms Turlag's (trekking association) tourist cabin, Jægervasshytta, which at 10 metres amsl and only three kilometres from the road at Jægervann Lake, is relatively easy to reach. Although the cabin has only four beds, there is a wide semi-loft or gallery which provides extra accommodation. There is a splendid and highly recommendable trail from Jægervasshytta through the Stortinddal Valley over to the Russedal Valley and Lyngen on the east side of the mountain massif. This trail takes you to an elevation of 400 metres and close to the tremendous glacier faces oozing from the summits Trolltind and Taffeltind.

It is also possible to drive out to Nord-Lenangen and walk along the beautiful and fertile Nordlenangsbotnen, surrounded by dramatic mountain peaks some of them hung with enormous glacier faces, in striking contrast to the flat, green valley below. Further south in the Lyng Alps, Lakselvdal Valley is a good starting point for a walk to Elvevoll, or alternatively through the pass Piggtindskaret and the Tverrdal Valley to Storfjord. The area also contains a few scattered, unlocked cabins owned by the regional society or the local hunting/fishing association.

El Dorado for mountaineers

The mountains in the north drop abruptly to the sea and it is clear to anyone viewing the Lyng Alps from the E6 road that this range of jagged summits must attract mountaineers. The starting point for glacier trekking or mountain climbing is the Jægervann Lake in the west and Koppangen at the end of the road in the east. As elsewhere in Norway, the climbing pioneers here were on the whole Englishmen, although the isolated top of the characteristic, pyramid shaped mountain Piggtind in the south-west was left in peace until 1920 when the first to conquer it were in fact three Norwegian mountaineers. A successful winter climb to the summit did not occur before 1971.

However, as the rock in the area around Lyngen is loose and cracks easily, the mountains are little used for rock climbing in the summer. The dominant mountain sport activities are winter climbing and summit ascending and in recent years this wonderful scenery has become popular for summit ascents on skis. This activity has developed parallel to the classic skiing trips in the lower elevations and is of equal interest to winter tourists, not only Norwegians, but also skiing enthusiasts from Finland, Sweden and even further afield.

Conservation area

With such natural qualities it was no surprise that the Lyngsalpan Landscape Protection Area totalling 961.2 square kilometres was established in 2004, and is divided in two by the Kjosen fjord arm and Lyngseidet. The purpose of the protected landscape is to preserve one of Norway's most characteristic mountain regions containing glaciers, moraines, valleys and geological deposits, with the biological diversity, cultural monuments and cultural influence featured in the landscape.

Concerning the biological diversity the bird life makes the biggest impression and includes nesting pairs of all of the nine normally found diurnal birds of prey and all the eight owl species in the county have been observed here.

87

Reisa National Park
Magnificent wilderness

Reisa National Park in Nord-Troms is synonymous with magnificent scenery. Powerful waterfalls plunge into a wild and narrow canyon, wolverine and lynx wander through and the salmon swim steadily towards their spawning grounds further up the watercourse.

One of the biggest attractions in the Reisa National Park is the Mollisfoss Waterfall. Photo: Tom Schandy.

This national park in Nord-Troms is synonymous with magnificent scenery. Photo: Torbjørn Moen.

The Reisa Watercourse is very similar to the Alta Watercourse with steep mountain sides towering up from the flat floor of the valley. Reisa was protected as a national park in 1986 and many people consider it to be the largest area of natural beauty in the entire Arctic Fennoscandia.

Wild waterfalls

While the fittest people hike mile after mile into the magnificent "Alaska landscape", most choose a simpler solution to travel up the watercourse, by river boat. One of the biggest attractions in the national park is the 269 metre high Mollisfoss Waterfall which plunges vertically down into the gorge. In fine weather a rainbow adorns the bottom of the waterfall providing a wonderful photo motif for the river boat tourists. However, Mollisfoss Waterfall is not alone as several other places in the valley large and small waterfalls cascade over the edge of precipices.

Several kilometres beyond Nedrefoss, where the river boat has to give up, the Imofoss Waterfall, mighty and untamed, tumbles into a dark ravine. Below the falls there are splendid potholes, one of which is over 10 metres deep with a handsome arched bridge of granite, a unique natural formation.

Botanical gems

When it comes to biological diversity, Reisa National Park and the surrounding mountains are the most valuable regions in Arctic Fennoscandia. The natural conditions with both acid and limestone-rich rocks provide wide variation in the plant life. There are also strong fluctuations in climate ranging from maritime in the north to continental in the south. All belts of vegetation are represented from the greenhouse-like conditions deep in the crevices to extreme conditions in the mountains, with a total registration of 525 vascular plants.

Many exciting and rare plants are attached to the river. Natural-ly erosive, the river constantly changes its course, building up levees and banks where plants such as the oatgrass species Trisetum subalpestre, arctic lychnis and Siberian lettuce grow. Apart from the Reisa Watercourse, the only other place these plants are found in Norway is in the Alta Watercourse.

The botanical gems do not only grow by the river, but also in the mountains and this area is one of the most exciting in the whole of Scandinavia. Approximately 230 alpine plants are found in Scandinavia and of these 193 are registered in this national park, many of the species not being found at all in Southern Norway. Among these are flame-lipped lousewort, white arctic bell heather, alpine arnica and arctic rhododendron. However, the most exclusive species is the small, green blunt-leaved orchid, which grows just outside the national park. It is otherwise only found in a very few mountain regions in the entire Arctic Fennoscandia and the nearest known occurrences are in Eastern Siberia and beside Lake Baikal.

Birds of prey and predators

The Reisadal Valley is also of great significance for birds of prey and predators. The high rocky crags in the valley support the densest occurrence of rock nesting birds of prey second only to the Alta Watercourse, including the common kestrel, gyrfalcon, rough-legged buzzard and golden eagle. The white-tailed eagle can also be observed regularly in the national park.

Reisa National Park is also well-known for its large predators, with a separate occurrence of wolverine, in addition to the possibility of seeing lynxes and bears. Several place names contain the Lappish word for the arctic fox, "njalla", which indicates that this species was previously characteristic in this area. Unfortunately the arctic fox has suffered a substantial decline in the whole of Norway and one needs a good deal of luck to spot an arctic fox these days.

Altogether approximately 140 bird species have been observed in the watercourse. Many of them are rare and vulnerable, such as the whooper swan, lesser white-fronted goose and bean goose. Both the red-throated diver and black-throated diver nest here and in years when there is an abundance of small rodents, the northern hawk owl is one of the most common owl species.

❧ FACTS ❧

Reisa National Park totals 804 square kilometres, bordering with Raisduottarhaldi Landscape Protection Area.

Attractions:
- Mollisfoss Waterfall
- Imofoss Waterfall
- Birds of prey
- Rare plants, including the blunt-leaved orchid
- Magnificent landscape

Maps:
Individual maps in the main map series for Norway 1: 50 000.

Access:
Easiest approach via Storslett and Saraelv. Here you can board a river boat to Nedrefoss. Alternatively you can walk the Arctic Fennoscandia Route to Kautokeino. This starts at Saraelv where you can park your car. Accommodation available at the no-service tourist cabin, Nedrefosshytta inside the park.

88

Finnmarksvidda Plateau

Undulating plains, fishing, the midnight sun and the northern lights

The Finnmarksvidda Plateau is a flat piece of Norway offering enormous outdoor experiences. In the summer you can fish for trout and salmon under the midnight sun, hunt willow grouses in the autumn and in the winter you can join a dog-sleigh trek over the plateau with the colourful splendour of the northern lights dancing across the sky.

The Finnmarksvidda Plateau comprises the inner and central parts of the Finnmark County, an enormous area covering 36 per cent of the county, in other words 17,000 square kilometres and substantially larger than, for example, the Hardangervidda Mountain Plateau in the south of Norway. While the latter is a mountain plateau more or less without trees at approximately 1,000 metres amsl, the Finnmarksvidda Plateau lies at around 300 to 500 metres' elevation with large areas covered in stunted birch forest. There are very few mountain tops and solid rock is on the whole only visible along some rivers and streams.

Domesticated reindeer and halo on the Finnmarksvidda Plateau. Photo: Trym Ivar Bergsmo/NN/Samfoto.

The land of the Lapps

For many people the Finnmarksvidda Plateau is synonymous with the Lapps and Finnmark does in fact mean "the Land of the Lapps", a people who are associated with reindeer and several theories exist about when they began to keep these animals. Some people maintain that reindeer have been kept from time immemorial, while others claim that in the 1600's the Coastal Lapps in Northern Norway began to keep a few reindeer as "decoys" during the reindeer hunting, and otherwise for transport and milk production. Gradually the Lapps gathered larger herds of domesticated reindeer and began a nomadic existence. Unfortunately the domestic reindeer stock has become much too large and has resulted in excessive grazing, reduced slaughter weight and increased calf death. Moreover the reindeer business has become extremely commercialised with snowmobiles taking over from reindeer for transport, not to mention an infinite number of ATV's, tractors and 4-wheel drives, which means that large parts of this plateau comprise anything other than an unspoiled natural wonder. However, if one can get away from the snowmobile and ATV routes there are still many great experiences here.

Fantastic fishing

Folk from the south of Norway to a great extent connect Finnmark with fantastic trout, char and even salmon fishing. The areas around the headwaters of the Tana Watercourse in Kárásjohka and Anárjohka are legendary for fishing, providing great opportunities to catch trout weighing 1 to 3 kilograms. A week here with a fishing rod and the midnight sun is for many people the biggest nature experience in the entire world. That is if one can put up with the mosquitoes, because the ones in Finnmark are famous for coming in size XL!

The Tana is a unique salmon river and has no equal either in Norway or Europe when it comes to the volume of caught fish. For example, in 2001 245.5 tons of salmon were taken from Tana, 125.9 tons on the Norwegian side and 122.6 tons in Finland. What makes the river unique is that the salmon run 300 kilometres inland. Tana has the world record for an Atlantic salmon caught by rod, 35.89 kilograms, admittedly from 1928, but every year it is possible to catch salmon here that weigh over 20 kilograms.

Summer and winter hiking

Apart from the fishing there are wonderful hiking routes. A marked path goes from Alta to Karasjok and the staffed lodge, Mollesjohka, which is a meeting point for all traffic on the plateau. The scenery is dominated by this wide open expanse together with the immense lake, Iesjávri, with all its nooks and crannies, and you have the feeling that you are on the roof of the plateau. You can eat a good meal at Mollesjohka, take a sauna followed by bathing in the snow, with the veil of the northern lights flickering overhead. Quite an exceptional experience, especially for people from the south of Norway.

Mollesjohka is not the only place offering accommodation on the Finnmarksvidda Plateau as the Norwegian State own several mountain lodges between Alta and Karasjok. They are simple but staffed and offer accommodation for mountain trekkers. Whereas the mountain lodges in Norway originally date back to the 1100's, the mountain lodges in their present form have existed in Finnmark since approximately 1840.

The Finnmarksvidda Plateau is famous for its fishing, and what could be better than a fishing trip in the midnight sun?
Photo: Lars Krempig.

89

Øvre Anárjohka National Park
In the embrace of the wilds

Norway's perhaps most inaccessible national park, Øvre Anárjohka, is located innermost on the Finnmarks-vidda Plateau. In these great wildernesses with mosquitoes humming around your ears, you can feel the slow breath of eternity.

The national park is a flat plateau with a number of rounded hills, and while half of it comprises marshes, lakes and barren plains, there are also large areas of pine and birch forest. The western part of the park containing mountains and marshes, is at a higher elevation than the eastern part and there are altogether more than 700 lakes in the park, many starting their journey to the sea far in on the plateau. The national park's largest lake, Gavdnjajávri, lies near the headwater of the upper Anárjohka. A special feature of the park are the so-called palsa mires, which are bogs containing a core of ice.

Overwhelming sensation of solitude

Anárjohka National Park is not organised for visitors, there are no marked trails or tourist cabins. You just have to manage on your own, a long way from the nearest civilisation, which means of course that you have to be well-equipped, both physically and mentally. In fact the silence and desolation of these enormous wildernesses can be uncomfortably pressing. A sensation of loneliness and a plague of blood-sucking mosquitoes is no perfect combination and many people can feel that the embrace of the wilds is especially strong. In his book about Norway's national parks, Professor Leif Ryvarden writes that there is no other place where he has felt the slow breath of eternity than here, and we, the authors of this book absolutely agree, after having spent a week in a tent at the foot of the Ulvefoss Waterfall in the east of the park.

Although only 15 metres high, the Ulvefoss Waterfall is one of the most well-known landmarks in the national park and it has its own regular pair of white-throated dippers. It is in fact possible to punt by riverboat all the way to the Ulvefoss Waterfall.

The 15 metre high waterfall, Ulvefoss, is one of the most well-known landmarks in Øvre Anárjohka National Park. Photo: Oddleif Nordsletta.

Company in the wilderness
If you like your own company then

The gyrfalcon nests in the river valleys in Øvre Anárjohka. Photo: Tom Schandy.

Øvre Anárjohka National Park is a magnificent place to be with the thought that you are absolutely alone in the wilderness. Maybe you come across the nest of a gyrfalcon in a river valley, a Siberian tit's nest in an old tree stump or are visited by one of the many Siberian jays, a species in its element in these wide-open pine forests. Nesting whooper swans are a common sight on the plateau as well as common goldeneyes, long-tailed ducks, common teals, black scoters and velvet scoters. You may see waders on the marshes, for example wood sandpipers, redshanks, whimbrels, bartailed godwits, spotted redshanks and jack snipes. The last three are typical eastern species that on the whole only nest in Øst- Finnmark.

Anárjohka is a paradise for those who like to fish and today many wilderness fishermen hire a seaplane that lands them on the national park boundary where they begin their trip. However, from the point of view of conservation this rather American practice is somewhat alarming, and we recommend that you enter the park under your own steam. This means a large heavy rucksack, but the reward is good fishing with grayling common in the rivers and trout on the plateau. There is a possibility of large pike in the holes under the waterfalls and in fact salmon travel several tens of kilometres up the Anárjohka River, salmon fishing being permitted as far in as the Ulvefoss Waterfall.

Bears exist in the national park and lairs have been registered, the animals being part of the large Norwegian-Finnish breed which wander over the border, and whereas the wolverine is not stationary, moose are quite common. Small rodents also populate the park, such as lemming, field mice, root voles and northern water voles, while the typical species for the park is the Siberian species of red-backed vole.

The plant life, also influenced by Siberia, includes long leaf speedwell, Siberian lettuce, two meadow-rues (Thalictrum simplex ssp. boreale and Thalictrum kemense) and tall (acutish) Jacob's ladder. In damper places one can find Lapland buttercup, northern golden-saxifra-

The Siberian tit thrives in the national park. Photo: Tom Schandy.

ge otherwise known as northern golden-carpet and red cottongrass.

Gold miners

More surprisingly perhaps are the seams of gold found in the national park; in fact there has been quite a Klondyke in these desolate districts. Gold miners first visited the plateau in 1735 but it took 130 years before anyone found any gold, which then led to a proper gold rush in Finnmark, gold being found in the sand along most of the rivers in the county. The national park was no exception and gold digging on a large scale occurred in the so-called Baltos field at Skiehããanjohka, 10 kilometres above its merging with the Anárjohka River. None of the gold miners became rich and the small amount of gold they found in the river sand was not really worth their efforts.

FACTS

Øvre Anárjohka National Park measures 1,414 square kilometres and is located in the south-east of the Finnmarksvidda Plateau.

Attractions:
- Wilderness
- Rich bird life
- Rare plants
- Good fishing
- The Ulvefoss Waterfall

Maps:
Individual maps in the main map series for Norway 1: 50 000.

Access:
From Karasjok, 90 kilometres on a gravel road to Basevuovdi Mountain Lodge in the east.
Just beside the park boundary is the sparse Andreas Nielsen Cabin which is open for visitors. From here it takes a good day's walk to reach the Ulvefoss Waterfall.
If you want to see some of the park you should plan for at least a week's walking tour.

90

Alta Watercourse
A deep canyon and extensive salmon fishing

The Alta River, one of Northern Europe's deepest and most beautiful river gorges is also one of Finnmark's great natural wonders, not only because of the exciting geology and nesting birds of prey, but also salmon fishing, sustaining a yearly catch of several tons.

For time immemorial the Alta River has carved its deep journey through the rolling landscape of the Finnmarksvidda Plateau, leaving behind one of Norway's most wonderful natural formations, and its untiring, meandering course creating enormous gravel and sand terraces has contributed to Alta Municipality's rather flat appearance.

The headwater of this watercourse, which is in fact called the Alta-Kautokeino Watercourse and is the third largest in Finnmark, is in several small lakes and vast marshes near the border with Finland, and it drains the entire west-ern part of the Finnmarksvidda Plateau. The two equally large main branches, the Kautokeino River coming from the west and Siebejohka from the east join just south of Kautokeino Village and continue their course in a valley landscape. After Virdnejávri (the power station reservoir) the river flows into a large, deep ravine which is now mainly dammed in connection with the Alta Power Station, and continues into the Sautso Canyon, before the river bed expands again the last few kilometres down to the estuary at Elvebakken in Alta. In fact the river is really only called the Alta River after Ladnejávri.

Norway's largest river gorge

The Alta River's impressive Sautso Canyon, 6 kilometres long and 300 to 400 metres wide, is considered to be Norway's largest river gorge, and a piece of living geology. The bedrock at the base of the almost vertical walls of the gorge gives way to slate alternating in red and green, while the youngest rocks which came from the west make up the top layer. As slate is brittle and disintegrates easily, the middle layer of Sautso's slanting sides form typical talus slopes.

These steep slopes provide a particular biotope favouring specialist species, including cliff nesting of birds of prey such as the rough-legged buzzard, gyrfalcon, common kestrel and golden eagle, and forms Scandinavia's densest concentration of these species. It

Norway's largest river gorge – the Alta River's Sautso Canyon. Photo: Jan Grønseth.

Every year tons of salmon are caught in the Alta Watercourse. Photo: Steinar Myhr/NN/Samfoto.

can be quite a strong nature experience walking along the top of the gorge looking down on a foaming river while birds of prey scream overhead.

Not only birds of prey but also the extremely rare endemic plant in the pea family, pendant oxytropis, makes its home here. It is of course protected in Norway and indeed its two European habitats occur along this watercourse within the boundaries of the Kautokeino Municipality, the one being in the limestone outcrops at Masi and the other, paradoxically, uppermost on the lime-rich talus slopes above the Alta Power Station's reservoir.

Controversial development of hydro-electric power

The Alta Hydro-electric Power Station has been in operation since 1987 and with its 125 metre high dam wall, the 18 kilometre long Virdnejávri Reservoir and the two kilometre long stretch of dry river bed, it constitutes a considerable encroachment. The development of hydro-electric power caused controversy leading to extensive demonstrations with use of civil disobedience at the beginning of the 1980's. The media coverage intensified when the police force was sent in which resulted in a delay in the development, with ensuing court cases in the years following until the Supreme Court ended the dispute. Today such a controversial project would never have been started and time has shown that due to the hydro-electric power development the salmon have problems during the winter.

It is worth mentioning that the vast watercourse above the Virdnejávri Reservoir as well as the tributaries above and below the dam wall have been permanently protected under the Conservation Plan II for Watercourses.

A realm of large salmon

Despite the development of hydro-electric power, the Alta River is one of the county's and country's best salmon rivers, the yearly catch totalling approximately 12 tons, and it is particularly well-known for containing large salmon. The salmon run 46 kilometres in land from the sea, stopping just short of the dam. The Alta Salmon Fishing Partnership owns the fishing rights and has a long and fascinating history dating back to 1725, forming the basis for the present day partnership. In order to become a member you have to be over 18 years old and own or work land in the district, which stretches from Hjemmeluft in the west to Tverrelvdal Valley in

the east. Furthermore, a landowner must live in the district and a farmer must live on his farm, where at least 2,500 kilograms of hay or 10,000 kilograms of silage must be harvested. In the Alta district this concerns farms totalling at least 0.7 hectares (1.75 acres).

The Alta Salmon Fishing Partnership distributes the much sought after fishing licences, the Alta River being considered one of Norway's most popular salmon rivers. The river is divided into five stretches for salmon fishing, the best stretch being Raipa, where in a good year approximately 300 large salmon are caught.

Even without a fishing licence you can experience this splendid river valley by joining a guided trip on board a traditional Alta riverboat, visiting the Gabofoss Waterfall via small falls and rapids – a very special experience.

91 ▶ Loppa
The westernmost point of Finnmark

Far west in Finnmark and far out to sea is the green island of Loppa, parts of which were established as a nature reserve in 1983 with the purpose of protecting a magnificent bird cliff. However, the island can also offer outdoor pursuits, not least of which are hunting and fishing.

Loppa, a small island lying far out in the Loppa Sea off the westernmost tip of Finnmark, is well worth a visit. This extremely fertile island in the Loppa Municipality has for a long time supported a population where hunting and fishing has provided sustenance.

In times when the boats were small and without motors it was important to live near the fishing grounds and Loppa was a popular place for fishermen to make their homes.

There has been a trading post on the island since 1570 and the

Magic evening light on Loppa Island far west in the open sea. Photo: Lars Krempig.

church is mentioned for the first time in 1589. However, today there are very few residents and although they still collect seagull eggs and cloudberries and hunt ptarmigan, this is to a much lesser extent than in former times. There is still a rich abundance of seabirds and cloudberries on the plateau, where also the willow ptarmigan is a tempting prey for bird hunters. The hunting regulations on Loppa Island are the same as for the rest of Finnmark. Anyone can buy a licence that applies for all land owned by the organisation Finnmarkseiendommen, which comprises 96 per cent of the whole of Finnmark. The hunting season for ptarmigan is 10 September to 15 March with some restrictions within the Loppa Nature Reserve.

Loppa has a wonderful sandy beach and although the water can be chilly, a dip in the Loppa Sea can be tempting on warm sunny days.

Bird cliff

The western part of Loppa Island consists of the Loppa Nature Reserve the southern part of which is a 200 metre mountain wall rising abruptly from the sea where most of the seabirds thrive. Further north the terrain is gentler with grassy slopes and rocky ledges. The bedrock consists of hard sandstone called quartzite which is not particularly nutrient rich for plants, the lushness of the area being due more to fertilization from the seabirds.

The reserve contains most of the species which nest on bird cliffs, for example, razorbills, Atlantic puffins, common guillemots, black-legged kittiwakes, black guillemots and shags. The

Atlantic puffin, numbering a few thousand pairs, is of course the most popular with its colourful beak and it digs out gropes in the grassy slopes or nests under stones in the screes. The razorbill resembles a miniature penguin, with its pointed beak and upright stance. Unlike the puffin that hides its nest, the razorbill lays its solitary egg directly on a rocky

ledge, and precarious though it may seem the egg's pear shape means that it rolls on its own axis instead of off the ledge.

Arctic skuas, great skuas, lesser black-backed gulls, mew gulls and arctic terns nest on the mountain above the cliffs, and in fact the great skua nested for the first time in Norway on Loppa Island in 1975, spreading to several places

Most of the bird species that nest on bird cliffs are found at Loppa. Here are two razorbills silhouetted against the midnight sun. Photo: Lars Krempig.

along the coast since then. It is now estimated that around 10 pairs nest on Loppa, but one should be cautious in the vicinity of a great skua's nest which it defends by dive-bombing intruders in fighter plane style. Arctic skuas are more numerous with approximately 100 pairs and they also attack intruders near their nests, perhaps being equally well-known for their pirate-like tricks of threatening other birds to release their food.

Fifteen years ago approximately 35 pairs of the northern subspecies of lesser black-backed gull nested here, but today this is reduced to only a few pairs, and the bird is on the Norwegian list of directly endangered species. It has a pelagic way of living, that is to say that it collects its food on the surface of the sea, while the southern subspecies also collects food on the shore and cultivated soil. The latter is gradually moving north and nests alongside its more endangered relative.

❧ FACTS ❧

Loppa Island and Nature Reserve in the far western reaches of Finnmark County.

Attractions:
· Bird cliff
· Cloudberries
· Old coastal settlement
· Ptarmigan hunting

Map:
1735 IV Loppa 1: 50 000.

Access:
With Alta as the starting point you can drive or take the bus to Øksfjord (127 kilometres) and then continue by boat, the ferry running almost daily. Possibility of accommodation at the guesthouse, Lopphavet Gjestehus.

92

Seiland
Lush island with glaciers

Seiland is one of the most untouched areas of nature in Finnmark and with its 582 square kilometres it is the county's second largest island and the country's seventh largest. Seiland can offer dramatic mountain scenery and huge glaciers, and received status as a national park in 2006.

Seiland, the large island lying south of Hammerfest between the mainland and the island Sørøya in the north, is almost divided in two by two deep fjords. The Jøfjord penetrates 11 kilometres into the island from the north, and separated by only 5 kilometres the 9 kilometre long Store Kufjord cuts in from the south. On the west of the island vertical mountain walls soar straight up from the sea and there are few or no skerries or beaches. The island emerges as an inaccessible fortress in the middle of the ocean and has, of

Seiland has dramatic mountain scenery including Norway's northernmost glaciers. Photo: Lars Krempig.

A walking tour in Seiland scenery. Photo: Lars Krempig.

course, no marked trails or tourist cabins. The scattered settlements in the north-east and south-west are well away from the recommended area for the national park.

Norway's northernmost glaciers

Seiland is a mountain realm with many summits exceeding 900 metres and two enormous areas of glaciers. Whereas the Nordmannsjøkul Icecap on the west side of the island is only three square kilometres, the Seilandsjøkul Icecap on the east side covers a total of 14 square kilometres. These glaciers, the northernmost on Norway's mainland, are in dramatic decline and the Nordmannsjøkul Icecap will probably disappear completely in the course of a few years.

The Seilandsjøkul Icecap can be scaled from several sides, the highest point at 995 metres amsl being of rock and marked by a small cairn. The glacier contains most of the glaciological formations found and is considered a museum for anyone interested in how the Ice Age formed Norway. On the south side of the glacier is a marvellous kettle landscape which has been formed by ice clumps that once were buried under earth and gravel, but on melting left large holes.

Lush island

Even if Seiland is a dramatic island with steep mountainsides, it is unusually lush due to the easily disintegrated rock types which provide nutrient rich soil for plant life, not least assisted by the large amount of sunshine and the damp climate. This results in grass, in some places one metre high, covering the steep slopes and this is perhaps not what one would expect to see so far north. However, as most of the island is north of the arctic tree line, there is very little forest except for in the valleys on the south of the island.

The flora on Seiland is exceptional including the rare Stjernøy poppy (Papaver radicatum ssp. macrostigma), its name deriving from its first occurrence on the island of Stjernøy, which neighbours Seiland in the south-west, but there is some dispute as to whether this is a separate species or just a subspecies of the arctic poppy. Other interesting species worth mentioning are alpine arnica, low sandwort, hawkweed saxifrage, ice grass, hairy lousewort, woolly everlasting, white arctic bell heather and maiden saxifrage. Another characteristic plant is wild chives which can in places create dense meadows of several thousand plants. Originally from the Siberian coast, this species has spread westwards to many fjords on the coast of Finnmark, including Seiland.

Birds of prey

With regard to the wildlife on the island the most significant is the occurrence of birds of prey. In 2002 a study ascertained 28 white-tailed eagle nests, eight of which were certain nesting sights and six probable. Nesting sites for gyrfalcon, merlin and rough-legged buzzard were also found as well as a probable nesting site for the common kestrel and recently also nesting golden eagles. Apart from birds of prey Seiland does not have a particularly rich bird life or wildlife, although there are scattered occurrences of red-throated divers, black-throated divers, long-tailed ducks and goosanders, as well as otters along the shoreline. Seiland, its nature framed by majestic mountains, is an exciting and little-known part of Norway.

✿ FACTS ✿

Seiland, island in Finnmark. Became National Park in 2006.

Attractions:
- Glaciers
- Landscape of sheer mountain sides
- Birds of prey
- Plant life

Map:
1835 I Seiland 1: 50 000.

Access:
The easiest access is via the coastal boat service from Alta to Hakkstabben a small populated place on the south of the island. This is the best starting point for a walk to the Seilandsjøkul Icecap. You can also take the ferry from Hammerfest and Kvaløya to Kjerringholmen on Seiland, from where you can drive to Hønsøybotn, but from here you have to walk.

93

Stabbursdalen National Park
Fantastic fishing in the world's northernmost pine forest

Stabbursdalen National Park offers salmon fishing in the world's northernmost pine forest surrounded by pristine and varied nature and a unique fauna, with many bird species finding their northern limits here.

Whereas several of Finnmark's wildernesses are off the beaten track, a visit demanding careful planning, the Stabbursdalen National Park awaits you only 20 kilometres from Lakselv Airport and lies adjacent to the E6 road. Despite its easy access and numerous cars in the car park, you soon feel that you are entering a pristine wilderness.

Stabbursdalen National Park, established in 1970, totalled originally only 97 square kilometres but a substantial expansion in 2002 brought it up to 747 square kilometres. It includes pine and birch forests, rapids, waterfalls, gorges, marshes, heaths and desolate expanses of stony ground, in other words extremely varied scenery and something for everyone.

A world record
The national park contains a world

The world's northernmost pine forest grows in the national park. Photo: Tom Schandy.

The salmon run in the Stabburselv River all the way up to the Njáhkáfoss Waterfall. Photo: Tom Schandy.

Salmon fishing

The anglers usually gather under the Stabbursfoss Waterfall. Fishing for salmon in the Stabburselv River differs greatly from fishing in the large well-known rivers. One must after all walk several kilometres to reach the river and camp in a tent in the middle of the world's northernmost pine forest. Whereas the heaviest salmon weighed in at 29 kilograms, the usual weight is 10 kilograms and during one season up to two tons of salmon can be caught in this watercourse.

The river also contains sea char and sea trout, the record for the latter being nine kilograms. The "Lombola" holds pike and burbot, but no-one knows why only these eastern species and not others, like common whitefish, grayling and perch, have come to the Stabbursdal Valley.

record, the world's northernmost pine forest, which grows in the south of the park. It is a low-grown and sparse forest but there are scattered trees of gigantic dimensions that date back 500 years.

Although no-one has ever lived in the Stabbursdal Valley, the park area has always been important for the subsistence of the population of coastal Lapps with their long traditions of hunting, fishing and collection of animal fodder. There is still evidence of the pit traps for hunting wild reindeer before the keeping of domestic reindeer took over in the 1600's.

After leaving your car in the parking area in the pine forest, a footpath quickly brings you to the so-called "Lombola" which is the Norwegian version of the Lapp word "luobbal" which means the widening of a river to resemble a large inland lake. The "Lombola", consisting of three tortuous lakes, or large backwaters, is connected by short stretches of river where common goldeneyes and goosanders thrive and make their nests in

old pine trees. If one is lucky it is possible to catch sight of other species of duck, such as Eurasian wigeon, northern pintails, tufted ducks and red-breasted mergansers.

Northern limit

Birch and pine forests lining the "Lombola" give the moose a home and whereas the pines have been here 4,500 years, the moose has only had this habitat since the middle of the 1950's. However, the national park does not have the most northern occurrence of moose, as this is found a few kilometres further north. On the other hand the park is the northern limit for many species like the capercaillie that holds its courtship displays here every spring, the berry-eating waxwing, three-toed woodpecker, pine grosbeak, great grey shrike, lesser-spotted woodpecker and Siberian jay. A number of plants also reach their distribution boundaries in the park, including the maiden saxifrage with its most eastern and Northern European outpost, the

northern limit for the one-flowered wintergreen and the alpine arnica, while the tall (acutish) Jacob's ladder is at its northern and western limits here.

The Stabbursdal Valley's splendour lies in its contrasts. Along the Stabburselv River in the lower region there are large gravel and sand terraces, while a few kilometres further up is the Stabbursfoss Waterfall, sporting the only technical encroachment in the park, a salmon ladder to help salmon reach up river, and thanks to such ladders, the salmon run almost up to the great Njáhkáfoss Waterfall.

After the Stabbursfoss Waterfall there is an immense ravine lined with sheer vertical mountain sides and vast talus slopes. The gully comprises the last 4 kilometres before both river and valley disappear in a stony desert in the mountains. The 60 kilometre Stabburselv River is one of Norway's few large unspoiled watercourses. The characteristic rugged mountain range, Gaissene, stretches from the Stabbursdal Valley and south-

---

🌿 FACTS 🌿

The Stabbursdalen National Park in Porsanger in Finnmark, with a protected area of approximately 747 square kilometres and additional bordering landscape protection areas totalling 189 square kilometres.

Attractions:
- The world's northernmost pine forest
- Angling, especially salmon fishing
- Northern bird species.

Maps:
1935 II Stabbursdal Valley and 2035 III Lakselv 1: 50 000.

Access:
Approximately 15 kilometres north of Lakselv along the Road E6. Gravel road to the west approximately 2 kilometres south of the bridge over the Stabburselv River.

94

Stabbursnes in Porsanger
Endangered lesser white-fronted geese and thousands of knots

The Stabbursnes Nature Reserve beside the Porsangerfjord in Finnmark is a vast delta of sand and gravel washed down by the Stabburselv River since the last Ice Age. This is a resting place for up to 30,000 red, arctic knots on their way to their nesting grounds, as well as the last remaining living examples in Norway of the lesser white-fronted goose which is on the verge of extinction.

The mouth of the Stabburselv River is on the north side of the actual promontory with vast beach and shoreline areas both to the north and south. The sea beyond is extremely shallow and the nature reserve, established in 1983, comprises part of Norway's largest uninterrupted areas of shallow water. In 1985 it was given the status of being a Ramsar region, that is to say wetlands of international significance.

The reserve is located right beside the E6 road only 15 kilometres north of Lakselv in Finn-

Valdakmyra. Photo: Ingar Jostein Øien.

Almost the entire Scandinavian stock of lesser white-fronted geese rests in Stabbursnes Nature Reserve during the spring migration. Photo: Ingar Jostein Øien.

Between 20 and 25 May almost 30,000 knots rest in the reserve. Photo: Ingar Jostein Øien.

mark County and in the two periods 1 May to 30 June and 10 August to 20 September entering the marsh, Valdakmyra, is prohibited. However, a pair of binoculars or even a telescope will give you a good view from the vantage point above.

The endangered lesser white-fronted goose

The prohibition for Valdakmyra is not without reason, as this is the resting ground for one of the most endangered bird species in the whole of Scandinavia, the lesser white-fronted goose – a small goose with a white forehead. Although Stabbursnes Nature Reserve is the most reliable place to see this species, the numbers are declining yearly.

Whereas at the beginning of the 1900's the lesser white-fronted goose was a numerous and common bird species in the mountain regions from Nord- Trøndelag/ Jämtland and northwards, the numbers today are reduced by 95 to 99 per cent, and there are only 30 to 45 pairs in the whole of Scandinavia. Over the last 10

years the number of lesser white-fronted geese using Stabbursnes as a resting ground during the spring migration has been approximately 20 to 35 pairs with 7 to 10 young birds, and this constitutes almost the entire Scandinavian stock.

Every year ornithologists in The Norwegian Ornithological Society catch some lesser white-fronted geese to fit them with a satellite transmitter, in order to learn more about the species' movements both in the breeding grounds and not least along the migratory routes south and winter grounds at the Black Sea and the Caspian Sea. This means of collecting knowledge about the birds is extremely important for preservation measures, especially when one is aware of illegal hunting along the migratory routes in Russia.

The lesser white-fronted geese arrive at Stabbursnes in the middle of May and continue on to their breeding grounds on the Finnmarksvidda Plateau during the first half of June. After the nesting season, they return during the second half of August staying at

the reserve until the first half of September.

Pink sky

If you visit the Stabbursnes Nature Reserve between 20 and 25 May, in addition to lesser white-fronted geese, you will witness a spectacular sight that occurs here and a couple of other places in Norway – not less than 30,000 red knots resting in the reserve and a simultaneous take off of all these birds colours the sky pink. Ringing has revealed that knot do not migrate to Siberia as one previously thought, but to Iceland and Greenland. The knot does not nest in Norway.

Dunlins and bar-tailed godwits occur in large numbers as do oystercatchers, ringed plovers, turnstones and ruffs, the latter also nesting in the area along with northern lapwings, Eurasian curlews and Temminck's stints. The areas of shallow water are popular with mergansers and diving ducks, not least large quantities of common eider.

The reserve contains some interesting flora including all the

important arctic plants which grow along the Finnmark coastline. Fourleaf mare's tail grows prolifically in pools of stagnant water and there are quite large occurrences of creeping saltmarsh grass.

In other words Stabbursnes absolutely deserves being considered as an international wetland worthy of protection.

95

Reinøya in Porsanger
Remarkable dolomite landscape

Reinøya Island lying in the middle of the Porsangerfjord south-west of Børselv in Finnmark has a remarkable landscape. The striking dolomite rock formations of pillars and portals adorning this seven kilometre long island could have come from another planet.

Spectacular and beautiful nature on Reinøya Island. Photo: Torbjørn Moen.

Reinøya Island is protected as a nature reserve; no-one lives here and there are no regular services to the island. If you want to visit, you have to arrange your own transport or join an organised tour. Reinøya Island is quite inaccessible and a little bit mysterious.

With its steep cliffs, naked rocks, gaping portals and dolomite pillars the island landscape is quite different to the rest of Norway, although there are also idyllic tarns, and small lush valleys and depressions with distinctive plants.

Dolomite landscape

Strolling around in this dolomite landscape is almost like wandering on another planet as the island is built up of dolomite, a magnesium rich calcite, which is the usual mineral in limestone. Apart from the fact that dolomite is harder than calcite they are identical in appearance, both of them originating from remains of shells from shellfish, corals and coralline algae, but limestone can also be created by direct precipitation of seawater.

The most famous dolomite landscape in Europe is the Dolomite Alps in Italy with tall rock formations in this magnesium-rich mineral. The dolomite occurrence in Porsanger is in fact among the largest in North Europe occurring in a long zone stretching from the Stabbursdal Valley via Kolvik and Reinøya Island to the mainland just north of Børselv.

As limestone and dolomite are both easily worn away by water, the ocean and breakers have sculptured these peculiar portals and pillars in the island's white and greyish cliffs.

Limestone provides nutrients for a fertile plant life and it is, therefore, not surprising that Reinøya Island has an abundance of the lime-loving mountain avens thriving in the lime-rich soil. When these blossoms have faded, the flowers of the large pink replace them, a plant which has probably arrived from the east and flowers in abundance on the island's shores. Reinøya is also a habitat for the fragrant orchid, hairy bittercress and dwarf bulrush. The island's name derives from its previous use as summer grazing for domestic reindeer, although today sheep have more or less taken over.

Trollholmsund

Difficult as it is to reach Reinøya Island, Trollholmsund is more accessible lying approximately 35 kilometres north of Lakselv on the road to the North Cape. Seven or eight dolomite pillars stand on the shoreline, petrified characters from an old Lappish legend of trolls who wandered over the plains with an enormous chest full of gold and silver. As they neared the fjord they tried to hide the chest and while they searched for a cave that was big enough, the sun rose, turning the trolls to stone.

❧ FACTS ❧

Reinøya Island, a 13 square kilometre nature reserve with occurrence of dolomite in the Porsangerfjord in Finnmark. Dolomite pillars are also found on the mainland at Trollholmsund.

Attractions:
· Special landscape built of Porsanger dolomite

Map:
2035 I Børselv 1: 50 000.

Access:
Reinøya Island is difficult to access without your own boat, so transport must be hired. However, Trollholmsund lies approximately 35 kilometres north of Lakselv, right beside the road to the North Cape.

Dolomite sculptures in Trollholmsund. Photo: Tom Schandy.

96

Magerøya and the North Cape
The northernmost point

The North Cape is one of Norway's most popular tourist destinations, but Magerøya Island has several natural wonders besides the steep-sided plateau facing the Barents Sea. On the Duken Mountain there are plants growing that otherwise are at home in Siberia and Gjesværstappen teems with bird life including Atlantic puffins, northern gannets and white-tailed eagles.

Although the wide open expanses on the island of Magerøya are barren, there are glittering lakes, green marshes and tussocks of red moss campion. There is in fact enough vegetation that the herds of domestic reindeer thrive here in the summer.

Rare plants and screeching sea birds
Magerøya's white mountain, Duken, with its bright wall of dolomite lies on the east of the island. Around it many rare plants grow which otherwise belong to Siberia and Svalbard, the rarest of them being purplish braya which does not grow elsewhere on the mainland. Low sandwort, a native of Greenland and North America, also thrives on Duken and the plant life is therefore an exotic meeting between east and west.

The bird cliff, Gjesværstappan with its tremendous colonies of sea birds, lies on the west of the island. It comprises three hump-like rocks, rather resembling a three-humped camel, rising out of the sea: Storstappen (270 metres amsl), Kjerkstappen (160 metres amsl) and Bukkstappen (90 metres amsl). It is forbidden to go ashore on Storstappen in the nesting period, but one can join a boat trip around the bird cliff to observe the large flocks of Atlantic puffins, razorbills, common guillemots and black-legged kittiwakes. The elegant northern gannet also nests on these bird rocks, one of its otherwise few Norwegian nesting grounds, while white-tailed eagles cruise above, hunting for suitable prey.

The North Cape Plateau
Most of the visitors to Magerøya are not there to see the sea birds or the rare plants. Their target is the North Cape, where Europe ends. It is a dramatic experience as the flat plateau drops vertically 300 metres into the swell of the Barents Sea. Whereas today the visitors arrive by bus, they previously came by sea, putting into shore at Hornvika beside the remarkable cliff called "Hornet" – The

Most of the visitors to Magerøya are targeting the North Cape, the place where Europe ends. Photo: Tom Schandy.

Knivskjellodden is the northernmost point on Magerøya, and in fact is 2 kilometres further north than the North Cape. Photo: Tom Schandy.

Horn. From Hornvika there were 1,000 steps up to the plateau.

While it was Stephen Burrows who named the cliff The North Cape, an Italian called Francesco Negri is considered to have been the first tourist there. In 1665 he wrote: *"Here where the world ends, my curiosity also ends, and I return home satisfied"*. Following this several dare-devils have walked up the steep terrain, one was King Oscar II in 1873 and another King Rama V of Thailand in 1907. Since 1965 the approach to the North Cape has been made

easier after the opening of the North Cape Road.

Today the North Cape is one of Norway's prime tourist destinations and you are seldom alone. The 200,000 tourists that visit Magerøya and the North Cape every year hope to see the midnight sun which illuminates the plateau day and night from 11 May to 31 July and at exactly midnight it hangs off the north edge of the cliff. However, no-one can guarantee the weather and unfortunately many travel home without seeing the midnight sun.

Most people assume that they are as far north as possible, but they are wrong. The North Cape is not the northernmost point on Magerøya. To the west Knivskjellodden sticks out into the sea and is two kilometres longer. So if you do not want to join hundreds of tourists taking photographs put on your hiking boots and walk the 10 kilometres to the end of this promontory. There are few other people and you can philosophise over the mysteries of life in peace and quiet as you walk beside the swell of the Barents Sea.

97

Slettnes and the Nordkinn Peninsula
The land of pirates

Northernmost on the Nordkinn Peninsula in Finnmark is the Slettnes Nature Reserve with status as a Ramsar region. The abundant bird life supports Europe's largest colony of pirates, the dreaded arctic skua, which breeds here, probably topping all other sites in Europe for the number of nesting pairs. Kinnarodden, the northern promontory of the Nordkinn Peninsula, is the European continent's northernmost point on land.

The Nordkinn Peninsula is a barren arctic landscape facing an open and exposed coastline, with no skerries to protect it against the cold and windswept Barents Sea. A summer month should have an average temperature of over 10 degrees Celsius, so defined in meteorological terms it is never summer here, as the temperature at Slettnes Lighthouse has never exceeded 9.6 degrees Celsius.

The Slettnes Nature Reserve has Europe's largest colony of arctic skuas. Photo: Tom Schandy.

The lack of trees, abundance of stones as well as the midnight sun creates a very special atmosphere. However, the plant life is not so scarce with over 350 different species of alpine and sea plants growing side by side.

If you drive 3 kilometres northwards from Gamvik, you arrive at Slettnes Lighthouse which is one of the world's northernmost lighthouses on mainland, lying as far north as the northern tip of Alaska. The lighthouse is inside the Slettnes Nature Reserve, one of the most important nesting grounds in Scandinavia for waders, and features a number of large and small lakes surrounded by marshes totalling altogether 12 square kilometres. The area is dominated by sandstone and phyllite as well as well-developed elevated shorelines lying in rows on the slopes rising up from the sea.

Unique wetland

Over 100 bird species have been observed at Slettnes, 66 of which are closely linked to wetlands, waders being perhaps the most interesting group with 24 different species nesting here including little stint, red-necked phalarope, European golden plover, ringed

The wetlands at Slettnes are popular for divers, ducks and waders. Photo: Tom Schandy.

The little stint is one of 24 nesting species of waders at Slettnes. Photo: Tom Schandy.

Several unusual species have also been observed including the grey plover, sanderling, curlew sandpiper, pectoral sandpiper, semipalmated sandpiper, knot, Eurasian woodcock, bar-tailed godwit and wood sandpiper. Numerous glaucous gulls can also migrate and spend the winter here, resting flocks of over 300 individuals having been observed on several occasions. Slettnes is, of course, one of the most significant wetlands known in Norway and Scandinavia and was protected in 1996, followed in 2002 with status as a Ramsar region. In 2001 the WWF Slettnes Eco-Station was established which follows the developments in the reserve.

Kinnarodden promontory
When you are satisfied with the bird life observations you should visit Kinnarodden, which, lying at 71 degrees and 8 minutes north, is the European continent's nor-thernmost point on land, and not the North Cape on Magerøya. However, the 23 kilometre walk in demanding terrain to Kinnarodden is for the experienced hiker, and is estimated to take seven hours. In the spring of 2004 the Gamvik Municipality surveyed and marked the paths to the promontory with stone cairns, but all the same you are recommended to take map, compass and even GPS equipment as the fog can quickly engulf these areas on the edge of the Barents Sea. A seven hour tour can quickly become a two-day trip needing a tent and it is perhaps wise to plan thus.

plover, dunlin and whimbrel. The area's enormous colony of arctic terns forms an ideal basis for Europe's largest colony of arctic skuas. More than 300 pairs nest here, that is to say 600 adults which live by stealing food from other birds. In addition there are non-nesting juveniles, the so-called "club",

making altogether somewhere between 800 and 1,000 arctic skuas living like pirates, chasing terns and gulls until they release or regurgitate their catch in order to escape their tormentors. Which is exactly what the arctic skua wants them to do, as it stops the chase and picks up the food.

FACTS

Slettnes Nature Reserve is located in the Gamvik Municipality in the north of the Nordkinn Peninsula in Finnmark.

Attractions:
- Arctic tundra landscape
- Bird life with Europe's densest colony of arctic skuas
- The European continent's northernmost lighthouse
- Kinnarodden, the European continent's northernmost point

Map:
2237 II Mehamn 1: 50 000.

Access:
Road 888 to Gamvik and Slettnes, alternatively a Widerøe flight to Mehamn. The Coastal Liner Express (Hurtigruta) docks at Mehamn, 20 kilometres from Gamvik. Continue your journey by bus or hired car. A tour to Slettnes can easily be combined with joining the Coastal Liner Express to the North Cape.

The European continent's northernmost lighthouse is at Slettnes. Photo: Tom Schandy.

98

Varanger Peninsula
Moon landscape and arctic tundra

The Varanger Peninsula has a distinctive arctic landscape unequalled elsewhere in Scandinavia. It is mostly barren, stone desert with scattered oases of unique plants and birds. You might even spot a snowy owl.

The Varanger Peninsula, the northernmost piece of Norway's mainland, lies between the fishing villages Berlevåg and Båtsfjord in the north-west and the towns Vadsø and Vardø in the south-east. In the autumn of 2006, 1,804 square kilometres of this peninsula was protected as the Varanger Peninsula National Park, with the aim of preserving the unique arctic landscape only otherwise found on Svalbard, Greenland or the northern regions of Canada.

Rocky ground and moon landscape
These barren wilds have their charm and in many places the geological formations are striking.

A winter's day in the Sandfjord beside Berlevåg. Photo: Bård Løken/NN/Samfoto.

The road to Hamningberg on the far east of the island crosses what is often compared to a moon landscape. It is scant and desolate, but at the same time starkly dramatic with geological gambols framed by the Barents Sea. Along the coast the stratified rocks have been squeezed and thrust into vertical positions enclosing the road with their ragged spires and creating an aggressive landscape.

Although the Varanger Peninsula was covered in ice during the last Ice Age, the inland ice did little to change the main features in the landscape. This was due to the fact that glaciers in arctic regions are often frozen to the ground at their base and therefore preserve the ground surface instead of scouring it away. However, despite little change of this monumental landscape by ice, there are other geological Ice Age phenomena here for example, such as the moraine rings which are circle-shaped moraine deposits formed on rocky ground. While there are a total of 3,000 of these circles on the Varanger Peninsula, they are only known to exist in small numbers a few other places in the world.

The peaceful mountain plateau is intersected by narrow river valleys which can be up to 200 metres deep, spreading from the interior of the peninsula towards the sea. In the very north, the plateau ends in an abrupt descent to the coast, where the waves have gnawed their way and created a wild stretch of coast in vivid contrast to the tranquil landscape above.

Oases of life

Despite the quantities of stone the varied climate and geological conditions on the peninsula sustain an abundance of plants, including arctic species such as the Finnmark poppy, a subspecies of the Svalbard poppy, and thyme-leaved sandwort which only occurs otherwise in Europe on Svalbard. Other arctic species include the Svalbard snow cinquefoil, sulphur-coloured buttercup and northern golden-saxifrage (golden carpet), while field fleawort, yellow oxytropis and the large pink have invaded from the east.

Bird enthusiasts will also find the Varanger Peninsula exciting, the area being considered one of the best in the country for observing the rare and noble snowy owl. It does not normally nest here but is common as a vagrant bird on the plateau during the summer season. The gyrfalcon is another

Over 400 pairs of northern gannets nest in colonies at Syltefjord. Photo: Tom Schandy.

rare and endangered bird of prey on the plateau and is accompanied by more usual birds of prey like the golden eagle, white-tailed eagle, merlin, rough-legged buzzard and short-eared owl. In years with plenty of small rodents a common sight is the silhouette of the long-tailed skua.

Ornithologists from the whole of Europe make a pilgrimage to these regions in the summer to twitch rare northern and eastern species off their lists. Europe's smallest wader, the little stint, is a celebrity along with the bar-tailed godwit, jack snipe and spotted redshank. During the winter the sea surrounding the peninsula is dappled with large flocks of the stunningly attractive ducks, Steller's eider and king eider, both of which nest in Siberia. Syltefjordstauran in the north is one of Norway's largest bird cliffs housing over one million birds including a colony of 400 pairs of the elegant sea bird, the northern gannet, which has settled here since 1961. While it is relatively tricky to get to Syltefjordstauran, lying right beside the road east of Vadsø there is Ekkerøy where 40,000 pairs of deafening black-legged kittiwakes nest.

The Varanger Peninsula is also a key locality in Norway for the endangered arctic fox. Several dens have been registered, but most of them are either not in use or have been taken over by the red fox. In order to rescue the Scandinavian arctic fox an extensive project has been started which includes helping them to survive the winter by putting out food for them. At the same time research is being carried out involved in reducing the number of red foxes, as this species competes with the arctic fox for both food and den localities.

During the winter one can observe large flocks of king eider in the sea surrounding the peninsula. Photo: Tom Schandy.

99

Hornøya and Reinøya
Bird sanctuary at the easternmost point of Norway

Hornøya Island in Finnmark is Norway's easternmost point and it combines with its neighbour Reinøya Island to form an exciting nature reserve which includes a high density of sea birds. On an overnight stay at the Vardø Lighthouse you can experience the bird life close at hand illuminated by the midnight sun.

The nitrogen-loving common scurvy-grass finds good growing conditions on the Hornøya Island due to the large quantities of bird droppings. Photo: Tom Schandy.

The Hornøya and Reinøya Nature Reserve, established in 1983, is an important nesting ground for several species of seabirds. Tourists can only go ashore on Hornøya, but they have the opportunity of experiencing most of the bird life. From 1 May to 15 August all activity in the reserve is prohibited, but it is permitted to move about freely under the bird cliffs, and to use the footpath, which in fact nearly traverses the Atlantic puffin colony, from the landing stage to the Vardø Lighthouse. You then have the possibility of photographing this bird close at hand perhaps even with a fish in its bill.

Brünnich's guillemot and other sea birds

Reinøya Island and Hornøya Island have steep cliffs with nesting seabirds, black-legged kittiwakes being the most dominant with approximately 23,000 pairs. Otherwise there is an abundance of Atlantic puffins numbering approximately 5,000 to 10,000 nesting pairs in the entire reserve. While there are around 500 nesting pairs of razorbills, the common guillemots number 1,000 to 1,500 pairs. However, it is the occurrence of Brünnich's guillemot which makes this reserve rather special, as this colony is the easiest to access in the whole of Europe. This high arctic species nests in large numbers on Svalbard and other arctic areas, Hornøya being one of the few nesting habitats on the Norwegian mainland. However, you have to study every guillemot carefully as the Brünnich's guillemot has a white stripe on its bill, which is the only apparent difference from the common guillemot.

The commandant and the gulls' eggs

One of Europe's largest gull colonies populates the flat parts of Reinøya, with an estimated 50,000 pairs of herring gulls and 600 to 700 pairs of great black-backed gulls. Despite this being a nature reserve, 100,000 eggs are collected on the island. Since the olden days Reinøya came under the Vardøhus Fortress where the Commandant had the right to collect eggs, and this right still applies, both the Commandant and Vardø Municipality being able to give permission for egg collecting to a maximum of five people at a time on Reinøya and Hornøya respec-

Norway's easternmost point is Hornøya Island. Photo: Tom Schandy.

tively. Hornøya's egg-producing capacity is 20,000 to 30,000 eggs per year which applies to eggs from herring gulls, great black-backed gulls and mew gulls, in accordance with the rules and regulations in the game laws.

Every year researchers and tourists visit Hornøya to study the bird life, and only until recently the tourists had to be satisfied with just day visits by boat from Vardø, until the Vardø Lighthouse on Hornøya Island was opened to take overnight guests, thanks to an agreement that the society called Friends of Hornøya have made with The Norwegian Coastal Administration. This means that if you are lucky with the weather you can study the bird life all night in the light of the midnight sun, quite a special experience when you consider that you are as far east as Istanbul in Turkey. In the

height of summer the surroundings of the lighthouse are adorned with the nitrogen-loving common scurvy-grass which has marvellous growing conditions due to the large quantities of bird droppings. The Vardø Lighthouse, Norway's easternmost, was erected in 1896 and after almost 100 years of manned operation it was made automatic in 1991. It is now protected under The Norwegian Cultural Heritage Act.

The two islands have an abundant bird life but the one that attracts the most attention is probably the Atlantic puffin. Photo: Tom Schandy.

Pasvik
Borderland wilderness

Pasvik is a wilderness on the border between Finland and Russia, as far to the north east as you can come in Norway. In the light summer nights bears pad around in Norway's largest primeval forest, a habitat for rare birds and plants which are otherwise found in Siberia.

Pasvik is almost boringly flat with its long sparse pine forests, thousands of small glittering lakes and wide open marshes. But do not be deluded by the monotony as this is wilderness with a capital W, containing the largest area of genuine primeval forest in Nor-way, that is to say, forest which has never suffered human interference. The Pasvikdal Valley has 100 square kilometres of un-spoiled pine forest, mostly within the Øvre Pasvik National Park. This forest is the western offshoot of the taiga, the vast belt of coni-ferous forest stretching more or less uninterruptedly to the Bering Strait in the Pacific Ocean. The majority of the forest this far north is dense, with thin tree trunks but in between there are trees 300 to 400 years old, larger and with enormous trunks.

The national park contains Tre-riksrøysa, the point where Finland, Norway and Russia meet and this is in fact the only place in the entire world where three different time zones intersect on land. From the car park at Grensefoss, approximately 5 kilometres from

Norway's largest area of primeval forest is in Pasvik, photographed here in the midnight sun. Photo: Tom Schandy.

Pasvik is the only place in Norway where the exclusive great grey owl regularly breeds in years with plenty of small rodents. Photo: Tom Schandy.

the border, there is a path up to Treriksrøysa on the Krokfjell Mountain, but it is important to observe that it is strictly prohibited to cross the border into Russia.

Eastern and western species

A special feature in Pasvik is the interface between eastern flora such as arctic bramble, swamp willow, red cottongrass and the white-flowering, strongly aromatic Labrador tea, and northern mountain plants like arctic saxifrage, snow cinquefoil and alpine mouse-ear. A total of over 384 plant species are registered in the Pasvikdal Valley and 190 of these occur within the national park boundaries. Locally rare species are the wild black currant, arrowhead, amphibious bistort, herb paris, blunt-leaf sandwort and whorled water milfoil.

The bird life in Pasvik is unique, as this is the meeting place for eastern and western species. Rare Siberian birds like the jack snipe, spotted redshank, little stint, great grey owl and arctic warbler all nest here, in addition to a number of other waders in the valley such as ruff, greenshank, wood sandpiper, whimbrel and common snipe. In recent years Pasvik has witnessed the nesting of the rare little gull which with its black cap and grey-black underwing can resemble a small black-headed gull. Another more exclusive species worth mentioning is the elegant white smew.

Whooper swans are also a distinguishing feature in Pasvik. They announce their arrival in March and April with loud trumpeting fanfares and stay until the ice forms in the late autumn. April and May see large flocks of bean geese resting on the water together with Eurasian wigeons, northern pintails, common teals, smews and common goldeneyes. The wetlands here as well as the vast expanses of marshes in the valley make Pasvik one of Scandinavia's richest wetland systems for waders, ducks and geese and the area is of course a so-called Ramsar region, that is an area of wetlands internationally worthy of protection.

Pasvik's forests provide habitats for many other interesting species. The Siberian jay is characteristic along with the Siberian tit. Bohemian waxwings, otherwise only seen in Southern Norway during the winter, nest here and in years with plenty of small rodents, the handsome great grey owl can be observed, Pasvik being the only place in Norway where this bird breeds regularly. A total of more than 212 different bird species are registered in Pasvik and every year bird watchers from the whole of Europe come here to find the rare Siberian species.

Bear country

The Pasvikdal Valley is home to many fascinating species of mammals, one of the most prominent being the muskrat. Coming originally from Eastern Asia it was introduced for fur farming in Russia and has since spread to Pasvik, and since 1990 it has become common in the lakes and watercourses with rich vegetation throughout most of the valley. In both appearance and behaviour it resembles the beaver, it builds small lodges, lives off water vegetation and therefore helps to stop the lakes growing over.

However, the big attraction in Pasvik is the brown bear. No other area in Norway has a denser population of them and it is the only place in the country where there is regular breeding, although it must be emphasised that the stock is also shared with Finland and Russia. As many as 35 different bears can visit Sør-Varanger and Pasvik in the course of the summer, but not necessarily all at the same time. The bear is not alone as a predator in Pasvik, as there are also occurrences of wolverine and lynx and some winters a wolf from Russia can wander through.

FACTS

Øvre Pasvik National Park measures 120 square kilometres. Also in the valley are Pasvik Nature Reserve (19.1 square kilometres, Norwegian part), Øvre Pasvik Landscape Protection Area (5.24 square kilometres) and Gjøkvassneset Nature Reserve (0.87 square kilometres).

Attractions:
- Norway's largest area of primeval forest
- Rare birds from Siberia
- Muskrats
- Brown bears
- Trerikrøysa

Maps:
Individual maps in the main map series for Norway 1: 50 000.

Access:
Øvre Pasvik is easy to reach by car from Kirkenes. Drive to Vaggatem. You can park at Sortbrysttjern if you are going to hike in the national park.

Pasvik has Norway's densest population of bears. Photo: Tom Schandy.

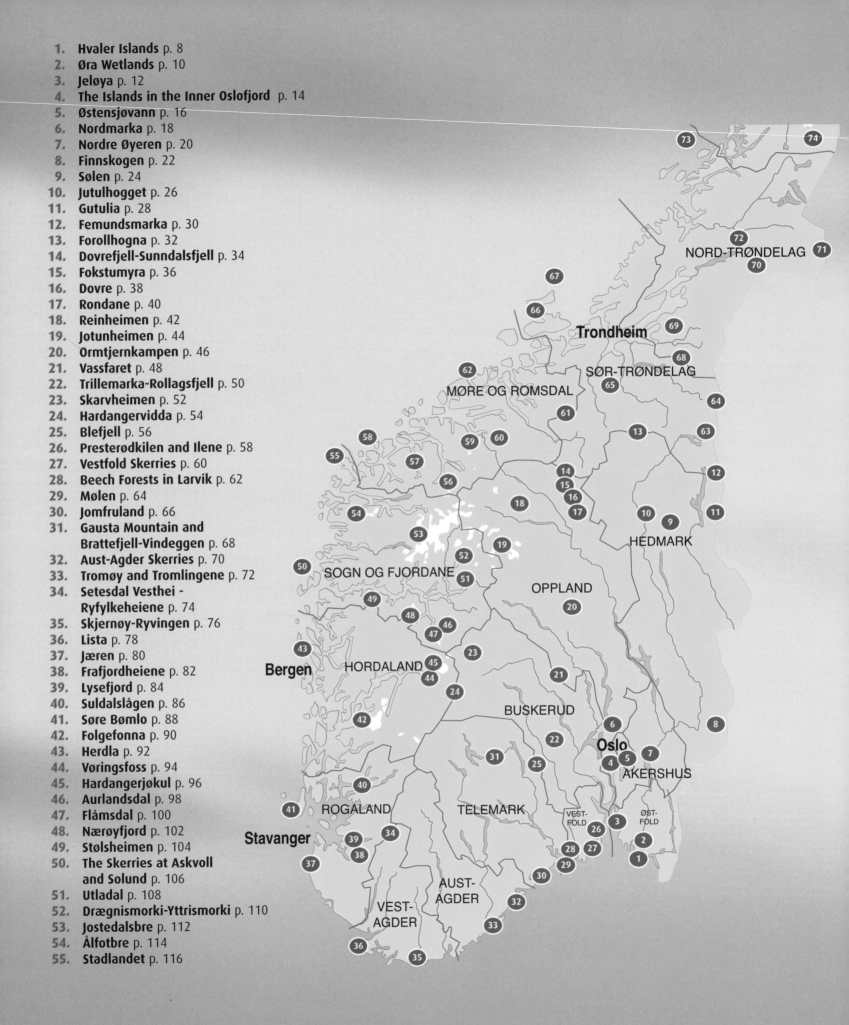